The World Atlas of
HORSES
& Ponies

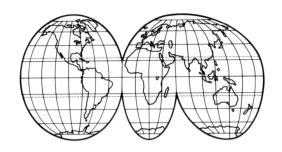

The World Atlas of
HORSES
& Ponies

Edited by Peter Churchill

CRESCENT BOOKS

NEW YORK

Consultant Editor
Peter Churchill

Contributing Authors
Max Ammann
Jenny Baker
Averil Douglas
Judith Draper
Professor H. Epstein
Jane Fuller
Jane Kidd
Steven Price
Penny Rohan
Pat Thorne
Andrew Wyndham-Brown

Designed and produced by
Chris Milsome Limited
11 Great Marlborough Street,
London W1V 1DE

Project Editors
Phillipa Algeo
Lesley Firth
Alan Wakeford

Editorial Director
Chris Milsome

Managing Editor
Susan Ward

Assistant Editor
Michael Doggart

Designers
Karen Bowen
Mel Petersen

Picture Researcher
Tessa Politzer

Researcher
Colin Crewdson

Production
Chris Fayers

First English edition published in 1980 by
Sampson Low,
Berkshire House, Queen Street,
Maidenhead, Berkshire SL6 1NF

Typesetting by Filmtype Services Limited, Scarborough
Separations by Photoprint Plates, Rayleigh
Printed in Italy by New Interlitho SpA, Milan

Library of Congress CIP Data
The World Atlas of Horses and Ponies
    Includes index
    1. Horses. 2. Ponies. 3. Horse breeds.
    4. Horses – Geographical distribution – Maps.
    5. Ponies – Geographical distribution – Maps.
    I. Churchill, Peter, 1933–
    SF 285.W89 1979   636.1   79–14320
    ISBN 0–517–29210–6

This edition is published by Crescent Books,
a division of Crown Publishers, Inc.

CONTENTS

THE STORY OF A SURVIVOR

Most experts accept that the tiny equus that crossed the Bering Strait from the American continent into Eurasia was the forefather of the modern horse. But was it? This short-striding, strong-bodied, horse-like creature could have been the founder of the sleek, tall, slender-legged riding horse that is seen in the Thoroughbred, the Anglo-Arab or the Furioso. Equally it could have been the ancestor of the onager a half-pony, half-ass creature, the ass or the zebra.

Long before man began to settle in fixed communities, and before the great empires and civilizations of antiquity developed, huge herds of ponies, onagers, asses and zebras roamed the steppes, plains and forests of Eurasia and Africa. Of all the animals depicted in cave paintings, the equid, in one form or another, seems to have been the most popular. At this time the onager was hunted for its meat by Man who followed the migration of these herds.

Was then the first equid domesticated by Man an onager, nothing more than an overgrown donkey? There is some evidence to support this as there was an abundance of onagers on the plains that surrounded the first townships. In many writings before the end of the third millenium BC, the equid was represented by a symbol (an ideogram) that meant 'mountain ass' or 'eastern ass'. In the second millenium BC, however, there are references to the 'real' horse or, as the ancient Chinese referred to it, the 'heavenly' horse.

Some experts believe that Man's first settlements were in the Middle East. At that stage the ability of the horse to carry people or loads was not appreciated and the animal was hunted for its food value. It would have soon learned that the scent of Man meant danger. To the east and north of the first settlements the Zagros mountains enclosed the east and upper Anatolian plateau and it is thought this could have been the secret home of the 'true' horse. Here in relative safety it could feed on the wild cereal, particularly wheat, growing in the region.

The first section of the book deals with the story of this durable survivor. It tells how the horse developed into its present form and how it has been used by Man in agriculture, trade and industry, art and sport, and as cavalry in armies. The second section describes the three main types of horse – the Heavy Horse, the Light Horse and the Pony. This is followed by the atlas. The world has been divided into ten regions and specially-drawn maps showing the physical features locate the major breeds, famous studs and breeding areas. A general survey of each country is also given and this is supported by a breed list which gives a comprehensive guide to where different breeds and types of horse are found in the world today. Technical terms relating to horses are explained in the glossary.

Below: *The Oklahoma Land Rush of 1889 – the horse is used in the race for land and riches.*

Evolution

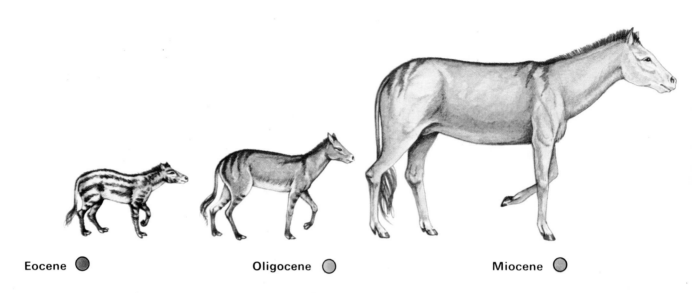

Eocene ●   Oligocene ●   Miocene ●

South America

North America   Orohippus   Eohippus   Ephippus   Mesohippus   Parahippus   Merychippus

Old World

All great stories are true stories and all good stories contain elements of mystery and adventure. Such is the story of the horse; the story of a survivor. For the horse arrived on this earth with no visible means of defence, never having had any horns or sharp teeth, nor the ability to roar or bark. One of Nature's pacifists, the horse has always been a vegetarian living off the land rather than the flesh of other creatures; never the aggressor but always the hunted.

And yet this peaceable animal has survived tremendous upheavals such as the breaking up of land masses, long treacherous migrations, the coming of Ice Ages and the uses and abuses of prehistoric man. By a seeming miracle of evolution this timid creature was guided and shaped to play the vital role of man's partner; together they would create great civilizations and build, conquer and destroy vast empires. For centuries the horse has been man's companion and servant.

The earliest horses

The story of the horse began some 60 to 40 million years ago during the Eocene period. In that swampy prehistoric world, herds of strange creatures roamed and foraged from one area to another. Among them were tiny dog-like animals living in small herds and recognizable as early members of the *Equus* family. These were the browsing, pad-footed *Eohippus* (Hyracotherium) and *Orohippus*, and from the evidence gained by studying fossils and remains, it is apparent that they lived in present-day America, south-east England and western Europe. But *Orohippus*, the less common of the two, seems to have been confined to North America.

Although closer to the dog in form, these creatures did have some remarkable similarities with the larger wild horse that was yet to come. The muzzle, nostrils, eyes and ears were horse-like but it is, perhaps, the eyes that provide the most important clue to the animals' character.

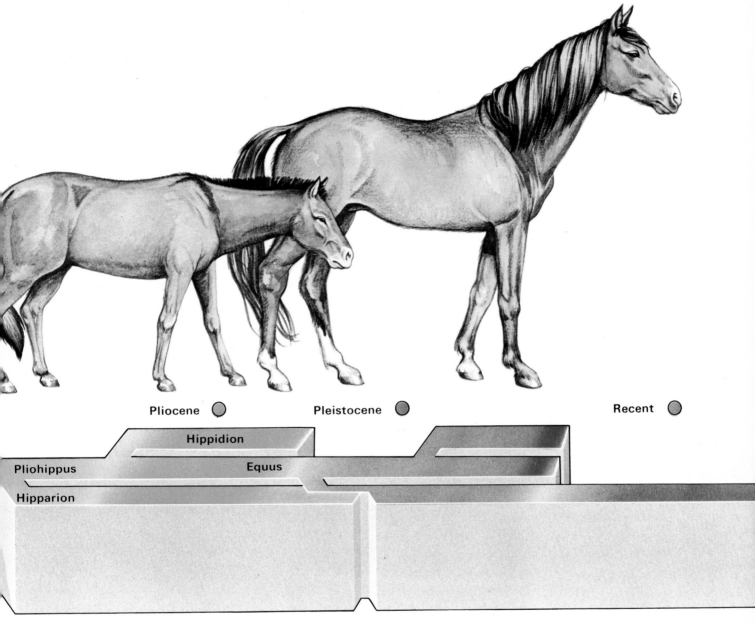

Pliocene ●   Pleistocene ●   Recent ●

Hippidion

Pliohippus

Equus

Hipparion

These were set to the side of the head, which is a trait distinguishing the hunted from the hunter, which has eyes set to the front. These creatures in their various evolutionary forms roamed the world long before man came on the scene.

Where and when the horse was first tamed and ridden is not known. But there is ample evidence to show that cave men recognized and knew horses as a separate species. This can be seen in the first flowering of man's creativity in early cave painting. Here the horse seems to have been one of the most popular subjects, often being the focus for elaborate religious and hunting rituals. As the representations became more frequent, so the form and size of the horses portrayed changed and grew.

The domestication of the horse
The potential of the horse, as a draught animal suitable for use in agriculture and for carrying people and goods, was not realized until about

4000 BC. As a result of conquest and trading, both nomads and settlers came to appreciate the advantages of being able to ride the horse. In this way, two separate horse-cultures were established that exist to this day. On the one hand there is the tradition of the open air and the natural, while on the other there is the culture of the enclosed and the artificial. To the nomad, the horse was as vital to his existence as the wind and rain and it was treated accordingly. To the settled urbanized and agricultural societies, the horse was but one facet in what was becoming an increasingly complex existence. It was both a means of transport and an asset in times of war.

The artificial or 'scientific' horse-culture spread from ancient Egypt through the great courts of Europe to England and North America, while the natural horse-culture remained outdoors on the Asiatic steppes, in Arabia, North Africa, Spain, the pampas of South America and the great plains of North America.

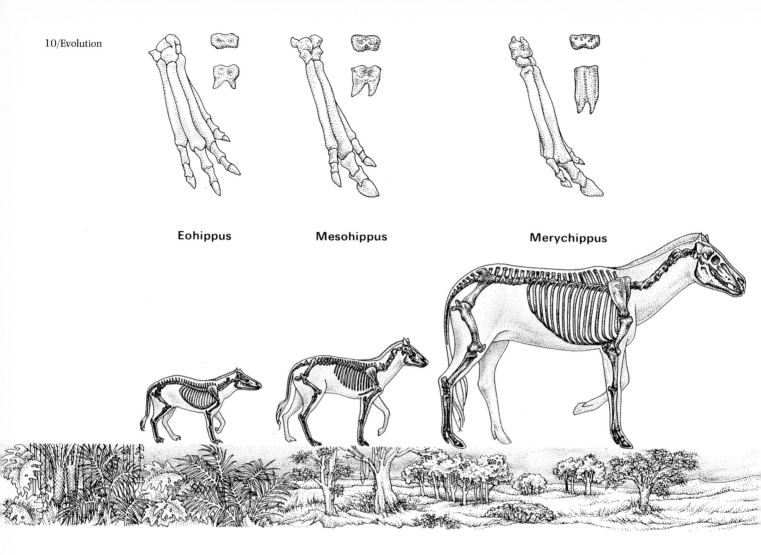

Eohippus **Mesohippus** **Merychippus**

The earliest fossils and remains from which reconstructions of skeletons have been made are of *Eohippus* and *Orohippus*, dog-like creatures standing some 26cm (10in) in height and living in small herds during the Eocene period around 60 to 40 million years ago.

Eohippus was the more common of the two and evidence suggests that it lived in America, south-east England and western Europe. *Orohippus* on the other hand seems to have been confined to the regions which are now North America. These early members of the *Equus* family had some recognizable horse features but they had padded feet with four toes on their forefeet and three toes on their hind feet. Vestigial 'splints' of a fifth toe remained on the forefeet, and either one or two on the hind feet.

First developments
One of the earliest changes in the anatomy of *Equus* can be seen in *Orohippus*. Towards the end of the Eocene period, climatic changes encouraged the growth of forests and plants, and these became richer in minerals and vitamins, thus providing better nourishment for bones and teeth. The little *Orohippus* responded to these changes by increasing in size and reaching a height of 40cm (16in).

By the Oligocene period, some 40 to 25 million years ago, the primitive *Equidae* had disappeared from Europe, but the *Equus* family continued to develop in what was later to be the New World of America. Two genera, *Epihippus* and *Mesohippus*, lived in herds in the forests of the central, eastern and southern areas of the land mass that became the continent of the Americas. They varied in height from 51 to 71cm (20 to 28in) and began to take on a shape nearer that of a recognizably horse-like creature. The legs became longer, the withers and shoulders more pronounced, although still lower than the croup; the neck became longer and more muscular, and a short mane appeared.

The development of the hoof
Whereas the four-toed feet of *Orohippus* had been able to support its slight body as it browsed through soggy woodland, the taller, heavier *Epihippus* and *Mesohippus* needed a much stronger foot. Gradually one toe disappeared and the remaining three became more elongated, the middle toe especially, but all three toes were still functional and reached the ground. This development, together with the growth of harder pads, enabled these primitives to begin to acquire one of the horse's most important and exciting attributes: that of speed. It is interesting to note that the modern equine embryo at six weeks of age still has this three-toed conformation.

During the Miocene period, 25 to 10 million

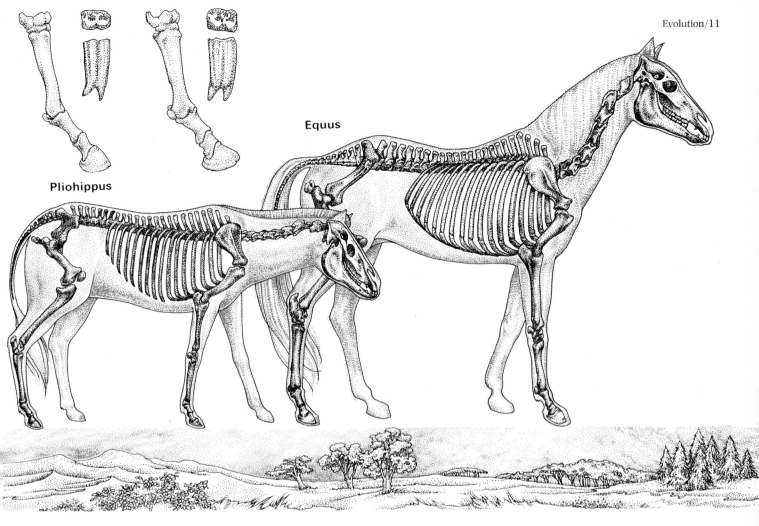

Pliohippus

Equus

years ago, the forests became thicker and larger and the plains more lush with vegetation. The small bands of primitive ponies had yet to start their long, arduous journey to Eurasia but herds of *Parahippus* and *Merychippus*, animals with straight, strong backs, standing at 92cm (37in), did reach the east and west coasts of North America, while others wandered as far north as the Rockies, and south to what is now the Panama Canal. *Merychippus* was one of the first members of the *Equus* family to take to the plains and become a predominantly grazing animal. The most important new tools of *Merychippus* were its high-crowned teeth with a good cement covering, which were better suited for cropping grass. The need for increased speed over firmer ground also forced *Parahippus* and *Merychippus* to make greater use of their central toe; eventually this became bigger and harder with a smaller toe set to either side. By the end of the Miocene period, the outer toe had almost disappeared.

Between five and two million years ago during the Pliocene period, two more advanced members of the *Equus* family emerged in Europe, Asia and North Africa. These were *Hipparion* and *Pliohippus*, taller at some 113cm (45in) and more angular than their earlier cousins. In stature and form, they were nearer the modern horse and it is from them that the solid hoof evolved. The modern horse in fact appears to have developed

from this stock, any remaining modification taking place between the Pliocene and Pleistocene eras. This group of horse-like animals is regarded as an indicator for the Pleistocene. In the South Americas, severe cold drove the herds to eventual extinction. But in Europe a recognizable, grass-eating, solid-hoofed pony, varying in size according to its environment, was awaiting domestication.

After the Ice Ages
It seems that only four basic types of equine survived the Ice Ages, the horse (*Equus caballus*), the ass (*Equus asinus*), the zebra (*Equus hippotigris*), and the onager (*Equus hemionus*).

The glaciers which retreated some ten thousand years ago left behind them a shifting pattern of seas, mountains, plains, forests, deserts, rivers and plateaux. The soil and vegetation of each region varied in vitamin and mineral content and thus affected the size and development of the grazing creatures that lived off the land. A temperate climate and a medium altitude tended to encourage a greater size of horse, and a severe climate and a high altitude tended to produce ponies rather than horses.

The horse family, wandering the four corners of Eurasia, divided into two basic groups: the Northern or Coldblood horse and the Southern or Warmblood horse.

Above: *The most important dental change seems to have occurred in* Merychippus *and around this time the* Equus *made the transition from browser to grazer.*

The story of the horse is not just the story of a survivor; it is also the story of an adventurous traveller, both solitary and as the companion of man on expeditions of discovery, conquest and migration. Some 100 million years ago the present-day land masses were joined together as two massive super-continents. But forces deep inside the earth caused these super-continents to break up and fragments of land drifted apart, taking with them various groups of mammals.

Between ten million and one million years ago, as the Americas drifted away from Europe and Africa, the ancestors of the modern camel and the horse crossed the remaining land bridge across the Bering Strait into Eurasia from the Americas. *Plesippus* was the first true solid-hoofed member of the *Equus* family to travel through or settle in Northern India, China, northern and southern Europe, central Europe, North Africa and the Middle East. As the world experienced these gradual climatic, geographical and geophysical changes, so six great zones of animal life emerged. Each zone, the Nearctic realm, Neotropical realm, Palaearctic realm, Ethiopian realm, Oriental realm and Australian realm, was divided by natural barriers of oceans, deserts, or mountains. The wandering herds of *Equus* tended to stay within these bounds and thus there emerged a distinct collection of varying types. Environmental factors determined the type and shape of the horse or pony that developed.

Northern and Southern Horses
Soil structure varied enormously from one area to another, its mineral and vitamin content dictating the feed-value of the herbage growing on it. An area with heavy rainfall and good natural drainage by means of rivers, streams, or low-lying coastlines produced lush green grass and forests. The herds of primitive horses living in such areas did not have to move very far in their daily search for food. So developed the *Equus giganteus*, a heavy, ungainly, slow-moving horse that lived in Scandinavia about ten thousand years ago. The type is also known as the Forest or Diluvial Horse, whose remains have been found in north-west Germany and it is thought that this could be the ancestor of the Shire and Percheron horses of today.

But in an area like the Zagros Mountains that enclosed the eastern and upper Anatolian Plateau, the climate was comparatively dry. Herbage was sparser so the herds of early horses had to be constantly on the move in search of food. Wild cereals grew in these areas, and they provided a natural high-protein diet which resulted in the development of a lighter, more agile and more alert type of horse.

All the herds of horses and ponies living in the Far East, India, the Asiatic steppes, North Africa,

Above: *The Onager, half pony, half ass, was used by early settled Man.*

Above: *The Ass, one of the oldest members of the Equus family.*

Above: *The African zebra, probably a relation of the ancient Onager.*

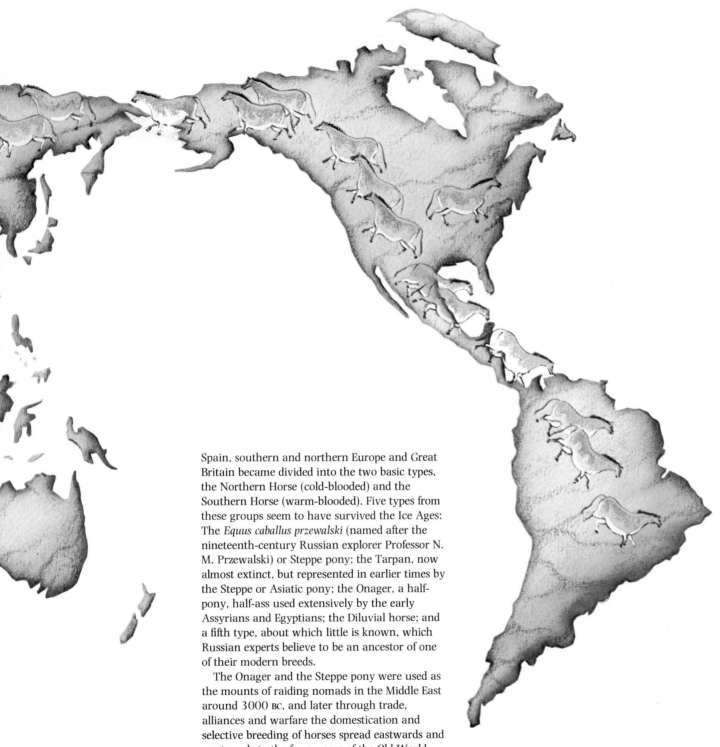

Spain, southern and northern Europe and Great Britain became divided into the two basic types, the Northern Horse (cold-blooded) and the Southern Horse (warm-blooded). Five types from these groups seem to have survived the Ice Ages: The *Equus caballus przewalski* (named after the nineteenth-century Russian explorer Professor N. M. Przewalski) or Steppe pony; the Tarpan, now almost extinct, but represented in earlier times by the Steppe or Asiatic pony; the Onager, a half-pony, half-ass used extensively by the early Assyrians and Egyptians; the Diluvial horse; and a fifth type, about which little is known, which Russian experts believe to be an ancestor of one of their modern breeds.

The Onager and the Steppe pony were used as the mounts of raiding nomads in the Middle East around 3000 BC, and later through trade, alliances and warfare the domestication and selective breeding of horses spread eastwards and westwards to the far corners of the Old World. Through the centuries, the horse became many things to many people: a prized possession, an essential vehicle, a god-symbol, a focus for man's need for myth, magic and power.

Return to the New World

Some forty thousand years ago Mongoloid groups crossed the Bering Strait going east to the Americas. Several hundred years later their descendants, both nomadic and town-dwelling Indian tribes, had spread across the continent south to Tierra del Fuego and high into the Arctic Circle. They were clever hunters, brave warriors and fine craftsmen, but because they were isolated from the emergent world in Eurasia, they had no horse-culture. In the sixteenth century, however, the Spanish *conquistadores* won possession of Mexico. The Europeans brought with them horses, guns and sophisticated tools which completely altered the traditional Indian way of life. The Plains Indians proved to be natural horsemen and successful hunters and they provided some of the greatest cavalry the world has ever seen. The horse had travelled through time and evolution to be brought back to the prairies by man.

Early training & trading

Above: *A west Asian horsebit with elaborate cheekpieces dating from 900–700 BC. It was most probably used as an Onager driving bit.*

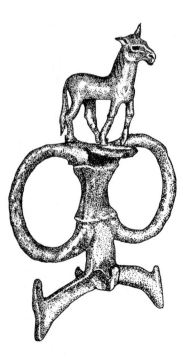

Above: *A harness rein-ring from Ur c. 2500 BC.*

We do not really know where or when the first steps were taken to domesticate the wild horse. We do know that an agricultural revolution took place over many thousands of years, a gradual progression through trial and error. For a variety of reasons men made the transition from hunting and gathering economies to those based on agriculture and animal husbandry. Townships speedily developed as communities came together to organize agricultural activities and security.

At Catal Hüyük, one of the earliest Neolithic settlements in Anatolia, archaeological evidence indicates that cattle, sheep, goats and dogs were domesticated first and that much later the horse became the centre of a major cult.

Meanwhile, out on the plains, nomadic pastoralists were developing a trading economy in livestock. In the region east of the Caspian Sea known as the Kirgiz Steppes, there are extensive grasslands varying in fertility from arid areas in Turkestan to rich prairies in south-western Siberia. It is thought that somewhere in these plains, a very long time ago, horse-culture began.

The first horse-dealers

It was from these vast steppes of Asia that bands of marauding Indo-European peoples wandered over the Old World, making lightning raids on townships or trading missions. Many of them settled in the various lands to work as mercenaries and horse-trainers. Other groups went further afield into India and China. These first horse-dealers not only sold horses to kings and princes, but also arranged for grooms and riders to stay behind and teach their clients how to handle the animals. These horsemen were possibly the first owners of the 'Heavenly Horses' said to be worth a Chinese Emperor's ransom.

Nomadic people left ample evidence of their horse-culture along the trade routes that stretched from China to ancient Britain. The Chertomlyk Vase, which can be seen in the British Museum, depicts the nomads' method of 'natural' horse-taming by reward and encouragement. Fine snaffle bits made of wood have been found, and even when they discovered iron these ancient nomads still made and used simple snaffle bits. One of the most famous examples was found in the River Thames, in Great Britain, and some fine bits dating from 2000 BC, beautifully carved from bone, were found in southern Russia. A tradition of intelligent horsemastership thus existed long before the urban civilizations were to leave us written evidence of their knowledge of equestrian techniques. These traditions continued through to the Celts and the Proto-Greeks, and in later times the Goths, Vandals, Huns, Moors and Mongols.

By 3000 to 2000 BC men were driving the horse but not yet riding it. The wheel had been invented, although it was the Hurrians of North Syria, bartering their horses for fine silks, grain and jewellery, who first used a spoked wheel that revolved around its own hub on a greased axle.

The first written records which throw some light on the way horse-culture developed among the townspeople of the Old World date from 3000 BC. The clay tablets and temple registers of the southern cities of the Sumerians show the animals entering and leaving rich temple estates. A legal code was drawn up concerning the theft of cattle and other beasts, and a letter from the royal chancellery lists the horses and mules (most probably onagers) purchased for the royal stables. The general attitude towards animals in ancient Mesopotamia does not seem to have been any kinder than it is today in many parts of the world, but horses seem to have been treated with a respect suggesting that they were imported and very expensive.

The first treatise on horsemanship

In 1500 BC Kikkulis, horsemaster to the kings of the Hittites, established the first written rules of horsemanship and stable management. He had chipped out on tablets the principles governing the training and feeding of stabled horses and wisely counselled the use of 'kindness to gain co-operation' rather than force. The rise, after 1350 BC, of the Assyrian Empire and Urartu, the main centres of which fell within the area now called Turkestan and Armenia, depended greatly on the horse. The Urartians, direct descendants of nomadic barbarians, were a highly organized people, cultured and natural horsemen. They were locked in mortal combat with the Assyrians almost from the beginnings of their rise to power. Horses were plentiful in Urartu and local horses were bred from stock. Much of the conflict between Urartu and Assyria arose from disputed control of trade routes through Parsua. It was through these that the Assyrians imported horses from the Medean steppe for their massive cavalry units.

In early Egypt the horse was reserved for the privileged classes only, the ox and the ass being the beasts of burden and haulage. This custom also prevailed in ancient Greece; horses were rare on the streets of Athens. The Greeks rode and drove horses and their techniques, like most of their art, were inherited from the Mycenaeans. Their horses came from Thessaly. Xenophon, the Greek officer, philosopher, politician and horsemaster, wrote his treatise on the training of cavalry horses in 401 BC. With the emergence of the Roman Empire there was an upsurge in the use of horses, despite the basic reliance of the Roman armies on infantry. The horse-culture of the military that resulted was to last right up to this century.

Left: *A dramatic horse race decorates a vase. Horse racing was part of the Olympic Games over 2,600 years ago. Although the bridles are of a relatively advanced design, the riders have no saddles or stirrups.*

Below: *The hunt of Assurbanipal, King of Assyria. The Assyrian reliefs contain the finest representations of horses in ancient art.*

'Art for art's sake'

Above: *The Duke of Newcastle, one of England's most successful 17th-century riding masters.*

Above right: *The famous* Cadre Noir *of the French cavalry, giving one of their fascinating displays of classical equitation.*

In Renaissance courts of the emerging countries of modern Europe, 'military' horse-culture was being developed by the high-booted 'scientific' horsemen with their luxurious saddles and heavily ornamented stirrup-irons. The chivalrous cavalryman, on his muscular, thick-set horse, was still killing his enemy with as much efficiency as the Assyrian, but this activity was carried out with more style and manners than before.

The Riding Master now became one of the most influential members of the royal court through his mastery of riding and training horses. *Haute école*, with its graceful but unnatural movements, was the system for training a *cheval de guerre* as well as being an entertainment for aristocrats.

The first impetus for the scientific movement came from Italy. The sixteenth-century riding-master Federico Grisone was the originator of artificial equitation. It was Signor Grisone, from his riding school in Naples, who first advocated the use of the combined aids. The aids are the signals given by the rider through his legs, hands and position in the saddle by which he communicates with and controls his horse. Although it could not be said that Grisone with his severe methods and bridles excelled in the 'kindness and co-operation' philosophy expounded by Kikkulis and Xenophon, he was one of the first exponents of the use of the rider's lower leg as an 'accelerator' instead of the sharp

spur. His teachings spread throughout the courts of England and Europe. The Neapolitan School, and its first off-shoot the Spanish School, became the system for training the *cheval d'école* and the *cheval de guerre*.

Many famous riding masters followed Grisone, some of them continuing his teachings, others introducing their own variations. Pignatelli became a director of the Neapolitan School and was one of the first to use pillars as an aid to advanced training. The horses were tied up between two pillars, sometimes mounted, sometimes not, and forced to arch their necks and increase the activity of their hind legs.

Antoine de Pluvinel (1555–1620), riding instructor to Louis XIII, was one of the few to teach kindness and co-operation as the basis to good riding. William Cavendish (1592–1676), an ardent royalist, established a famous riding school at Antwerp during a period of exile, and published there his first work on horsemanship entitled *Méthode et Invention Nouvelle de dresser les Chevaux*. He accepted a peerage as Duke of Newcastle and retired from public life to devote the rest of his days to his estates and the training of horses. François de la Guérinière (1688–1751) was one of the last great directors of the riding school at Naples and the first man to say that *all* horses must be given training in obedience and flexibility. These were the sources of the techniques used in later military riding academies, and the foundation of what we now call dressage (from the French word, *dresser*, to train), a demonstration of the horse's suppleness and discipline.

Today we can see examples of classical riding and training as it was performed in the sixteenth century and earlier, in the methods of the Spanish Riding School in Vienna and the Cadre Noir at Saumur.

As the use of fire-arms became more widespread, so the *cheval de guerre* and the *cheval d'école* began to lose their military importance. The great nations were still at war of course, but cavalry became less and less decisive on the battlefield. For hundreds of years there was little change or innovation in equitation, but by the turn of the nineteenth century the military riding academies of Saumur, Pinerolo, Madrid, Weedon and West Point, with their rigid equitation manuals, became the guardians of mainstream riding techniques. Thanks to them the horse has returned to its natural habitat, the great outdoors, for sport has taken the place of warfare as a major justification for keeping and breeding the animal.

The forward seat
One dashing young man from the home of classical equitation, Italy, was to cause a riding revolution that was to underpin the theories and science of modern competitive riding. This man was Captain Federico Caprilli (1868–1907). Caprilli was an Italian cavalry officer and an instructor at the Cavalry School in Pinerolo, in 1904. As an impatient young lieutenant he worked out a new and greatly simplified *sistema*, later known as the Italian Seat, the Forward Impulse and finally the Forward Seat (*Principi di Equitazione di Campagna*, 1901). This was to take equitation away from the established traditions of severe bits, the violent jerking of the horse's head, the excessive use of wheeled-spurs and the horseman's dependence on the reins. The principle of Caprilli's system was that the horse should be interfered with as little as possible and that, although under the rider's control, it should move with the freedom and natural balance of a riderless animal.

The Forward Seat spread all over the world. West Point and Madrid rewrote their army riding manuals and produced some of the finest international riders the world will ever see.

This then is the background to the dramatic forms of entertainment and equestrian sport we see today. European riders have remained the masters of the art of dressage and the West Germans, British, Americans, and Australians now dominate the world of showjumping and Three-Day Eventing.

Above: *One of the famous Lipizzaner stallions of the Spanish Riding School in Vienna. In their 18th-century bi-corn hats, brown frock coats and high riding boots, the riders and their horses give a display of classical equitation based on principles that have existed for over 400 years.*

The horse in agriculture

The prehistoric settlers in the great valleys of the Nile and the Euphrates, fertile regions with ample vegetation, made the earliest known transition from hunting and gathering economies to agricultural economies. They harnessed the ox and the ass (originally the onager) to plough their rich fields.

Horses were not used for several reasons. First, they had to be imported, making them expensive. Second, no heavy breed of horse was known to these early people and the horses they did know were too small and light for work on the land. Third, the horseshoe had not been thought of, so the horse would have been of little use on certain types of land. Fourth, the horse-collar had not been invented, although a light breast-girth was used for chariot horses.

For many centuries slow-moving oxen were considered the best animals for all farming enterprises in most parts of the world. Even when horses had largely replaced oxen, however, the southern states of America and some Latin countries considered the half-bred cousin of the horse, the mule, far superior to both. Horses were initially bred on farms to be sold for use in war and for transport. Teams of oxen were still being used in some parts of Britain as late as 1911.

The horse began to be used on the land after the invention of the horse-collar, an achievement attributed by many experts to the Chinese. It does not seem to have come into general use in Europe until medieval times, although the earliest-known illustration of horses being used for land cultivation is to be found in the famous Bayeux Tapestry representing the landing of William the Conqueror in England in 1066. The tapestry shows a farm worker with a horse-drawn harrow.

Horse power

At first horses were used for ploughing, harrowing and carting, while the farmhands did the sowing, reaping, haymaking and threshing. Ploughing was the most important job of the horseman's year, for on it depended the sowing of the seed and the quality of the harvest. In Europe a horse, or pair of horses, pulled a single-furrow plough at a speed of about one and a half miles (2·4km) an hour, guided by the ploughman walking behind.

With the development of newly-discovered continents, vast acreages came under cultivation in America, Canada, Australia and New Zealand. Multi-furrow ploughs were developed with a seat from which the ploughman guided his big team of horses. One man with a five-horse team pulling a two-furrow plough could till six acres a day. Thirty-horse teams pulling combine harvesters were once a common sight on the vast, fertile prairies.

Left: *The heavy horse was, in fact, quite late on the agricultural scene. Until the invention of the horse-collar in the Middle Ages, it was oxen and mules that worked on the land.*

Right: *Harvesting the Californian way. The vast acreages of the New World demanded more power and machines like this combine harvester photographed being pulled by nearly thirty horses about eighty years ago.*

Below: *A 'four-horsepower' threshing machine.*

Thousands of heavy horses were exported from Europe and Great Britain. The Clydesdale became the favourite choice of Canadian and Australian farmers. The Percheron was very popular in America for many years until the Belgian heavy horse was imported at the beginning of this century.

With the invention in the late eighteenth century of the horse-walk, otherwise known as the horse-whin, horses could provide the power for barn machinery, threshing, elevators and other stationary machines as well as for ploughing, cultivation, sowing, reaping and carting.

The horse-walk was constructed completely of iron and consisted of a crown wheel 90cm (36in) in diameter, mounted at ground level with two long arms extending outwards to which the horses were harnessed. As the horses walked round and round turning the crown wheel, the machinery was driven via a pinion wheel and gearbox and ground-level drive-shaft.

The horse-whin was universally used for over a century and underwent considerable development in the United States and Australia, where whins of up to eight-horsepower drove the big barn machinery.

Perhaps the oldest role the horse has played in agriculture has been in the controlling and herding of livestock. About 160 years ago light stock horses were bred in New South Wales from stallions and mares imported by the first settlers

who were to farm the new lands of Australia. These horses became known as Walers. Many Australian farmers still prefer to use horses on their sheep and cattle stations. In the United States and Canada the ranchers and arable farmers developed special breeds of horses to suit their particular demands.

The Canadian Cutting Horse has a reliable performance record on the ranch, while the American Quarter Horse, with its good temperament and stocky physique is ideally suited to controlling the big beef herds of the western states of America. Two other excellent working horses are the Kentucky or American Saddle Horse used by the southern farmers and the Tennessee Walking Horse, a breed that can half run, half walk which was first used for inspecting crops. The latter's work on plantations gave it the alternative name of Plantation Walking Horse.

Fortunately there are still enough heavy horse enthusiasts throughout the world to keep the breeds alive, while in some parts of the world the horse has never stopped working on the land. In the late 1960s there was a worldwide revival of interest in the working horse and now, some ten years later, the demand for heavy and light working horses exceeds the supply. The agricultural horse will never regain its previous supremacy, but the high cost of fuel and the predictions of oil shortages have encouraged parts of the world to revert to horse power for specific jobs on the farm and ranch.

The horse in war

Above: *A bronze statuette of Alexander the Great. He rode mainly Thessalian-bred horses.*

Top: *This section of the Bayeux Tapestry shows Harold and a hunting party with its pack of hounds. Hunting is one of the oldest equestrian sports and still thrives today in Britain, Ireland, America, Canada, Australia and parts of Europe.*

Above right: *Medieval knights in battle, from the 14th-century Codex Balduineus. Although horses were an important element of armies, the Middle Ages saw equitation and horsebreeding drop to one of its deepest declines.*

Bottom right: *A German cavalry patrol in World War I. Many of the breeds of light horse in use today originated from bloodlines used in modern cavalry.*

During the fourth millenium BC, the horse became an accepted part of the daily lives of men in both urban and pastoral cultures. Evidence comes from Sumeria, where a heavy war-car was pulled by onagers by 3000 BC, and from the Tripolye culture in the Ukraine, from 3500 BC. Knowledge of horse-keeping spread during the great migrations of the Indo-European peoples from about 1900–1000 BC. Bands of people such as the Hittites, Hurrians and Iranians disrupted the more settled life of the early civilizations and their trade routes.

In times of war the horse had a subsidiary role at first. Warriors from the cities and townships would drive their horses or onagers and chariots to the battlefield, climb out, fight the battle and, if still able, climb back into their chariots and return home. Some leaders even employed a driver to take them into battle, for most of the early civilizations considered riding a horse to be undignified.

Evidence of riding becomes more frequent towards the end of the second millenium. There is a Hurrian relief from Tell Halaf, about 1400 BC, which shows a mounted warrior, and Mycenean potsherds from Ugarit, in Syria, show formations of riders. Assyrian artists have left some of the earliest graphic examples of the ridden horse being used as an organized military unit. The Hittites and the Assyrians were the first to field thousands of well-disciplined charioteers and mounted men. From 1350 BC onwards empires expanded or disappeared under the charging hooves of squadrons of charioteers and cavalrymen.

Scythian horsemen were well known to the classical world, but by the fifth century BC the Greeks were becoming pre-eminent, especially after they had blocked the expansion of Persian power. Like the Romans later, the Greeks tended to place their warring strength in legions of infantrymen, using the horse, chariot and wagon to supply the fighting men with transport and communications. The all-conquering armies of Alexander the Great proved an exception to this rule, Alexander himself immortalizing his own steed, Bucephalus, by naming a city after him in India. The Romans, however, lost touch with Alexander's earlier lead, and depended more on infantry muscle in their conquest. They were surprised by the effectiveness of the chariot when they invaded ancient Britain. Like the Greeks, the Roman officer-classes liked to see themselves portrayed astride muscular snorting steeds.

The Roman Empire was finally divided in 363 AD under pressure of barbarian movements, and successful invasions, led by the Visigoths, of Vandals, Saxons, Franks, Burgundians and Ostrogoths soon followed. A generation afterwards the continent of Europe came under the menace of Attila the Hun. The Huns were a basically Mongoloid mixture of nomads from Central Asia, and were the most feared and ruthless horse-warriors of the time. Their steeds went into the fray wearing protective rope 'bandages' on their front legs. These pagan horsemen were defeated only at Châlons, 140km (86 miles) east of Paris, by the first heavy cavalry of the Visigoths under their king, Theodoric, who was in league with the Franks and the Roman legions.

At the beginning of the eighth century, after the death of Mohammed, Berbers and Arabs swept across the plains and mountains of North Africa to invade Spain. These forward-riding Islamic armies, mounted on light, fast, hot-blooded eastern horses, were soon joined by other peoples, also Muslims. Together these Moors, as they became known, created vast empires from Spain to the River Ganges. The success of the Moors owed much to their agile eastern horses, on which they could attack and manoeuvre with speed. By crossbreeding with the indigenous horses of the conquered lands they passed through, these animals influenced the development of many of the native breeds of Europe as they are today. Some five centuries later the nomadic hordes of another famous race of natural horsemen, the Mongols, reduced the vast empires of Islam to ruins, leaving millions of corpses in their wake.

For centuries the cavalry was the most powerful force of war although dominance swung back to the infantry from time to time. For

example in 1066 the English infantry remained unbroken for several hours when opposing the charging Norman cavalry at Hastings. William the Conqueror's horsemen were forced to throw their light lances through the air like javelins. Subsequently the heavier lance and the cumbersome armour of the Middle Ages evolved to reassert the superiority of the cavalry. This was again undermined by the development of the long-bow shown, for example, at Crécy in 1346.

After the Middle Ages

Eventually the light and the heavy horse had to give way to some extent to man's inventiveness in warfare. The bow, the pike and the musket played an increasingly important role as did the cannon and the tank later. Ships were built to explore and conquer other parts of the world, notably the Americas. The Spaniards introduced horses and guns to the North American Indians, descendants of the Mongoloid people that had crossed from Asia to America centuries before. Although the Indian on horseback made a superb hunter and warrior, by the mid-1800s the American cavalry and the repeating rifle reigned supreme.

Before the colonists won the American War of Independence (1775–1783) and the white settlers discovered the goldfields of California, the Indians dominated the plains with their spectacular horsemanship. For a long time the Indian rode without a saddle, using a thong around his horse's lower jaw for control. The Indian brave and his horse moved as one; the rider would slide down the side of his horse to hide from his enemy and shoot from under its neck.

In Europe, Napoleon's spectacular rise to power was almost completely due to his brilliant use of cavalry. But in 1815 his French cavalry met their match in the British and Prussian cavalry led by the Duke of Wellington, in the battle of Waterloo, which left 45,000 dead and wounded.

One of the last, and certainly one of the most romanticized important cavalry charges was the infamous charge of the Light Brigade during the Crimean War in 1854, where mistakes of judgement and communication combined to cause terrible slaughter.

In *The River War* the young Winston Churchill described the Lancers' charge at Omdurman, in the Sudan, as two living walls crashing together. In two minutes, 65 men, 5 officers and 119 horses had been killed or wounded.

The Australian Waler, one of the finest saddle horses in the world, served at Waterloo, in the Crimea, and in India, Palestine and Syria during World War I. By the time of World War II, however, the horse had fortunately moved behind the battle-lines in most armies.

The horse in industry and transport

Above: *The Road Coach or Stage Coach. In order to attract business the coaches were often painted in bright colours with the details of their journey and stopping places marked on them.*

Above right: *The grim world of the miner and pit pony. The implementation of 'lift cages' at collieries in the 19th century enabled the use underground of animals such as Shetland, Welsh, Dartmoor, Fell, Norwegian and Iceland ponies. But later mechanization made them redundant.*

The huge juggernauts that thunder day and night along the motorways, autobahns and freeways of our world are the modern versions of heavy land transport. Before the invention of the petrol engine or the steam engine, the pack-horse trains of the sixteenth to eighteenth centuries, with their massive lumbering wagons, were the lifelines of a nation's trade.

The Romans, with their efficient road system, were the first to make horse-powered transport and communications a vital part of their economy. In the cities, too, horses played their part. The Rome of 21 BC had a fire service of 600 men: fire-fighting equipment would be rushed to a fire on a horse-drawn *currus*, or tender, while the firemen ran behind.

The horse became essential to trade in the Middle Ages with the adoption of the horse-collar which enabled it to haul loads of three tons or more, deliver tradesmen's goods, drag timber from the forests and generally increase the economic mobility of society.

One of the most beneficial innovations that horse-drawn transport brought to life in the nineteenth century was the national and international postal service. In the days before railways some 140 long-distance mail coaches carried mail to all parts of Britain. All outward-bound coaches from London left promptly at eight o'clock and, except for changing horses at staging-posts, they travelled non-stop to their destination. All the coaches belonged to the Postmaster-General but they were pulled by teams of horses owned by 'jobmasters'.

Jobmasters maintained very large stables and supplied a variety of horses on contract hire to government departments: the Post Office, the Fire Service and the Police, as well as to private companies and individuals.

In the country big, heavy, wide-wheeled vehicles called stage-wagons were used to transport goods. The first to offer a regular service ran between Shrewsbury and London carrying a five-ton load. The roads were so bad that it took an eight-horse team eight days to complete the journey.

Meanwhile in America, the famous Conestoga wagon had been designed to carry freight over long distances. It originated in Pennsylvania and had a boat-shaped body with a canvas hood. It was the forerunner of the lighter prairie schooner used by early pioneers to open up the West.

Barge-horse, vanner, pit pony and bus horse
The development of canals revolutionized industrial transport. Between 1792 and 1820 over 6,400 kilometres (4,000 miles) of inland waterways were completed in Britain therefore greatly improving freight handling. The barge-horse, which continued to be used until well into the twentieth century, was usually a smallish cart-horse of Shire breeding, which, once trained, became highly skilled. Pulling a barge with a 50-ton load aboard by means of a long tow-rope, it would walk the tow-path unaided, knowing every lock and tunnel on the route.

The railways also used a heavy horse to shunt railway wagons and carriages, and for pulling wagons along factory spur lines. They also employed many thousands of lighter horses for delivery and carrier work. These were called vanners and usually worked in pairs to pull big covered vans.

A most important servant to industry before mechanization was the pit pony, which replaced the women and boys whose job it was to pull coal tubs in harness to and from the workings.

Pit ponies were usually small, thick-set, strongly-built animals ranging from 11hh (112cm) to about 14.2hh (148cm) and they came mostly from the Welsh, Dale and Fell native breeds. They wore specially-designed compulsory protective harness and were stabled underground under the care of expert horsemen. Every colliery maintained a farm or had other arrangements whereby the ponies were brought to the surface in batches to enjoy a periodic rest.

A law of 1911 which controlled the hours of work, underground stable management and veterinary care ensured that the pit pony experienced the least hardship of all horses used in industry.

The golden age of coaching lasted only from 1815 to 1840, when the railways took over, but horse-drawn public transport continued to be used in towns until the internal combustion engine replaced it.

In country districts wagonettes of varying sizes became 'country buses' carrying from twelve to 28 passengers and pulled by pairs or unicorn (three-horse) teams of big half-bred horses.

In towns and cities horse-buses not only became bigger but increased in such numbers that traffic congestion was a constant headache. The London General Omnibus Company had no less than 15,000 horses and 1,200 buses operating; another company owned 5,000 horses and there were several smaller companies. The London bus trade alone required 5,000 replacement horses a year, many of which were of the half-bred cart-horse type.

Today heavy breeds like the Shire have a certain popularity and there are some commercial enterprises, particularly breweries in Britain and Europe, which claim that the heavy horse is still economical for certain short-haul transport.

Below: *Fire horses. Horse-drawn fire engines were widely used throughout the 1860s and 1870s in Great Britain and America.*

The horse in sport

The domestication of the horse increased the mobility and efficiency of society, and for some this gave more leisure time.

The earliest records show that a form of mounted polo was played in Persia in 525 BC. The nomadic peoples of the steppes played a similar game, often using a small animal as a 'ball', and this perhaps pre-dated the Persian game. In ancient China too, polo was one of the most popular games.

Hunting, as a sport, and racing are also among the oldest equestrian pursuits. The Romans and Greeks loved chariot-racing, which the Greeks included with flat-racing in the Olympic Games over 2,600 years ago. Flat-racing was also popular in Roman-occupied Britain.

From the eleventh century, jousting became the popular pastime of medieval knights. Indeed it seems that this was the first equestrian sport to produce its own book of rules, and there is evidence of friendly tournaments being played as far back as the ninth century.

In more modern times, as the techniques of warfare changed, new mounted sports evolved. The era of the great military riding academies, Saumur, Pinerolo, Madrid, Weedon and West Point, contributed to the creation of Three-Day Eventing. First known as the *Militaire*, the sport was an exercise in testing an officer's charger in fitness, obedience and endurance. Military riders were also the originators of showjumping, the first international show being staged in Turin, Italy, in 1901.

As the new settlers in the Americas and Australasia prospered, the cowboy and the stockman turned their skills into competition events. The rodeo is now America's second largest equestrian spectator sport after flat-racing, while Australians flock to barrel-racing and campdrafting contests.

The sport of kings

Organized racing started in England in the reign of James I with matches between two or three horses run in gruelling heats. Charles II created the round course and some form of organization at Newmarket in the east of England, now the headquarters of British flat-racing. In 1752 the Jockey Club was formed and is still the governing body of racing in Great Britain. The General Stud Book, which registers the family pedigree of full Thoroughbred horses, was started in 1791.

The oldest of the five British classic races is the St Leger, first run on Town Moor, Doncaster, in 1776, and open to three-year-old colts and fillies. The Blue Riband of the British turf is the Derby Stakes, first run on Epsom Downs in 1780. The race today is over 1½ miles (2·4km) and is open to three-year-olds. The first of the classics each season is the Two Thousand Guineas, a race for

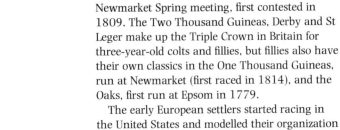

three-year-olds run over one mile (1·6km) at the Newmarket Spring meeting, first contested in 1809. The Two Thousand Guineas, Derby and St Leger make up the Triple Crown in Britain for three-year-old colts and fillies, but fillies also have their own classics in the One Thousand Guineas, run at Newmarket (first raced in 1814), and the Oaks, first run at Epsom in 1779.

Left: *Jousting was not only a way of fighting but also a popular spectator sport in the Middle Ages.*

Below left: *Peyton and Fashion in their great match for $20,000 on the Union Racecourse, Long Island, USA, on 13 May 1845. British settlers brought the Thoroughbred and the sport of racing to America.*

Below: *Trotting racing on snow in Austria. In many countries this is a sport as popular as flat-racing.*

The early European settlers started racing in the United States and modelled their organization on the British system, as have most countries in the world. The American Triple Crown is made up of three principal races for three-year-olds; the Belmont Stakes, the Kentucky Derby and the Preakness Stakes. The Belmont Stakes, run at Belmont Park, New York, was first run in 1867. Eight years later the Kentucky Derby was first run on the fast dirt-track of Churchill Downs in the heart of the famous Blue Grass Country, the main Thoroughbred breeding centre in America. Pimlico, situated in the State of Maryland, is the home of the Preakness Stakes, first run in 1873. The Coaching Club American Oaks, the Acorn Stakes and the Mother Goose Stakes make up the three-year-old fillies' Triple Crown.

There are some 700 race-tracks in Australia, and each state has its own classic programme for three-year-old colts and fillies. The Australasian Thoroughbred is celebrated throughout the world for its stamina. Most of the major races like the Melbourne Cup and Caulfield Cup are run over distances of $1\frac{1}{2}$ to 2 miles (2·4 to 3·2km).

Since World War II showjumping has grown into a major international sport with its own superstars, human and equine. National teams from many countries now travel the international circuit to such shows as Madison Square Garden (New York), the Royal Winter Fair (Toronto), the Royal Sydney Show, and the Royal International Show and Horse of the Year Show in Britain.

Three-Day Eventing or *Concours Complet* has been a popular sport in continental Europe for a long time but in recent years the British and American riders have gone right to the top of this demanding sport. Dressage, too, is more of a European sport but its following in America, Britain and Australia is growing each year.

The chariot-racing of ancient times was not all that different from the exciting modern sport of Trotting and Pacing. Harness-racing today, especially in America, France, Germany, Australia and New Zealand, is big business, with meetings held in vast stadiums, often at night under floodlights.

Throughout the world people are now enjoying the pleasure the horse can give, not only by participating in sporting events but also through riding holidays, pony trekking, trail-riding, driving marathons, ranch holidays and gypsy caravan holidays.

The horse in exploration

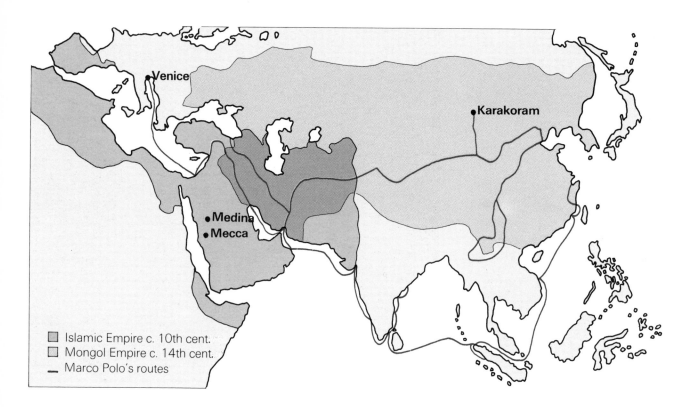

Islamic Empire c. 10th cent.
Mongol Empire c. 14th cent.
— Marco Polo's routes

Christopher Columbus (1451–1506)

The horse has accompanied man on voyages of exploration, conquest and pilgrimage since time immemorial. Often horses would be left behind by their masters when they reached their destination, or stolen by local tribesmen or even lost in a battle or a skirmish with robbers. Many returned to the wild state and formed herds while others interbred with indigenous horses or ponies.

The earliest explorations made with horses must have been the nomadic movements of the steppe peoples: clay models of sledges have been found in the Ukraine from about 2000 BC. The establishment of trade routes between the cultures of the Middle East, southern Europe, India and China must also have played a large role.

In the eighth century the Arabs surged out of the Arabian peninsula to conquer the Middle East and North Africa, spreading the Islamic faith. On arriving at the northern coast of Morocco they loaded their fine, light horses on to boats at Ceuta and set out to invade Spain, ultimately to establish the Ummayad Emirate, the empire of Islam that extended from the borders of China to the Atlantic Ocean. The warm-blooded eastern strain of horse, Arab and Barb, became one of the most sought-after mounts of the empire and wherever it went it left the influence of its potent bloodlines. The Moorish horsemasters themselves brought the science of selective horse-breeding, which they had practised for centuries, to the countries they conquered or to the people they converted to Islam.

But it was a very different type of horse that another army of religious soldiers was to take on the long ride in the opposite direction to the Holy Land. These were the European Christian knights who set out on the Crusades from France, Germany and Britain, motivated both by religious belief and the search for loot. They were mounted on slow-moving cob-type horses. Many of the knights found their cumbersome mounts no match for the agile eastern horses of the armies of such great Muslim leaders as Saladin. However, horses were of utmost importance to their crusader owners; since they were so difficult to replace, a knight who lost his horse would be reduced to the ranks of the foot soldiery.

In medieval Europe many people undertook a less hazardous mounted pilgrimage at some time in their lives to one of the great cathedrals which contained the relics of saints.

In the thirteenth century the Mongol armies of Genghiz Khan, mounted on the tough, hairy ponies of the steppes, swept out of the east to create the Mongol Empire. The Golden Horde, as they were known, seized control of a huge territory between the Adriatic and the China Sea, and created such terror that reverberations spread throughout Europe. Only one man appeared to think that these wild men could be befriended. Marco Polo, a Venetian merchant, set out eastwards in 1271 armed only with letters from the Pope and from Kublai, a Mongol ruler, which had been given to him by his father who had travelled east fifteen years earlier. Many of

The long journey taken by Marco Polo and his companions (left) was depicted on a 14th-century Catalan map (below). Marco Polo's account of his travels became the guide book of subsequent explorers.

the missionaries who accompanied him did not complete the journey, but Marco Polo trekked all the way to Peking. The journey of 14,000km (8,700 miles) took three-and-a-half years and crossed areas of Asia not seen by any other European until the twentieth century. Subsequent explorers took Marco Polo's book as their guide.

In 1492, as the last of the Moorish states in Europe fell, and its ruler, Abu Abd Allah or Boabdil, left Granada, Christopher Columbus was making his celebrated voyage to America.

Exploring the New World
The Spanish explorers, with their beautiful Andalusian horses, set up breeding centres in the West Indies. Then in 1519 the *conquistadore*, Hernando Cortés, took eleven Spanish and Pinto stallions and five mares (gelding was not practised in those days) to the American continent. The Mexican Indians and the tribes of the western plains of America quickly showed their talents for natural horsemanship. Some horses they found running wild after escaping, others they stole from white men or other tribes.

The Comanche were the greatest horse thieves of them all, and horse raiding soon became a way of life to the Plains Indians. For boys it was also a form of initiation into manhood. A youth had not proved himself a man until he had stolen a horse from an enemy. A horse was the Plains Indian's most prized possession and he created songs and poems in praise of its strength, endurance and courage.

European settlers soon followed the *conquistadores* to create new townships on the Atlantic seaboard, and they too brought horses. In Europe the horse was used mainly for riding but in the New World of the Americas horses had to be versatile. There was light farm work to be done, haulage and clearing of the forests, transportation, carriage work and saddle-work, and often one horse carried out several if not all these jobs on each homestead. The North American pioneers unexpectedly inherited some fine 'native' horses, left behind by the earlier Spanish explorers. They crossed these with good stallions imported from England and after generations of breeding, finally produced versatile types of horse. Many of the famous breeds of the United States, such as the Quarter Horse and the Morgan, evolved in this way.

It could be claimed that the reputation of the American West was built on the broad back of the Quarter Horse. This strong, stocky cattle horse was ideally suited to the rigorous frontier life. It could work all day and then be left to forage for itself at night. Although the name Quarter Horse is associated with the West it was, in fact, an easterner, brought by settler families in the 1840s when they streamed across the plains to California, Nevada and Oregon.

The Spanish had been to California in the 1700s but a severe drought had ravaged the coastal areas and forced them to abandon their horses. The horses survived and multiplied, and become known as the California mustangs.

Above: *The conquistadores and their horses were thought to be gods from the sea by the Mexican and South American Indians. Many, such as Cortés, used to attach bells to their horses to emphasize the legend.*

Hernando Cortés (1485–1547)

THE TYPES OF HORSE

Below: *Horse racing, the sport of kings and the downfall of princes.*

The horse family divides basically into eight different groups: the onager, an ass-like creature used as a pack animal and driving 'horse' by the ancients; the ass or donkey; the mule; the pony; the cob, an animal with the body of a horse and the legs of a pony; the zebra of Africa; the light horse and the heavy horse.

The light horse and the heavy horse are the two branches of the *equus* family dealt with in this section of the atlas. These are the two basic types common to most parts of the world. The light horse includes the Thoroughbred, the Arab, and the clean-bred riding ponies seen in the show rings of the world. All three are vital to the breeding programmes of the majority of equestrian nations today. The heavy horse was the working animal of the world both on land and on the highways. Before the Industrial Revolution it formed an important element of the economies of many countries.

But within this framework are many varying types which are not strictly speaking breeds, while many breeds of horse have been purposely taken to new environments. To save over-complication the story of the light horse and the heavy horse has separate sections.

The Thoroughbred and the Arab along with the Shire, Percheron and Clydesdale are found throughout the world. And many countries have developed types and varieties suitable to their own conditions and requirements from these and other breeds where there were no native breeds available or adaptable enough. Such breeding programmes continue today in many countries, especially where the incentives of racing and showjumping are strong.

A 'type' is a horse or pony developed through a mixture of selected bloodlines, such as Arab or Thoroughbred, to produce an animal suitable for a particular practical use but not meeting, perhaps, the strict definitions of a stud book, for example, the Hack and the Hunter or the original Australian Waler. The Hack is a riding horse often thoroughbred or near-thoroughbred with an unblemished and perfect conformation, and impeccable manners. For showing purposes the Hack is usually categorized as Large, 15hh–15.3hh (152–160cm); Small, 14.2hh–15hh (147–152cm) and Ladies, 14.2hh–15.3hh (147–160cm), suitable for a lady riding side-saddle. Some of these types may themselves become breeds if they are bred in isolation for long enough, as shown by the Australian Waler.

A breed is a light or heavy horse or pony either developed and registered in a stud book to strict bloodlines or an animal indigenous to a particular country with a pure-bred bloodline and mental and physical characteristics constant throughout the generations.

The Light Horse

Several different strains and varieties of light horse, riding pony and working horse are found in most countries of the world. In order to simplify a very complex subject, section II concentrates on the development of the sporting and working horse or pony found almost anywhere as a universal type or strain. Thoroughbred horses and Arab horses have been and continue to be the most influential in the creation of the modern sporting horse but to understand the development of these horses we must travel back about four thousand years.

Around that time horses used by the grassland cultures of the steppes were bred from stock, with each mating and crossing carefully recorded. The warm-blooded Barb and Arab were then introduced to the urban centres of the Near East.

Eastern stallions, from Constantinople, were first imported to England in the reign of James I and later Charles II encouraged the importation of more eastern stallions and mares. Three in particular entered the record books as the creators of the Thoroughbred. These were the Byerley Turk, the Darley Arabian and the Godolphin Arabian. These three stallions can be found in the male line of all Thoroughbreds but to say that they created the modern Thoroughbred is over-simplifying a very complicated process. For in the breeding of racehorses, and almost all clean-bred strains of horses and ponies, the various in-crosses and out-crosses are just as important as the more apparent sire and dam line.

Bloodstock historians seem to divide into two basic schools of thought, those who say that the Thoroughbred's most formative influence was the Arab and those who stress the Englishness of the breed. The Duke of Newcastle, for instance, one of the leading stud owners of the 17th century, was convinced that eastern blood was the best, and most of his brood mares were of foreign origin. But around the same time Gervase Markham, the son of a Nottinghamshire breeder, was convinced that foreign blood was unnecessary.

The answer is probably somewhere between the two views, for fine examples of running horses were bred in Britain, especially in Yorkshire, long before the fashion started for importing eastern stallions. The Thoroughbred might best be defined as an admixture of eastern blood and home-bred native stock, influenced by the favourable climate and soil of England.

However, eastern-blood influence did produce the first truly great racehorse. Flying Childers was bred by Leonard Childers of Doncaster in 1741 and described as 'the fleetest horse that ever ran at Newmarket, or, as generally believed, was ever bred in the world'. Flying Childers was a son of the Darley Arabian out of a mare (Betty Leedes) that traced back to Arabian and Barb blood.

Flying Childers was not the only famous son of the Darley Arabian. Bulle Rocke went to the United States in 1730 and so did Medley, Messenger and Diomed with the later importations. These dynasties were foremost in creating the mighty American Thoroughbred. British thoroughbred stock was also imported into France in the mid-19th century, the French Thoroughbred being called the *pur sang anglais* in recognition. The British Thoroughbred stallion Rockingham was sent from South Africa to stand at stud in New South Wales and begin the long process of developing the Australian Thoroughbred.

The Thoroughbred's influence is found today in practically all native strains of sporting horses around the world and the Hanoverian and the Selle Français in particular are good examples of how thoroughbred blood can be used to improve a breed.

The influence of Arabian blood is equally important. The Arab can be found in most countries today either in the pure form, in an adapted form, or as the Anglo-Arab, but by modern standards the Arab horse tends to breed too small in height to meet the demands of competition riders and trainers. Yet the Arab has gained a well-deserved reputation as improver of other bloodlines. The classical Arab should be short-backed, with long sloping shoulders, a broad chest, finely textured mane, large widely-spaced eyes, broad forehead tapering to the muzzle with large nostrils, clean legs, well-defined tendons and a high-set tail.

There are many strains of Arabian horse today. Stud books of the breed are kept in Argentina, Australia, Britain, Bulgaria, Canada, Egypt, France, Holland, Hungary, Japan, Pakistan, Poland, Romania, South Africa, Spain, Turkey, the USA, and the USSR. One of the oldest strains is the Polish Arab, a clean-bred line first introduced to Poland in 1570. The Royal Jordanian Stud has built up a breeding farm of superb horses with traditional narrow muzzles and high-set tails. They are all recorded *asil* (pure-bred) and show the *mitbah*, the curve on the crest of the neck and the *fiblah*, the concave or dished profile of the head, more pronounced in mares.

In modern Arabia, Kehailan is the principal strain with large pear-shaped eyes and dark eyelids, the hallmarks of the pure Arab horse. The Arabian is one of the oldest established breeds in Australia and the Australian Arab Horse Society is now the fourth largest in the world. Some 11,000 pure-bred Arabians are registered each year in the United States and during the last decade Polish-bred horses and Egyptian bloodlines have been imported by breeders to stand at stud on farms from Maine to California.

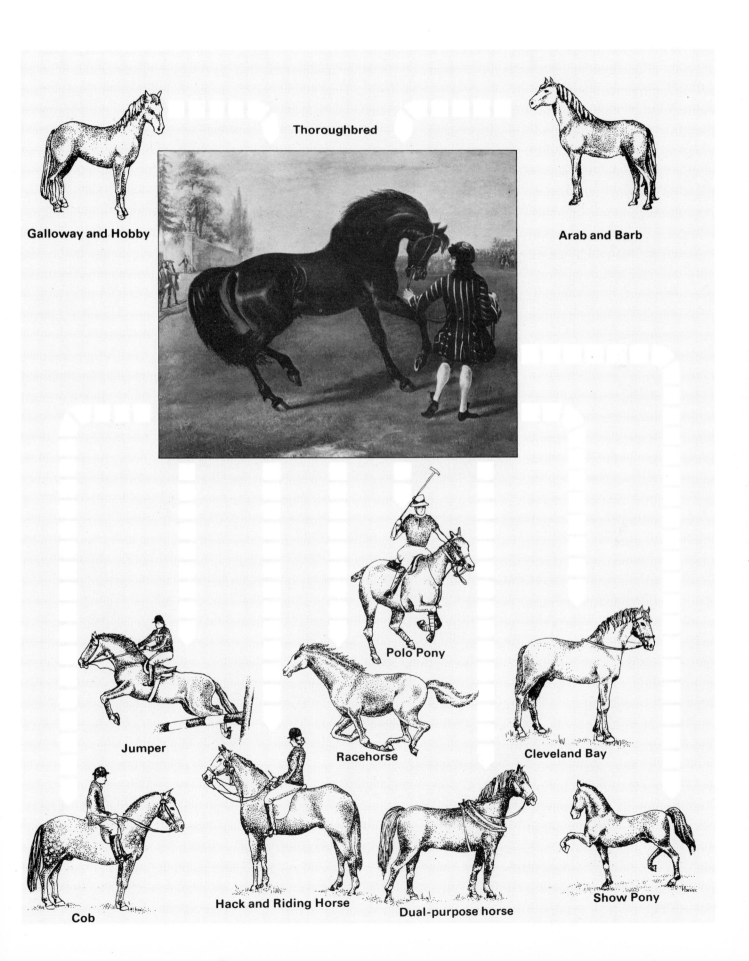

Galloway and Hobby

Thoroughbred

Arab and Barb

Polo Pony

Jumper

Racehorse

Cleveland Bay

Cob

Hack and Riding Horse

Dual-purpose horse

Show Pony

Famous examples

Bottom: *Lord Derby's Hyperion, winner of the English Derby and the St Leger in 1933. Standing only 15.1½ hh, no stallion has contributed more to the creation of the 20th-century racehorse than this small, good-natured animal.*

Below: *Eclipse, one of the finest racehorses of the 18th century. He did not start racing until he was five years old and was never beaten on the turf. He retired to stud in 1771.*

Secretariat

Over the years many Thoroughbreds have claimed the crown of greatness but one of the most successful three-year-olds in the history of flat-racing was the good-looking chestnut Secretariat. This American colt was bred by Mrs Penny Tweedy at her Meadow Stud, Virginia, sired by the great USA-bred Bold Ruler out of Something Royal in 1970. Secretariat was trained by French-Canadian Lucien Lauren at Belmont Park, New York, and ridden in all but his final race by Ron Turcotte. After a successful two-year-old career Secretariat took the American Triple Crown in 1973, the first horse to do so since the legendary Citation in 1948.

The colt, with a star on his forehead, won the Kentucky Derby in a record time of 1min 59⅗ secs before landing the Preakness Stakes and the third leg of the Triple Crown, the Belmont Stakes, by 31 lengths in track record time.

Secretariat finished his racing career winning the Canadian International Champion Stakes, bringing his total winnings to $1,316,808. The colt then went to stand as a stallion at the Claiborne Farm, Kentucky, syndicated to 32 breeders for over six million dollars.

Hyperion

The 'daddy-of-them-all' must have been Hyperion, for together with the stallion Nearco he

dominated classic bloodstock breeding in Great Britain in the middle of the 20th century. It is doubtful if any modern Thoroughbred has had the world-wide influence on breeding that the little Hyperion had. His name appears in the bloodlines of racehorses from Hong Kong to Florida.

This good-natured chesnut horse, standing only 15.1½hh (156cm), was bred by the 17th Earl of Derby in 1930. But what he lacked in inches he made up for in courage, perfect conformation and good action. Hyperion won the 1933 British Derby in the then record time of 2 mins 34 secs, from a field of 24 runners. Ridden by Tommy Weston and trained by George Lambton, he went on to take the Doncaster St Leger that year. He was leading sire of winners in England six times and two of his sons, Heliopolis and Alibhai, brought his bloodline into the American racehorse.

Arkle

The Duchess of Westminster's Arkle was one of the greatest steeplechasers in the history of the sport. He was foaled in 1957 and given the name Arkle after a Scottish mountain, like many of the Duchess of Westminster's favourite steeplechasers. Arkle was perhaps the best example of what the Anglo-Irish steeplechaser and jumping thoroughbred should look like. He was bred in County Dublin by the classically-bred stallion Archive out of a brilliant steeplechasing mare called Bright Cherry.

Arkle stood 16.2½hh (169cm) with a broad chest and deep body, the ideal conformation for a middle distance steeplechaser. In a brilliant career this equine superstar won 27 races worth £73,617 and was placed seven times in the other eight races he contested. In the hands of Pat Taaffe, one of the finest jump jockeys ever produced in Ireland, Arkle won the Cheltenham Gold Cup three times, in 1964, 1965 and 1966. A racing injury in 1966 forced him into retirement which he passed at his owner's stud in Ireland for the rest of his days.

Nautical

America's famous horse with the 'flying tail', Nautical was a classical example of mixed breeding producing an athletic sporting horse. He was a Mexican three-quarter bred Quarter Horse mixed with thoroughbred blood and an attractive Palomino in colour. He was so popular with showjumping fans in America and Europe that Walt Disney made a feature film based on his life and sporting career. He was ridden by Baltimore horse-breeder Hugh Wiley and in 1959 they won the Horse and Hound Cup, the King George V Gold Trophy, the Daily Mail Cup and the Saddle of Honour at the Royal International Horse Show.

Above: *The great American racehorse Secretariat won the US Triple Crown in 1973. His total career winnings for two seasons were $1,316,808.*

Top: *Arkle, an Irish-bred gelding, was one of the most famous steeplechasers of this century.*

The Heavy Horse

Top: *Lithuanian Heavy Draught*

Middle: *Rhineland Heavy Draught*

Bottom: *Italian Heavy Draught*

The heavy and draught breeds of horses are found mainly in Europe and may trace back to the Forest or Diluvial Horse of some 10,000 years ago or more. Cave paintings in the Dordogne area of France depict a heavy horse, not unlike the Swedish heavy horse, which is now believed to date back to the Ice Age.

The development of the various breeds is relatively modern. The romantic theory is that breeds such as the amiable Shire horse, with its strong legs covered in fine silky hair, is a descendant of the Great Horse of Europe and was developed as a war-horse. The theory supposes that as the medieval knights must have weighed about 30 stone (420lb/190·5kg) in full armour they would have needed a horse of Shire proportions. However, it was found that the horse-armour that has survived through the ages could not have been made for a Shire horse or

any other of similar build as it is much too small. It was the 'Hollywood' film makers who created the idea of knights being placed on their horses by means of a crane. This was nothing more than artistic licence and fantasy.

The medieval knights may have ridden a very stocky, strong little horse brought to many parts of Europe during the migrations of people such as the Goths and Lombards several centuries earlier. The war-horse of the Middle Ages and just before may have been a relation of the heavy and draught breeds of Europe; it certainly was not the Shire or his like that thundered across the battlefields or galloped down the jousting lanes to win the favour of a lady.

The most important factor in the development of the heavier working breeds of horses was the arrival of the horse-collar in the Middle Ages. This simple piece of equipment brought the horse into more general use for agriculture and haulage and in doing so started the long, slow breeding programmes that have produced such noble workers as the Shire, Breton, Percheron and Clydesdale. Lombardy and Flemish mares were used to start this process but in many of the heavy breeds other blood-strains, in some cases thoroughbred and eastern blood, were used over the centuries to produce the breeds we know today. They were the backbone of most economies before the coming of steampower, steel and the combustion engine.

During the first part of the twentieth century the number of horses in agriculture and commerce was at its peak but by World War II the number of horses used in these spheres had dropped drastically.

The decline continued after the war, although horses were still used in agriculture for a number of years and a few farmers still use them today instead of tractors. They are also used by a number of breweries for local deliveries, since apart from being cheaper they have the added bonus of providing good publicity. In other countries, other uses were found for the heavy horse. In Holland, for instance, the Poitevin was originally used to help clear the marshlands, a job for which it was well fitted with its very large feet. It was also used to breed the Poitevin Mule and the French Percheron, with its infusion of Oriental blood, besides being a carriage horse.

Pre-eminent among the horses now used for haulage is the Shire Horse. The Shire Horse Society, formerly the English Cart Horse Society, was incorporated in 1878 to improve and promote the Shire Horse. However between 1948 and 1950 the Shire population dropped by 27 per cent and the breed, fast overtaken by the tractor and motor vehicles, was being slaughtered by the hundred.

Ten years later, primarily because of the

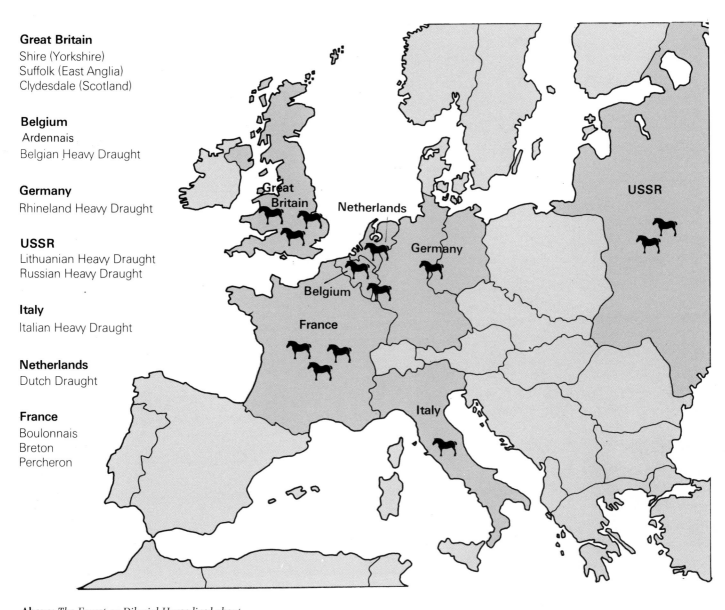

Great Britain
Shire (Yorkshire)
Suffolk (East Anglia)
Clydesdale (Scotland)

Belgium
Ardennais
Belgian Heavy Draught

Germany
Rhineland Heavy Draught

USSR
Lithuanian Heavy Draught
Russian Heavy Draught

Italy
Italian Heavy Draught

Netherlands
Dutch Draught

France
Boulonnais
Breton
Percheron

Above: *The Forest or Diluvial Horse lived about 10,000 years ago. A number of heavy horses are believed to have descended from it including those shown above.*

enthusiasm of the breweries, there was an unbelievable resurgence of interest in the Shire, even to the extent of Shire Horse Centres being opened to the public in several parts of Great Britain. Their popularity spread abroad and many have been exported to Australia, New Zealand and Europe. Not all the foreign heavy breeds have been so fortunate however; the Ardennais, Breton and Italian Heavy Draught in particular are bred nowadays almost exclusively for meat.

Right: *Field Marshall, a famous Shire horse.*

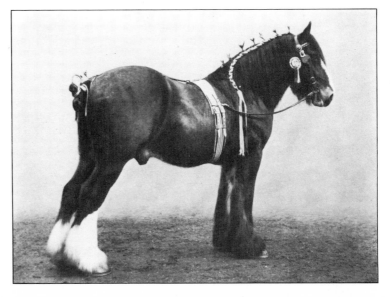

Famous examples

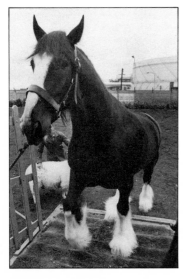

Harold

Harold was bred in Spondon, Derbyshire by John Potter in 1881 and was sold as a two-year-old to Charles Douglas, a Canadian who intended to export him to the United States. In trying to increase his value he decided to show him at the London Spring Show before selling him on. Harold did well at the show and was bought and kept in England by Sir Henry Allsopp, later Lord Hindlip, who also owned the champion stallion Enterprise of Cannock. After spending a couple of seasons at stud during which he matured and developed, his owner entered Harold for the 1886 Show, where he duly won his class, beating his stablemate, the erstwhile champion, Enterprise of Cannock.

Following this success Harold was sold again to Mr. A. C. Duncombe, while Enterprise of Cannock was sold on Lord Hindlip's death and exported to Wisconsin, a virtual replacement for Harold.

However, luck was not with him and during the Atlantic crossing a violent storm blew up and he and many other horses were killed.

In 1887 Harold, then standing 17.2hh (178cm) weighing 21cwt (1,070kg) and dark brown in colour, won the championship which had eluded him the previous year. The following year he came fifth to the 1886 champion Prince William. Harold together with Prince William and Hitchin Conqueror (both by William the Conqueror) are the three stallions from which every pedigree Shire horse, and many more non-pedigree Shires are directly descended in the male line.

This was Harold's last show before retiring to stud where he produced many good daughters and even better sons, his first prize-winning son being All Here who won the three-year-old stallion class out of a total of 61 competitors at the 1888 London Show.

Harold was put down in April 1901 and is buried at Duncombe's home at Calwich Abbey alongside Premier, Duncombe's other famous stallion.

Henry Cooper

Henry Cooper is a big, black Shire gelding aged fifteen years who stands 18.2hh (188cm) and weighs over a ton. He is owned by Young and Co Ltd's Brewery and has been delivering beer round the London streets since the Brewery bought him as a four-year-old. He has won many prizes and championships as well as being a member of Young's four-, six- and eight-horse teams where he usually takes the position of a 'wheeler'.

In addition to his usual activities he went to Münster, Germany, in 1972 to take part in the World Driving Championships, where Young's Brewery led the International parade of commercial teams.

Cicero

Cicero is a big 17hh (173cm) skewbald gelding, probably the most famous of the six drum horses in the two mounted bands of the Household Cavalry regiment. Although the drum horses are usually bought in Ireland, Cicero was spotted by the Crown Equerry, Sir John Miller, pulling a milk cart in Scotland. Cicero was born in Ireland in 1963 and had been sold to an Edinburgh dairy, but after being noticed by Sir John Miller he was sent to Holyrood Palace for HM The Queen's inspection and then to London.

On arrival in London he was lunged, taught to stand out, and driven in long reins before the foot reins were attached, and the practice drums introduced. The drums weigh 63lb (28·35kg) and are made of solid silver, so a powerful horse is needed. Cicero now regularly appears in ceremonial occasions and has taken part in the Trooping of the Colour Ceremony three times.

Above: *The traditional ceremony of the Trooping of the Colour in London, a pageant of mounted and foot soldiers to mark the official birthday of the reigning monarch of Great Britain.*

Above left: *A Shire horse of Young's Brewery Company competing at the East of England showground, the headquarters of the Shire Horse Society.*

Far left: *Wandle Henry Cooper enters his motor horse box en route for Münster in Germany.*

The Pony

The Development of the Pony

While the Steppe and Plateau horses are recognized as the joint founders of the warm-blooded horse breeds the different types of horses and ponies developed according to the varying environment of each region. European cave paintings show the types of ponies that existed in these early palaeolithic times in the northern areas of Europe between 40,000 and 10,000 BC, and as the tarpan and his descendants moved across the continent a number of them can be distinguished. In the Dordogne, for instance, there is a cave painting of what looks remarkably like our present-day Exmoor, while in the Pyrenees there is a painting of a pony very like a Fell pony. In Spain there is a painting resembling what we know as the New Forest pony and in Scandinavia there are Bronze Age rock drawings of ponies which resemble the Exmoor.

But it was not until the horse was ridden that man really began to play a part in its evolution. From the thirteenth century BC horses were kept in increasing numbers by the nomadic tribesmen on the Altai plain in Mongolia and in Siberia and Kazakhstan. These were probably the descendants of the Plateau horse, animals like those found by Przewalski. Bronze cheek pieces from the bridles found in the Pazyryk tombs in the High Altai, where horses were buried in and around the chiefs' tombs, show beyond any doubt that they were ridden. They were probably used to herd livestock, principally reindeer.

British Mountain and Moorland ponies

It is probable that a mixture of the Steppe and Plateau types has resulted in the Mountain and Moorland ponies despite theories about the influence of eastern blood. The subsequent development of Britain's nine native breeds has been brought about by selective breeding in which the best features have been retained and the worst points bred out.

Although all have their own characteristics, Britain's Mountain and Moorland ponies do have some qualities in common, for their surroundings ensure that all are tough, hardy and strong, with a constitution which enables them to live on the sparsest grazing. The smallest of them all, the Shetland, comes, as its name implies, from the Shetland Islands, and because of its remoteness it is probably the purest of the native ponies with no infusions of outside blood for the last hundred years. Its small size fits it well for its life on the harsh Scottish islands, but its strength is quite out of proportion to its diminutive size and until fairly recently it was used on the island crofts for hauling peat and seaweed, as well as for ploughing and for transport. During the industrial revolution, the Shetland was used extensively down the mines because of its size.

The Exmoor is another breed which has been little influenced by outside blood, for the high bleak moor in the south-west of England where it lives is inhospitable to any but the hardiest of animals. Mention is made of the Exmoor in the Domesday Book and it is probable that Exmoor ponies inhabited the moor as far back as the Bronze Age. The Dartmoor pony, although living fairly near Exmoor, is very different in appearance and is believed to have Arab blood in it, while the Welsh breeds, of which there are four types, two ponies and two cobs, are known to contain Arab blood.

The Fells and Dales ponies in the north of England have only been recognized as separate breeds over the last hundred years or so. They are believed to have changed little until the Romans came over to Britain, who, requiring a work animal in the area and believing the Fell and Dale to be too small, started to import Friesian horses from the Netherlands to cross with the native stock. Today the Fell and the Friesian do look very similar except that the Friesian is bigger. The Dale on the other hand tended thereafter to be more influenced by the Welsh Cob, or one in particular, a trotting stallion called Comet who stood in Westmorland for many years.

The Highland, of which there appear to be two types, the light Western Isles type and the heavier mainland pony, the Garron, although only one is officially recognized, derives from the original Celtic pony. It has had infusions of Arab, Percheron and Clydesdale and has a number of coat colours, including yellow, silver and grey dun with a black eel stripe down the centre of the back, and frequently with zebra stripes on the legs too, inherited from its early Przewalski-type ancestors.

The New Forest is the least pure of British ponies, as all kinds of ponies have been turned out in the Forest over the years. Only since 1938 has the Breed Society attempted to define the type. Ireland's Connemara has had a good deal of Spanish influence, both accidental, following the wrecking of several Armada ships in 1588 and deliberate, as later importations of Andalusian and Arab stock. Flourishing studs, particularly of Welsh, Dartmoor and Shetland ponies, now exist in many countries.

Of the non-British ponies, the extremely tough Icelandic pony, which has a peculiar fast gait known as the tölt, the Norwegian Fjord, resembling the Highland, the Døle Gudbrandsdal from Norway resembling the Fell and the Gotland are the oldest and purest breeds.

The Gotland is believed to have existed in a wild state on its island home in the Baltic since the Stone Age. The Dülmen pony and the Senner (now almost extinct) are the two native breeds of Germany.

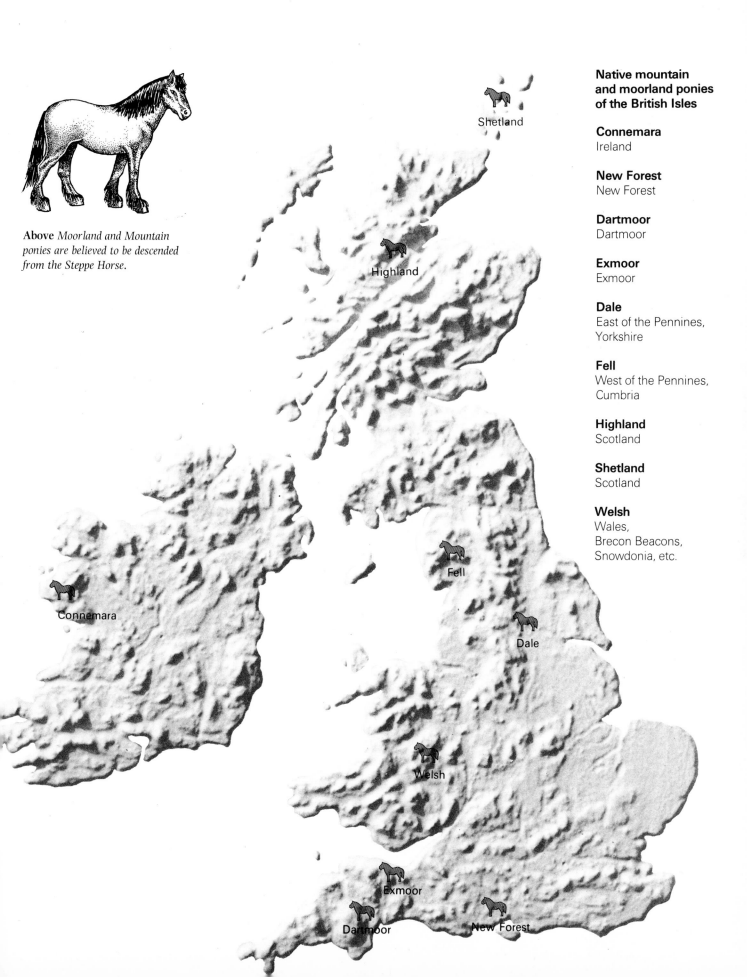

Above *Moorland and Mountain ponies are believed to be descended from the Steppe Horse.*

Native mountain and moorland ponies of the British Isles

Connemara
Ireland

New Forest
New Forest

Dartmoor
Dartmoor

Exmoor
Exmoor

Dale
East of the Pennines, Yorkshire

Fell
West of the Pennines, Cumbria

Highland
Scotland

Shetland
Scotland

Welsh
Wales,
Brecon Beacons,
Snowdonia, etc.

Shetland

Highland

Connemara

Fell

Dale

Welsh

Exmoor

Dartmoor

New Forest

Famous examples

Above: *Pretty Polly, one of the finest show ponies of its time. A show pony should have a small quality head, good sloping shoulders, a short back and sound limbs with a fluent flowing action. It should present a picture of elegance with perfect manners and good substance.*

Pretty Polly

Pretty Polly, foaled in 1945 in Ireland was by the Arab Naseel out of the Thoroughbred/Welsh cross mare, Gypsy Gold. Four years later she was champion show pony at Dublin before being bought by Mr Albert Deptford. In 1950 she won at her first four shows in England including the Horse of the Year Show at Harringey. Standing only 14hh (142cm) but competing against ponies of 14.2hh (147cm) she took first prize in every show in which she competed, except once when she came second at the Royal Show.

Pretty Polly retired to stud while still at the peak of her showing career and after producing Cusop Policy by the Welsh pony Bolged Automation, found her perfect mate in Bwlch Valentino and nine of her eleven foals subsequently became champions. Her most famous offspring were probably Polly's Gem, dam of three champions including Gems Signet, champion Riding Pony in 1972, and Pollyanna who became champion Riding Pony of the Year at Harringey in 1961 and was subsequently sold to America. There she crowned her achievements by taking the supreme championship at New York's Madison Square Garden. Pretty Polly lived to the age of twenty-eight.

Dyoll Starlight

Dyoll Starlight was foaled in May 1894 and bred by Mr Howard Meuric Lloyd of Llangadog in Wales. He was by Dyoll Glasallt, a dark brown pony with a wide blaze down the centre of his face and out of Dyoll Moonlight, a little grey mare described as a 'miniature Arab', and believed to be descended from the Crawshay Bailey Arab who ran out on the Brecon Hills in the 1850s. Moonlight had been bought by Mr Lloyd in 1891, and after using her in harness for several years he retired her to stud and Starlight was her second foal.

Mr Lloyd recognized Starlight to be a pony of exceptional quality and bought some mares to put to him and founded a stud (the Stud prefix being Dyoll – Lloyd backwards). Although he produced some good fillies it was for his colts that Starlight became famous, among them Bleddfa Shooting Star, who was a prolific winner in the show ring, and Greylight, who was exported to Australia.

Starlight had a highly successful show ring career himself, coming first at the Royal Show four years in succession from 1898 and returning in 1912 and 1913 to repeat his earlier wins. He was beaten, when over twenty years old, only by his own progeny, most of whom were greys, and eventually died aged thirty-five years, having virtually founded a new line of ponies.

Stroller

Stroller, the Irish-bred pony of 14.1½hh (146cm) was bought for Marion Coakes (now Mrs Marion Mould) when she was thirteen and he was seven, and, although he was difficult to school at home and impossible to take hunting because he got so full of himself, the pair soon started winning junior classes. At the end of 1962 they were included in the victorious Junior European team which went to Berlin and three years later when she was still only eighteen Marion became Ladies World Champion, and won the Queen Elizabeth II Cup for the first time at the Royal International Horse Show in 1965, the second occasion being in 1971. In 1966 Stroller helped to win three Nations' Cups and the following year won the Hickstead Jumping Derby and the Wills Hickstead Gold Medal, besides amassing for the second year in succession the highest number of points throughout the season at Hickstead.

His biggest success came in 1968 when the pair were selected to go to the Mexico Olympics, where, in spite of suffering from a decayed and broken tooth, and consequently being off work for a few days, Stroller produced a superb first clear round and had only two fences down in the second round, to earn the pair their individual silver medal; the first woman to win an Olympic individual jumping medal and the first, and probably last pony ever to compete in an Olympic competition with one of the only two clear rounds. In the team competition four days later, however, when Stroller was still suffering from his poisoned tooth, he stopped for the first time in his career. In the second round he stopped again, and fell on coming in for a second attempt, and Marion, hit by flying poles, was concussed. They jumped it at the third attempt but by then had run out of time and were eliminated. On their return to Britain Stroller's tooth was removed, but he took a long time to recover and it was not until 1969 that he really got going again, winning the Hamburg Jumping Derby and the Hickstead Grand Prix, besides being the only British horse to go clear in the winning Prince of Wales Cup team that year. Stroller retired in 1973 when he was twenty years old.

Above: *A superb example of the Welsh Cob, one of the most versatile of the 'Ride-and-Drive' breeds.*

Left: *Britain's Marion Mould (formerly Coakes) and her father's great Irish-bred showjumping pony Stroller jumping at the All England Jumping Course at Hickstead. Marion Mould, now one of the world's top lady riders, and the brave Stroller won the Ladies' World Championship in 1965 and the individual silver medal in the showjumping at the 1968 Mexico Olympic Games.*

THE ATLAS

Throughout the world there is a wide variety of breeds of horses and ponies. Some are exotic, some practical, some developed by Man, some now obsolete and some bred only for the show ring while others date back to prehistory.

In this section each breed is related to its country of origin but, of course, there are many breeds of horses and ponies that can be found great distances from their country of origin. Some of these transplanted breeds have been kept true to type while others have been changed by national breeders to meet the special requirements of their country's markets or to meet the demands of specialized horse-sports that are becoming popular in most countries.

The Thoroughbred, for example, is a uniquely British creation but in the bloodstock markets of the world there are now many variations on the English theme. The Australian and New Zealand Thoroughbred is well-known for its stamina, the American Thoroughbred for its precocity and tendency to mature early, the British and European (mainly French, German and Italian) Thoroughbred for its versatility and superiority in middle distance races of 7 furlongs to 1¼ miles (1·4 to 2km) and the Irish Thoroughbred for its durability and gameness. The Thoroughbred therefore merits a section on its own, but where a country or area has developed a particular horse that is very different from the original tap-root source, the English Thoroughbred, then details have been given in this section.

The Arab horse has been treated in the same way, for it is one of the most influential breeding bloodlines used as an 'improver' on the vast majority of the world's native breeds. The Arab in its many forms can be found almost everywhere and its blood is in the veins of practically every thoroughbred strain in the world.

One of the most popular riding horses in the world is the Anglo-Arab. Definition of this breed varies from country to country. For example, the Arab Horse Society of England defines an Anglo-Arab as a cross from a Thoroughbred stallion and an Arab mare or vice versa, or the subsequent crossing of progeny thus bred. The Anglo-Arab has no strains of other blood except that of Thoroughbred and Arabian. In Australia, Canada, and Sweden the same definition is followed. But in the USA not less than twenty-five per cent Arab blood nor more than seventy-five per cent Thoroughbred is demanded before a horse can be classified as an Anglo-Arab.

Many societies, especially the French and American, are now breeding larger Anglo-Arabs than in previous generations and this versatile horse with its classic head and stylish tail carriage is becoming increasingly successful in the show ring and in the demanding spheres of showjumping and three-day eventing.

Below: *The famous 'White horses from the Sea', the Camargue horses that live semi-wild in southern France.*

The Americas

This map of the basic physical divisions of the region locates the areas where major horse breeds originated. Present-day important breeding areas and studs are also indicated.

The horse returned to the western hemisphere at the beginning of the fifteenth century with Cortés, Pizarro and other Spanish *conquistadores*. Explorers and colonists brought more horses, many of which escaped or were stolen by Indians. Although Indians had no tradition of horsemanship, they quickly learned to become expert riders. Horses were used in hunting the huge buffalo herds that roamed between the Mississippi River and the Rocky Mountains and in inter-tribal warfare.

Meanwhile, settlers who came to the eastern seaboard before the Revolution brought their own Thoroughbreds and coach horses, hackneys and pacers, and heavier draught breeds.

ARCTIC OCEAN

PACIFIC OCEAN

ATLANTIC OCEAN

ALASKA (US)

CANADA

VANCOUVER
CALGARY

Rocky Mountains

Mississippi R.

Missouri R.

MONTREAL

Sable Island

VERMONT

SAN FRANCISCO

SALT LAKE CITY

U.S.A.

CHICAGO

NEW YORK

Ohio R.

Appalachian Mts

LOS ANGELES

WASHINGTON D.C.

Assateague
Chincoteague Island

AMARILLO

NEW ORLEANS

LOUISVILLE

LEXINGTON

Ohio R.

Kentucky R.

BLUE GRASS COUNTRY

GULF OF MEXICO

BAHAMAS

WEST INDIES

MEXICO CITY

CUBA

DOMINICAN REPUBLIC

PUERTO RICO

MEXICO

JAMAICA

HAITI

BELIZE
HONDURAS

CARIBBEAN SEA

GUATEMALA
EL SALVADOR
NICARAGUA
COSTA RICA

Panama Canal

PANAMA

SOUTH AMERICA

Ice/Tundra	
Mountains/Uplands	
Tropical forest	
Forest/Woodland	
Grassland	
Savanna	
Scrub	
Desert	

Key

- ● Towns/Cities
- ▫ Studs
- 🐎 Light Horse
- 🐎 Pony
- 🐎 Heavy Horse

The first Thoroughbred to arrive in North America was Bulle Rock, who was imported in 1730. This son of the Darley Arabian was followed by such noted stallions as Janus (foundation sire of the Quarter Horses) and Diomed.

As settlers moved west across the Appalachian mountains, they took their horses with them. The animals were not the finest ever bred, since what was needed was stamina and versatility; a horse might be required to pull a plough one day, serve as a saddle horse the next, and then be hitched to the family buggy for the Sunday trip to church.

The horse was an indispensable element in the West during the second half of the nineteenth century. The United States Cavalry fought many mounted skirmishes against Indians (the sole cavalry survivor of the Battle of Little Big Horn in 1876, between General Custer's Seventh Cavalry and the Sioux led by Sitting Bull, was a horse named Comanche). When huge tracts of land came under the control of the white man, large herds of cattle were assembled on ranches from Mexico to Canada. Ranch work was a dour and demanding existence despite its glamorous reputation. Cowboys needed a handy, hearty mount, and a horse with 'cow savvy' was the pride of every cowpuncher.

Light Horse

1. Anglo-Argentine
2. Anglo-Normando
3. Appaloosa
4. Criollo
5. Crioulo
6. Cutting Horse
7. Galiceno
8. Mangalarga
9. Morgan
10. Mustang
11. Palomino
12. Paso Fino
13. Peruvian Stepping Horse
14. Polo Pony
15. Quarter Horse
16. Saddler
17. Standardbred
18. Tennessee Walking Horse
19. Thoroughbred, United States

Pony

20. Assateague and Chincoteague
21. Falabella
22. Pony of the Americas
23. Sable Island Pony

The horse in America today

Even though the United States Army abolished the cavalry after World War II, and Clydesdales and Percherons have long been redundant, there are more horses in the United States today than there were at the turn of the century. The rapid growth of equestrian sports has raised the numbers to about nine million.

The United States has been called a melting pot, a country which has absorbed people from many lands. The same is true of its horses. Beginning with Andalusians and Arabians from Spain, horses and ponies from all over Europe came to the New World. Some were mixed to create new breeds for specific working or sporting purposes, and the result is a rich legacy.

Canada

Cutting horse

The most prominent Canadian horse today is the Cutting Horse which, like so many horse-breeds in the Americas, has spent much of its existence helping to control and survey herds of cattle on the ranches. Much of its work is now carried out by jeeps and helicopters but it has developed as a popular competition horse through the enthusiasm of the Canadian Cutting Horse Association and the National Cutting Horse Association of Canada. The ideal type stands between 15.2hh and 16hh, has strong shoulders, a short-coupled back, well-developed hindquarters and a compact and powerful conformation. Body colours tend towards black, brown, bay and other solid hues.

The breed's name comes from the cattle ranch activity of cutting, or singling a calf or steer from a herd in order to isolate the animal for branding, castration, innoculation, or merely to transfer it to another group. Training begins when the horse is three or four years of age. The rider first makes the horse move towards the calf to be singled out, guiding the mount to interpose itself when the calf tries to return to the herd. A horse with 'cow

sense' quickly learns what is expected and is taught to work off its hindquarters, swinging to either side or charging straight ahead. After a while Cutting Horses with good mental aptitude and physical ability work on their own; the rider merely points out which calf or steer is to be cut, then he sits back and watches as, with loose rein, the Cutting Horse performs in a manner that more than equals any other form of equine skill.

These versatile horses are equally at home at work on the stock farm, in pleasure riding, trail riding, rodeo and western show competitions. The following excerpt gives an idea of the drama and thrills of some of these contests: 'During the two and a half minutes ... a rider demonstrates the ability of his horse to out-think the cow with terrific short bursts of speed, agility of turns in mid-air, fabulous foot-work, and co-ordination between horse and rider that is unexcelled in any arena event'.

Canadian Pacer

The Canadian Pacer originally came from France, where in turn it had been imported from England. The breed traces its ancestry to the ambler, the type of horse sturdy enough to carry a knight wearing full armour yet sufficiently comfortable to provide a smooth ride. The comfort came from the amble, or pace, in which the forelegs and hindlegs on each side moved simultaneously (before the introduction of posting, or rising to the trot in the eighteenth century, trotting horses were not very highly prized).

Canadian Pacers were used to produce home-bred Standardbreds, and they figured prominently in the development of the American Saddle Horse through Denmark, foaled in 1839, who was the foundation sire of the American Saddle Horse. Harness racing is very popular in Canada, and over the past decade there have been notable drivers and horses. They include Herve Fillion, seven times leading money-winning driver and Fresh Yankee, the first North American-bred horse to earn purses in excess of one million dollars in a year.

Sable Island

Sable Island is a sandbank in the Atlantic Ocean off the coast of the province of Nova Scotia. A few small herds of ponies live here numbering from five to eight mares for every stallion. Slight in build and standing about 14hh these ponies are said to be descended from horses and ponies brought by settlers from New England during the early eighteenth century. Sparse forage, limited to grass and other plants which grow on the sand dunes, has restricted their growth.

Sable Island ponies are used by lighthouse keepers and their families – the main residents of the area – for riding and driving.

Below: *The Canadian Cutting Horse, popular these days in competitions.*

Left: *Sable Island Ponies roam the sand dunes of Nova Scotia.*

Below left: *A horse in top gear as it makes for the line during a harness race at Ladner, British Columbia.*

The United States

1. The Palouse river region of Oregon and Washington gives its name to the Appaloosa breed.
2. The islands of Chincoteague and Assateague off Virginia became the home of shipwrecked ponies.
3. The Rockies have become the last refuge of the wild Mustang.
4. A Californian family is believed to have bred the first Palomino.
5. The New England colonists developed several breeds which retained their popularity, including the Quarter Horse and Morgan.
6 & 7. Farmers in the south developed the Saddle Horse (6) and the Tennessee Walking Horse (7) for their comfortable gaits.
8. The famous 'Blue Grass' country, the home of the American Thoroughbred and the most important racehorse stud farms in the world.

Appaloosa

The Palouse River runs through northern Idaho and parts of Oregon and Washington. The Nez Percé tribe of Indians, so named by Europeans because they ceremoniously pierced their noses, lived in that region of the American West, sheltered from marauders by high mountains. Wandering tribes sold or traded horses to the Nez Percé, who were particularly attracted to those animals with spots on their rumps.

Spotted horses (as distinguished from those with coats of larger 'patches') were also much admired by other cultures. Spanish and Portuguese Andalusians bearing such markings were prized, as court painters such as Velasquez noted. American Indians attributed special magical powers to multi-coloured animals, and the Nez Percé selectively bred spotted horses to refine coloration patterns. In 1804 Lewis and Clark set out on their famous expedition

Above: An Appaloosa stallion. The Nez Percé Indians are thought to have developed the Appaloosa as a breed, but horses with similar markings can be seen in ancient Chinese and Persian Art.

Left: The legendary hunter and Indian-fighter William S. Cody ('Buffalo Bill'). When he moved into showbusiness his choice of an Appaloosa as an opening parade mount for his Wild West shows focused attention on the breed.

Not every spotted horse can qualify as a true Appaloosa. Coloration should normally consist of dark spots randomly sprinkled on a white patch over solid-coloured hindquarters. However, horses without these 'blankets' but with small spots all over their bodies are known as 'Leopards' and can be registered as Appaloosas. Other important distinguishing characteristics of the breed are the unique circle of white round the iris which gives it the appearance of a human eye, mottled skin around the muzzle, striations running the length of all four hooves, and a short tail. With regard to conformation, Appaloosas have pointed ears, a deep chest over sloping shoulders, and solid hips. They have strong legs and well-defined withers. Their weight averages slightly more than 450kg (1,000lb), and their height averages just over 15 hands (153cm).

The Appaloosa's stamina and versatility are in evidence to this day. Few long-distance endurance rides take place without at least a handful of spotted entrants, and in the American show ring Appaloosas compete in English pleasure horse classes, buckboard pleasure driving, Western pleasure horse and trail horse classes, as well as in breeding classes. Two competitive events require contestants to run horse against horse in the traditional Nez Percé manner in stump and barrel-races until all but one is eliminated. In the colourful costume class, the trappings and equipment of horse and rider, who are both turned out in traditional Indian costume, are judged along with the horse's performance under saddle.

Chincoteague and Assateague ponies

No one knows how a band of ponies happened to come to Chincoteague and Assateague, two small islands in the Atlantic Ocean off the coast of Virginia. One hypothesis holds that a ship carrying Shetland Ponies was wrecked there during the sixteenth century and that some of the animals swam to the shore. Another suggests that the wrecked vessel was carrying Moorish ponies bound for South America. The truth will probably never be known, but the result is a rather stubborn breed of ponies named after the two islands.

Standing at no more than 13hh (132cm), the animals tend to be pinto in marking and coloration, although recent infusions of Arab and Welsh Pony blood have produced browns, blacks, bays and greys, and more fine-featured animals.

Once a year, on the last Wednesday of July, the band of approximately 150 ponies is rounded up and made to swim from its home on the otherwise uninhabited Assateague, across a narrow channel to Chincoteague. There the ponies are examined and branded, and some of them are auctioned.

Above: *The Chincoteague Pony. The origin of these small ponies that live on the islands off the Atlantic coast of America is unknown.*

commissioned by Thomas Jefferson to explore the American heartlands acquired from the French through the Louisiana Purchase. Lewis noted in his journal that the horses favoured by the tribe were 'pied with large spots of white irregularly scattered and intermixed with . . . some other dark colour'.

Other white men played a decisive role in the history of the Appaloosa. Missionaries preached against the Nez Percés' preoccupation with horses, but although some tribesmen were swayed by their arguments and remained sedentary fishermen and farmers, others continued to breed and use horses, especially against encroachments of the white settlers. The Indians were outnumbered when hostilities broke out, and following a valiant fight and a thousand mile retreat led by Chief Joseph, the Nez Percé were defeated. Their horses either perished or were scattered throughout the West.

was a consistent winner at quarter-mile dashes and trotting races. When his owner died of consumption in 1797, Figure was bought by farmer Robert Evans and the 'mighty little giant' spent most of his time pulling logs and doing the roughest farm work.

As with many horses of the day, he was known by many different names, which changed almost as frequently as his owners. Known first as Figure, he was called the Morgan Horse after he had left Morgan's ownership, and later still the Goss Horse from the family name of his next owners, and finally and probably only posthumously, Justin Morgan.

It is thought that Justin Morgan was by a famous Thoroughbred racehorse called True Briton. This seems quite feasible, for it is known that around the time of Justin Morgan's foaling there was a stallion called True Briton. Many different claims have been made for Justin Morgan's pedigree. In the years following his death the issue was keenly fought over by supporters of various Dutch, French, Spanish, Canadian, Arab and Thoroughbred horses.

Justin Morgan's dam is even more obscure but it is claimed that she belonged on her male line to the same family, sired by the imported stallion Wildair. This could be true, for Wildair was in the same ownership as True Briton. If this is so Justin Morgan's dam is the direct maternal line from which the modern racehorses and stallions Nearco and Nasrullah were descended.

Another of the horse's attributes was his prepotency. His offspring resembled him in conformation, strength, speed and disposition, as did succeeding generations. Three of Justin Morgan's sons were especially important: Sherman and Bulrush were champion trotters of their day, while Woodbury was prized as a showy saddle horse. The eighteen-year-old Ethan Allen 50, of the Sherman line, defeated the top ranking trotter of the region in three consecutive mile heats, all under the time of 2mins 20secs.

Establishment of the breed

The offspring of Justin Morgan gradually became known over a wider area and their character was prized. One horseman, Erasmus Fuller, used the Morgan for his stage-coach run from St Albans to Richford from 1869–1872. 'My horses were practically all Morgan. I kept using them because I could depend on them. They were lively, bright, cheerful and intelligent driving horses ... all square trotters. You spoke to them and they were ready to start.'

By the 1850s Morgans were the most popular and widespread breed in America, and owned by several presidents. They became enormously popular in the mid-West, especially Ohio, not previously noted for its horses' quality. There an

Above: *General Sheridan's famous 20-mile ride to rally Union troops in Virginia during the American Civil War.*

Morgan

In 1791 a Vermont schoolmaster named Justin Morgan received as payment for a debt a two-year-old bay colt named Figure. The animal was physically unlike its Thoroughbred sire and dam, standing 14hh (142cm) when full grown and weighing scarcely more than 900lb (409kg). Despite his diminutive size, however, Figure displayed extraordinary strength and speed. He hauled loads no other horse could budge, and article in a local newspaper commented: 'All unprejudiced minds speak well of the Morgan, the only difference is in the degree of praise.'

The Civil War also helped to spread the breed's reputation. A Vermont regiment rode only Morgans and General Philip Sheridan made his famous ride to rally his troops at Winchester, Virginia, on a coal-black Morgan named Rienzi.

Some Morgans were crossed with other breeds and types; the Standardbred, American Saddle Horse and Tennessee Walking Horse all have Morgan blood in their ancestry. With the exception of the Thoroughbred, no other breed has had such an influence on the development of light horses in America as the Morgan.

At a time when crossbreeding posed a threat to the Morgan's distinctiveness, Colonel Joseph Battell established the Morgan Horse Register in 1894. His register provided the impetus for the Morgan Horse Club, which subsequently assumed maintenance of the stud book. The United States Department of Agriculture was also interested in maintaining the breed, and in 1905 created the Morgan Horse Farm (now run by the University of Vermont), which helped to provide cavalry horses during World War I.

Morgans are now somewhat taller than their progenitor, ranging from 14.2 to 15.2hh (147–157cm). The head is characterized by large prominent eyes and small ears, a small muzzle and a prominent jaw. The Morgan has a crested neck, considerable shoulder angulation and depth, a short back, muscular croup and a high-set tail. Legs are relatively straight with short cannon bones and medium pasterns.

In addition to conformation classes, Morgans compete as park horses (akin to American Saddle Horses gaited classes), in harness, as English and Western pleasure horses, and in pleasure driving and jumping (the last involves two fences set no higher than three feet, 96cm). Entries in a Justin Morgan class trot half a mile in harness, gallop the same distance under saddle, show at the walk, trot and canter, and finally pull 500 pounds (227kg) of dead weight a distance of six feet (183cm).

Below: *A Morgan mare with her foal. The round, balanced conformation of the breed can be seen in both of them. The Morgan is one of the most versatile light horses bred in the United States and has a remarkable ability to breed true to type with each generation. Its range and recognition can be accredited partly to its use during the American Civil War (1861–65).*

Mustang

The Spanish *conquistadores* and other explorers of the American south-west took horses with them. Those which escaped formed bands, and became known as mustangs, from a Spanish word for 'ownerless animals'. No particular conformation marked mustangs, although they usually stood under 15.2hh (158cm) and were sturdy enough to stand the rigours of range life. With few natural predators, bands flourished until there were millions of wild horses roaming the Great Plains from Mexico to Canada.

The mustang population was severely threatened by settlers. Hundreds of thousands of wild horses were rounded up for use in the Boer War and World War I, and more were slaughtered for pet food, fertilizer or leather. The remaining horses were driven westwards into the Rocky Mountains. From an estimated two million wild horses at the turn of the century, fewer than 17,000 remained in the late 1960s.

Public reaction to the slaughter was roused by such people as Velma 'Wild Horse Annie' Johnston and Hope Ryden, amid much press and television publicity. Congress was moved to action, and in December, 1971, harassment or slaughter of wild horses was made a federal crime. In spite of this mustangs continue to be hunted, and most recent estimates number them at fewer than 10,000.

Paints

Among the 16 horses brought to Mexico by Cortés in 1519, according to the expedition's historian there was 'a pinto with white stockings on his forefeet' and 'a dark roan horse with white patches'. These were the first multi-coloured horses to come to North America. Indians were particularly attracted by the painted horses ('pinto', from the Spanish word for 'painted', is used interchangeably with 'Paint', although the latter word properly describes the breed, and 'pinto' a type). They thought colourfully-marked horses had magic properties which would make a brave invincible in battle. The Cheyennes and Comanches, for example, favoured 'Medicine Hat' – mustangs boldly splashed with colour on the head and chest.

Although Paint Horses could have suffered the same decline as the mustangs, Wild West shows came to their rescue. Eastern audiences love the spectacle of cowboys and Indians, usually riding Paints, galloping around indoor and outdoor arenas.

Its distinctive coloration apart, the Paint Horse closely resembles the Quarter Horse, with a clean head, fairly long neck, deep chest, short backline and long croup, and straight, clean legs. There are two types of body coloration, *overo* and *tobiano*. An *overo* gives the impression of being a

Left: *The Mustang, with his long flowing mane and strong body, symbolizes to many the spirit of the American West.*

Right: *The Golden Horse of the West – the Palomino. The Palomino is not a breed but a type of horse.*

Below: *A group of Paints gallop across the plain in Virginia, USA.*

dark horse splashed from underneath with white, while a *tobiano* is predominantly white with dark markings (*tobianos* almost always have white legs). The markings can be brown, black, or roan.

The reason for the Paint's resemblance to the Quarter Horse is often no accident, since a Paint can have a sire or dam of that breed. Hence the great speed in Paint racing horses; times of under 12 seconds for 220yd (201m) and under 20 seconds for 350yd (320m) are not uncommon.

Some of the great Paint Horses of the past had names that came out of the American West: the great racer Painted Joe, a cutting mare called Calamity Jane, Wahoo King, whose name sounds like an Indian warcry, and Mr. J Bar, suggesting a ranch's brand. The Paint's versatility is shown in such Western events as barrel-racing (galloping clover-leaf patterns around three barrels), as well as pole bending, calf roping, and reining classes, the Western equivalent of dressage. In addition, they compete in English hunter, jumping and equitation classes recognized by the American Paint Horse Association, established in 1961.

Palomino

The sun and sand of the American south-west reflect the heritage and fascination of the Palomino, the golden horse. Like mustangs and Paints, they came from Spain, selected by owners of *ranchos* for their regal looks. The Palomino's name is a variation of the Spanish word for 'dove', thought to be the name of a Californian family which bred them. It is a difficult horse to breed. Two golden-coloured horses do not always produce a similar foal; the combination of a chestnut stallion bred to a lighter-coloured mare stands a better chance.

The colour qualification of a Palomino is strict; it must be as near as possible the colour of a newly-minted United States gold coin. If the coat is more than 15 per cent darker or lighter it is penalized, as is any attempt to dye it. A white mane and tail is permissible, and so are white markings on the face or lower legs. Mature Palominos should measure 14.1 – 16hh (145 – 163cm).

Because the Palomino is a type rather than a true breed, the animals are shown in many ways, such as Western pleasure horses, English pleasure horses, saddle horses, and fine harness. Harking back to their antecedents, Palominos are shown in a Spanish fiesta class in which horses and riders wear and carry costumes and appointments which evoke *haciendas* and *ranchos*. That elegance remains outside the show ring too. City and town streets brighten when a 'sheriff's posse' passes by in a parade, silver and gold trappings on saddles, bridles and outfits gleaming brightly. Trigger, Roy Roger's mount in countless films, was a Palomino as was Nautical, the famous showjumper.

Pony of the Americas

The Pony of the Americas is one of the most recent additions to the world's equine breeds. It was developed by Leslie Boomhower of Mason City, Iowa, who bred an Appaloosa mare to a Shetland Pony in 1956. Black Hand, the resulting colt, was the equivalent of a miniature Appaloosa and was the centre of attention whenever he appeared in a show ring. He became the breed's foundation sire.

Now more than 14,000 registered Ponies of the Americas live in the United States and Canada. Distinguishable by their Appaloosa characteristics of spots over a solid 'blanket' on their hind quarters, mottled muzzle, vertically striped hooves and white-rimmed eyes, they stand between 11 – 13hh (112 – 132cm) full grown. The breed is shown primarily in Western pleasure and performance classes, although the ponies also compete in harness as well as under English saddles.

Quarter Horses

Although Quarter Horses have come to be most closely associated with the American West, they originated along the eastern seaboard, in New England and the southern colonies. Before the import of Thoroughbreds at the end of the eighteenth century, racing was restricted to quarter-mile dashes along town and village streets or along paths cut through forests. Short, compact horses, descendants of Spanish horses stolen by Indians, were best at these sprints. They were able to jump off at the start like jack-rabbits, and a visiting Englishman described them as having 'inferior height of the forehand and in the loftiness of the withers ... while superior in the general development of the hindquarters ... and in the height behind'.

A Thoroughbred was initially deemed responsible for establishing animals of this conformation as a breed. Janus, a grandson of the Godolphin Arabian, foaled in England in 1746 and brought to America as a nine-year-old, had been particularly successful at four miles. But his sons and daughters were noted as sprinters, and excelled at quarter-mile dashes, so Janus was later declared to be the Quarter Horse's foundation sire.

Infusions of Thoroughbred blood continued to mould the breed. The celebrated Sir Archie sired a number of sprinters, his great-grandson becoming one of the best quarter-milers of the time. Foaled in 1843 and taken west a year later, Steel Dust became known as 'the fastest horse in Texas' by defeating horses of all breeds, types and backgrounds. Other outstanding sprinters of that era included Shiloh, Old Billy, Copper Bottom and Old Fred.

Although a match race might have been a pleasant diversion, the Western horse was primarily a work horse and the Quarter Horse was perfectly suited to cattle work. Calves needed to be singled out and herds kept together and driven many miles – the lightning acceleration of the breed and its ability to turn quickly proved to be more than equal to the task.

Quarter Horse conformation is now most distinctive. The head is short and broad, and set on a neck lower than most other breeds. The chest is broad and deep, while shoulders are sloping and withers are high. The hindquarters are noticeably higher than the withers, and the feet and hooves are well-formed below short cannon bones which contribute to speed and power. The Quarter Horse averages slightly over 15.2hh (152cm) and its weight is 499–590kg (1,100–1,300lb). The American Quarter Horse Association established a breed register to these standards in 1940 and now, with over a million animals, is the largest US breed association.

Quarter Horse racing has come a long way since village street sprints were run for a bale of tobacco. The world's richest race, the All-American Futurity, takes place every September at Ruidoso, New Mexico, where the ten finalists vie for a purse of over $1,000,000. Record times of under 22 seconds for the 440yd (402m) have become commonplace.

Below: *The Pony of the Americas. These ponies were first produced by crossing a Shetland Pony stallion with an Appaloosa mare. They are a recognized breed with their own stud book and registry.*

Above: *The American Quarter Horse is seen here using his powerful hindquarters to balance and control his sharp turn.*

Above right: *The elegant American Saddle Horse now one of America's most popular show ring performers.*

Most horse show classes for Quarter Horses are based on the breed's working background. Reining classes, the Western equivalent of dressage tests, involve trotting, loping (the Western word for cantering), rein-backs, figures-of-eight and turns on the haunches. Trail Horse Classes simulate such working chores as passing through gates, crossing water and wooden bridges, and being loaded into a trailer. Good manners and outstanding performance under saddle are important points in judging. Quarter Horses are also shown under English tack in jumping, English pleasure and polo classes.

Saddle Horse

Taken literally, 'saddle horse' describes any horse with a leather pad and a rider on its back. However, the American Saddle Horse is a breed, performing with a heady combination of elegance and brilliance, and is a favourite with the crowds at horse shows.

The Saddle Horse developed primarily as a work horse in the South, where people needed animals which could carry them across acres of cotton, rice and other crops as comfortably as possible. One, by the Thoroughbred Denmark (who was foaled in 1839) out of a mare of no particular pedigree, stood out for his showy yet comfortable gaits and his conformation, which included an arched neck and high-set tail. That was Gaines's Denmark, who sired hundreds of foals and was declared foundation sire of the American Saddle Horse.

Saddle Horses are trained to be either three- or five-gaited horses. The former perform at the walk, trot and canter, while five-gaited horses have two additional 'artificial' movements. The slow gait (or singlefoot) is something of a broken lateral pace, each foot striking the ground individually, and the rack is similar but faster. All Saddle Horse gaits are noted for elevated leg action: the legs are raised sharply and held in mid-air before striking the ground. The action is natural to the breed, although encouraged by special training.

Three-gaited Saddle Horses are also shown in fine harness classes in which they pull light buggies at the walk and trot.

Junior riders compete on three-gaited Saddle Horses in equitation classes for the ASPCA 'Good Hands' trophy, held at New York City's National Horse Show each November.

Right: *The American Standardbred
'Bonefish'. The breed was mainly
developed in New England where
trotting races have been popular
since colonial days. It is also widely
known as the American Trotter.*

Standardbreds

Among the first horses brought to colonial
America was a type originating in the
Netherlands. Like diminutive versions of the
Flemish Great Horse, they were solidly-built
animals well-suited for work which, in the New
England area, included carrying a rider under
saddle. The breed's propensity for pacing, more
comfortable than trotting in pre-posting days,
made them highly prized, especially in impromptu
races in the Massachusetts Bay Colony. Racing,
however, was frowned upon by the
predominantly Puritan citizens, and settlers who
wished to live in a more liberal climate moved to
Rhode Island. They took their horses with them,
and the animals became known as Narragansett
pacers. (One of these pacers played an important
role in American history by carrying Paul Revere
on his celebrated 1775 'Midnight Ride'.)

Until the end of the eighteenth century, racing
was confined to quarter-mile sprints or longer
distances. Trotting and pacer horses were second-
best until a superlative horse, Messenger, was
imported from England in 1788. A grey
Thoroughbred of the Darley Arabian line,
Messenger sired more than 600 foals, most of
which matured into fast trotters.

Trotters and pacers raced under saddle until
the nineteenth century when the buggy, a light

wagon stripped of excess weight, was invented.
Lady Suffolk, of the Messenger line, was the first
to pull a buggy over a one-mile distance in under
two and a half minutes, achieving equal
immortality as the subject of 'The Old Grey Mare'
folksong. A great-grandson of Messenger,
Hambletonian, was one of the most prepotent
stallions in history. Flourishing after the Civil
War, he sired more than 1,300 foals of which at
least 40 trotted the mile in under two and a half
minutes. Messenger was subsequently declared
the foundation sire of the Standardbred breed, the
'standard' being the ability to trot or pace a mile
in two and a half minutes or less. The stud book
reflected the trotting and pacing qualities of
Thoroughbreds, Narragansett Pacers, and
Morgans (Ethan Allen, a great-grandson of the
Morgan foundation sire, Justin Morgan, once
trotted a mile in two minutes and fifteen seconds).

The first sulkies, or two-wheeled driving carts,
were cumbersome affairs. Weighing
approximately 70lb (32kg) with 5ft (1·5m) high
wheels, these vehicles were precarious and gave
the driver minimal control. Then, in 1892, the
lower and pneumatically-cushioned bicycle wheel
made handling easier, and a bicycle-type seat
lowered the driver's centre of gravity, cut down
wind resistance, and consequently reduced race
times.

Left: *The Tennessee Walking Horse was developed by the prosperous Southern planters at the end of the 19th century to carry them between the plantation rows while inspecting the young crops. The Tennessee Walking Horse Breeders' Association of America was founded in 1935.*

The most famous Standardbred of his era – some say of all time – was the pacer Dan Patch. Foaled in 1896, he was unbeaten in three racing seasons, and thereafter toured the United States in his own private railway carriage, establishing track records wherever he went. He set a record of one minute fifty-five seconds for the mile in 1906, behind a pace-setting galloping horse. Another great Standardbred, Greyhound, trotted his way through the 1930s, achieving a personal best for the mile of one minute, fifty-five and a quarter seconds.

Hitherto a poor second to Thoroughbred racing, harness racing prospered after the introduction of arc lights permitted night racing. In former days such races began in a haphazard fashion, drivers positioning themselves and their horses as best they could. Now a mobile starting gate is used; entries trot or pace up to a barrier attached to the back of a car which increases its speed until, at the starting line, all horses are on gait and at the proper speed.

Other breeds of horse have more distinguishing conformation points than the Standardbred. It resembles the Thoroughbred although somewhat smaller in height, standing approximately 15hh (152cm), and being more sturdily built. Its weight ranges between 408–544kg (900–1,200lb), and its colour is unbroken.

Tennessee Walking Horse

Like its Saddle Horse kin, the Tennessee Walking Horse developed from Thoroughbreds, Standardbreds, Morgans and pacers. The breed's foundation sire was a Standardbred named Black Allen. Other early progenitors include a Thoroughbred-pacer mix named Copperbottom, and Free and Easy, a pacer especially well regarded by President Andrew Jackson.

The Walker is distinguished by its two unique gaits. The running walk is a four-beat movement during which the horse's hind legs over-reach the forelegs, often by more than 12in (30cm). There is much shoulder motion, but little lateral swaying. Walkers nod their heads in a pronounced fashion at each step of this gliding gait, which once took plantation-owners and foremen for miles at a clip. The 'rocking chair' canter was also developed to make hours in the saddle as painless as possible.

The Tennessee Walking Horse should have a neat, well-shaped head and a graceful neck. Its shoulders should be muscular and well-sloping and the body deep in the girth and well-ribbed in front of a short back. Legs should be flat and cordy. Height ranges from 15 – 16hh (152–163cm) and weight from 454–544kg (1,000–1,200lb). Nowadays, Tennessee Walkers are mostly limited to the show ring activities.

Mexico & the West Indies

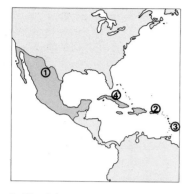

1. *The Galiceno is indispensable in the dry regions of northern Mexico.*
2. *The Paso Fino is bred on Puerto Rico.*
3. *Thoroughbred racing is especially popular in Barbados.*
4. *Cuba, conveniently situated, was used by the* conquistadores *as a horse breeding centre.*

In 1492, Christopher Columbus discovered the West Indies. He returned several times with consignments of Andalusian mares and stallions of mixed European, North African and Arabian origin. To prevent the horses from falling during the long, often rough journey, each horse had to be suspended inside its stall by means of a sail-canvas sling, slung under its belly and tied by lashing to a beam overhead. Therefore it is not surprising that the *conquistadores*, decided to set up horse-breeding stations on the larger islands of Cuba and Haiti from which to launch their conquests of North and South America.

In 1504, a young Spaniard called Hernan Cortés organized an expedition for the conquest of Mexico. One of his boyhood friends and fellow *conquistador*, Bernal Diaz del Castillo, kept a detailed record of these preparations. There were eleven stallions, including two pintos, and five mares, and on March 12th, 1519, Cortés and a complement of four hundred men arrived in Mexico, or New Spain as it was then called. The Indians were afraid of the Spanish horses and even more so of the cannon, and the conquest of the new land was swift and complete.

Having conquered the central valley of Mexico the Spaniards spread rapidly across the central plateau and within twenty years had explored far to the south in what is now known as Central America.

Northern Mexico today, the land of the Mexican *charro* (cowboy), is a continuation of the Great American Desert, with little rainfall and sparse vegetation. The greater part of the agricultural production of the region consists of stock-rearing, and as in the countries of South America, the horse is vital as a means of transport. Today this vast area is the home of some thirty-eight million cattle and seven million sheep, and the country's horse population is reckoned to be well over five million.

The Galiceno
The Galiceno is typical of the native Mexican horses today, most of which are related to the Spanish horse descended from those brought by Cortés. Standing 12–13.2hh (122–137cm), this is a tough, hardy and courageous animal, similar to the South American Criollo with its docile temperament and ease of handling. It is found in all colours, but piebalds, skewbalds and albinos cannot be registered. The breed has been established in the USA since 1959.

The West Indies
Few people realize the number and extent of the Caribbean islands which curve from North to South America over about 2,500 miles of ocean. All the native horses are typical of those of Spanish descent found throughout the South American countries, but the island of Puerto Rico has developed a breed of its own called the Paso Fino, similar to the Peruvian Ambler or Stepping Horse.

As with all the Southern American countries, horses and horse-sports are a popular and essential part of recreational and festival activities. Racing of Thoroughbreds, mainly descended from English stock and regularly strengthened by fresh injections of winning European blood, is especially popular in Trinidad and Barbados.

Four race meetings of three or four days each are held in February, May, August and November at the Garrison Savannah in Barbados, which is one of the few places in the world where sweepstakes in connection with racing are legalized.

The Barbados Turf Club has continued its policy, started in 1935, of keeping Thoroughbred stallions especially imported from England for the

purpose of improving the breed of local horse. The first stallion, a brown horse called O.T.C. by Obliteraty Telephone Call sired the winners of over $200,000 in the West Indies between 1939 and 1951. Other stallions which have had a considerable influence on the stock in the country over the years are Pride of India, winner of the Dewhurst Stakes at Newmarket, H.V.C., Elco, Blue Sails and Head Worker. H.V.C. was the sire of Ferry Boat, which although beaten in the Barbados and Trinidad Derbys by his stablemate Pepperpot, became one of the best horses ever bred in Barbados.

Paso Fino

Puerto Rico's now celebrated Paso Fino horses are descended from the Spanish Andalusian, and their 'island gait' has been evolved through a mixture of natural dexterity and training. Paso

The Patzcuaro Rodeo, Mexico **(far left)**. *The word rodeo was originally a term given to the round-up of cattle on the American prairies, but it soon became used to name shows where cowboys and gauchos exhibit their skills* **(above)**.

Fino horses do not walk, trot or canter, they perform the *paso largo* and *paso corto*, a broken pace in which the hind hoof strikes the ground a fraction before the front, with various high-stepping paces.

The paso fino gait is very slow with a steady unbroken rhythm, the paso corto is more relaxed, while the paso largo is a fast gait which can often outstrip the canter of other horses.

Paso Fino horses range from 13 to 15.2hh (132–157cm).

1. *The Criollo bred freely in a wild state on the Pampas grasslands.*
2. *Racing is very popular in Argentina. There are about forty racecourses, the most successful of which are at Buenos Aires and San Isodro.*

Below: *The Falabella Pony is one of the smallest breeds of pony in the world. These miniature horses have been bred by generations of the Falabella family in the Argentine and were originally down-bred from Shetland Ponies.*

Argentina

Criollo

The first horses to reach South America were brought over by Columbus on his second voyage in 1493 and disembarked at San Domingo, from where they spread to South and Central America and to Mexico. But the first importation to have real significance for the Argentine was the consignment of a hundred Andalusian stallions and mares, together with light draught and other transport horses, landed in 1535 by Don Pedro Mendoza, founder of the city of Buenos Aires. These animals were of the finest Spanish stock, with a good deal of Arab and Barb blood in their veins. Later when Buenos Aires was sacked by the Indians many of these horses escaped and were left to wander over the inhospitable Pampas, breeding in such numbers that fifty years later, herds of up to 20,000 were reported. The best of these tough animals, who could survive long periods with little water or food, were later caught and used by settlers, and named 'Criollos' or Creoles. They carried their owners or heavy packs across the endless plains of the Pampas or up the steep, rugged mountain passes over the Andes.

About a century ago, the tough Criollo was nearly ruined by being crossed with imported European and American stallions. This produced a faster, more elegant horse, but one which lacked the breed's celebrated resistance to hunger and disease. Then about seventy years ago, Argentine breeders combined to re-establish the true Criollo by strict selective breeding from the best remaining specimens. In 1918, a society was formed to promote the breed which now figures in the Argentine government stud book.

Criollo horses are noted for their longevity, especially if they are not broken till they mature, at around six or seven years of age. The most famous demonstration of the incredible stamina and toughness of the breed was the journey undertaken by the Swiss professor Aimé Tschiffely in 1925. With two native Argentinian-bred Criollo horses, Mancha and Gato, aged eighteen and sixteen respectively, he made a unique trek of 13,350 miles (22,695km) from Buenos Aires to New York, crossing mountains and deserts on the way. Gato lived to the age of thirty-five, Mancha to forty, neither ever having had a day's illness. Small wonder that the Criollo breed today not only makes up the largest part of Argentina's 4,000,000 strong horse population, but also flourishes throughout South America.

The Criollo now stands from about 13.2–14.3hh (137–150cm) and comes in many colours: dun with black dorsal stripe, blue or red roan, mealy bay, brown, black and skewbald.

Falabella

Named after the owner of the Recreo de Roca Ranch near Buenos Aires, the Falabella is a miniature horse developed some forty years ago, by crossing small Thoroughbreds and Shetlands. Never above 7.2hh (76cm), this breed can be of any colour including spotted. It is hardy, good-tempered and intelligent.

Anglo-Argentino

Often called the Argentine Horse (*Caballo Argentino*), a term previously only applied to the Criollo, the Anglo-Argentino breed evolved from the crossing of Thoroughbred stallions with Criollo mares, to produce ultimately a breed with approximately three-fifths to four-fifths Thoroughbred blood. These are strong, well-built animals, usually chestnut, bay or brown in colour, possessing the quality and speed of the Thoroughbred as well as the toughness and agility of the Criollo. The breed is divided into two categories, those under 1'6hh (163cm) which are mainly used as stock-horses or polo ponies, and those over 16hh (163cm) which are heavier in build and popular for showjumping and all riding activities.

Anglo-Normando

The Anglo-Normando originated in France, but

has long been bred in the Argentine. It is strongly built, courageous, with a placid if rather sluggish temperament, and while it lacks the quality of the Anglo-Argentino, it has more bone. Being rather long in the back, it does not stand up well to hard work on sandy or broken ground, but under normal conditions the heavier type of this breed makes a good driving horse, while the other, lighter type is popular with the army for cavalry and police use, and for showjumping.

Polo Pony

Most British and American players originally preferred to use small Thoroughbred ponies but Argentine breeders, realizing that the Criollo possessed the vital qualities of stamina, toughness and calmness, but lacked the quality and speed of the Thoroughbred, decided to set out to breed an ideal type of pony. From 1900 onwards, they kept up-grading their own native stock by continual importation of the best stallions, until by 1930, the Argentine pony was just as handsome as the English Thoroughbred, but tougher and with more bone.

Since 1939, when polo playing was suspended in all the major equestrian nations except the Argentine because of World War II, Argentina has been considered the main source of supply for the best polo ponies in the world. The high quality of the breed is carefully monitored by Argentine breeders, who insist that only mares which have proved themselves on the field can be used for breeding.

Arab

Towards the end of the last century, the brothers Alfonso and Hernan Ayerza brought back from the Arabian desert a few of the finest Arabs they could find. These became the foundation stock for their respective studs, and while in general the Arab has not been a popular breed in South America, in recent years breeders have begun to appreciate the Arab's iron-hard legs, endurance and fluent action. Arabs and Anglo-Arabs make an excellent cross with the Criollo and Anglo-Argentino. In 1972 there were some 600–700 registered and pure-bred Arabs kept in the Argentine.

Above: *A gaucho in Entre Rios, Argentina, oversees his stock from horseback.*

Top: *Polo is a fast, tough game that could possibly be one of the oldest equestrian sports. The ancient Persians and Chinese played a form of polo and in China it was the women who played the game.*

1 & 2. Different varieties of Crioulo-type horse have developed in different regions of Brazil: the Northeastern in the north east (1) and the Curraleiro in Goias (2).
3. The Mangalarga breed was founded in Minas Gerais province, north of Rio de Janeiro.
4. Horses were first introduced to Peru by Pizarro, who brought them to Lima, the capital.
5. The Venezuelan Criollo is sometimes called the Llanero from the llano *or plains of northern South America.*

Brazil, Peru & Venezuela

Brazil is the fifth largest state in the world – a country of plains and high plateaux. It has a huge and steadily-increasing horse-population which, according to United Nations' figures, is currently well over 9,000,000.

In 1500 a Portuguese, Pedro Alvares Cabral, sailed so far to the west to avoid the calms off the Gulf of Guinea that he eventually touched the South American coast. But it was not until Dom John's reign from 1521 to 1557 that colonization was encouraged. At first settlement was confined to the coastal areas, but over the years groups of impoverished *colons* formed themselves into small bands and set out to develop the rugged, mountainous interior, setting up outposts which became centres of agriculture and cattle-breeding. As in the other countries of South America, the nature of the terrain and the vastness of the area – a single 'paddock' or enclosure can be 10,000 acres (4,000 hectares) or more – were such that the horse was generally the most practical if not the only possible mode of transport. Even today, the army cannot be fully mechanized and is the main force behind the Brazilian horse-breeding industry, using large numbers of Arabian or Thoroughbred stock for cavalry purposes, and lightly-built Bretons of the old 'post-horse' type for draught.

Crioulo

The Brazilian equivalent of the Argentinian Criollo, the Crioulo traces back to a consignment of Portuguese Altérs landed near Santa Catarina on the Brazilian coast by Alvar Nuñez in 1541. Like the Andalusians of Don Pedro Mendoza, these spread and bred throughout Brazil, so different types of the breed can be found in different parts of the country. The Crioulo of today is rather smaller than the Criollo, and in north-east Brazil is known as the Nordestino, while in the State of Goias it is called the Courraleiro. The finest type of Crioulo, developed in the Rio Grande do Sul, is now being used to improve the quality of native horses in other parts of the country and makes an excellent cavalry, ranch and polo horse, as well as showjumper.

Right: *The Criollo is a South American breed of versatile horse used on the ranch and on the polo field. Some have made good showjumpers. The origins of the breed go back to the early 16th century.*

Mangalarga

During the nineteenth century, selected stallions from Spain and Portugal were imported into Brazil in an attempt to improve the native horses, and one of the best of these, named Sublime, established the Mangalarga breed. Larger than the Crioulo, standing about 15hh (152cm) the Mangalarga is an excellent working horse. It sometimes has a peculiar gait, half-jog, half-canter, called the *marcha* which it can maintain for hours on end. The breed has been successfully crossed with Arabian, Anglo-Arab, Thoroughbred or clean-bred European blood to provide high-quality riding horses. A separate variety of the Mangalarga, the Campolino is to be found in the State of Rio de Janeiro and the surrounding regions. It is well known for its quality and toughness, the result of careful selective breeding. Heavier than the Mangalarga, it is used both for riding and for light draught work.

Peru

For centuries the headquarters of the conquering Spanish armies, Peru used to receive more Andalusian and other Spanish breeds than any other country in South America. The first horses were brought to Lima by the city's founder, Pizarro, and regular reinforcements sent from Spain meant that pure-bred Andalusians were to be found in the area for hundreds of years.

As in the case of the Argentine consignment, some of these horses found their way into the wild and their descendants became the Peruvian type of Criollo, sometimes called Saltenos. Smaller than the Argentine Criollo, they are known for their soundness and fluent action. A larger variety, 14–15hh (142–152cm) is known as the Costeno and makes an excellent riding horse, while the more heavily-built and smaller mountain pony type known as the Serrano is used in the highlands as a pack-horse. The Morochuquo strain of the family, which seldom exceeds 13.2hh (137cm) but is more thick-set than most Criollos, is used as a pack-horse in the cold, forbidding Cordillera mountains.

Peruvian Ambler or Stepping Horse (*Caballo de Paso Peruano*)

Claiming descent from Spanish stallions, mainly Barbs, introduced during the conquest of Peru, the Caballo de Paso is similar to that breed in appearance, but slightly bigger with longer legs and higher tail carriage. Its unique gait, like that of the Mangalarga, enables it to cover vast distances over rugged country for hours on end, with the minimum of discomfort to the rider. The modern Stepping Horse is a handsome animal, 14–15.2hh (142–157cm), usually bay or chestnut and sometimes with a white blaze, but it can be found in all colours.

Throughout the countries of South America, the Criollo exists in all forms, shapes and sizes according to the manner in which it has adapted over the centuries to the rigours of the climate and the type of country in which it lives and works. Chile, Uruguay and Paraguay all have their own type of this remarkable breed, in use as a pack-horse or cow-pony. Venezuela too, with its tough climate of long droughts and hard winters, has developed its own type of Criollo, known as the Llanero. Smaller, finer and lighter than other Criollos, largely because of the rigours of the climate, the Llanero has retained the grace and lively action of its Andalusian forbears, but rarely exceeds 14hh (142cm). It is widely used as a pack-horse or cow-pony because of its stamina.

Competition riding is also popular in Venezuela, where jumping, cross-country and dressage events are held, mainly however on imported Thoroughbreds.

Above: *The Paso Fino, a breed of small riding horse developed in the Caribbean and South America. It is well-known for its lateral four-beat gait, giving a very comfortable ride. The breed can also be found in the United States.*

The British Isles

Ponies are indigenous to the British Isles and many of the herds, some still living in a semi-wild state in certain areas of Britain, can be traced back to early times. The Shetland Pony, for example, seems to have been domesticated in the Bronze Age, about 3,000 years ago. The original ponies, it is thought, came to northern Britain about 10,000 BC, and were of Tundra origin. Documents from the tenth and eleventh centuries mention herds of wild ponies living in a vast forest area in southern England. These could have been the forbears of the New Forest pony. From Roman times there are accounts of spirited little horses that roamed the Welsh hills which could have been the ancestors of the Welsh Pony.

From these ancient equine families, Britain's Mountain and Moorland ponies are descended. They consist of the Welsh – basically two types, pony and cob – the Shetland, Dartmoor, New Forest, Highland, Exmoor, Fell, Dales and Connemara ponies.

These native breeds have survived social changes, industrial revolution and the fickleness of fashion, and can now be found all over the world. The smaller type of Connemara pony, for example, is very popular in the United States and the Shetland Pony can be seen in the United States, Canada, the Falkland Islands, Holland, Sweden, Denmark, Belgium and France. Many of these countries now have their own stud books.

Great Britain's finest contribution to the equestrian world was surely the creation of the Thoroughbred race-horse. Running-horses, Hobbies and Galloways, have been bred and raced in Britain and Ireland since the fourteenth century. By the seventeenth century, eastern bloodstock was being used to improve home-bred horses and from this policy developed the modern Thoroughbred. These sleek equine racing-machines travelled to the new colonial lands to become the foundation stock of the American, Australian, New Zealand and French Thoroughbred.

Since the twelfth century, Irish farmers and breeders have been producing strong, sound horses and ponies, most of which were exported to England. Many years of shrewd breeding, mixing the Irish Draught Horse with thoroughbred or near-thoroughbred blood, has produced the Irish Hunter or Half-bred. Though strictly speaking a type rather than a breed, the Irish Hunter/Half-bred is one of the most successful light horses of modern times.

Ireland is a country of mineral-rich limestone soils and strong hunting traditions, and by virtue of these is the natural home of the steeplechaser, a thoroughbred by bloodline and registration but less glamorous than its flat-racing brother. Ireland has also more stallions of classic or top quality standing at stud than Great Britain.

Above: *Depicted in typical settings, some famous British horses form the basis of a set of postage stamps.*

Left: *A New Forest pony wanders through the trees in the winter evening sunshine. It is thought that herds of wild ponies have lived in this forested area of southern England since the days of King Canute (1017–1035).*

This map of the basic physical
divisions of the region locates
the areas where major horse
breeds originated. Present-day
important breeding areas and
studs are also indicated.

Heavy Horse
1. Clydesdale
2. Hackney
3. Irish Draught
4. Shire
5. Suffolk Punch

Light Horse
6. Cleveland Bay
7. Hackney Pony
8. Thoroughbred
9. Welsh Ponies and Cobs

Pony
10. Connemara
11. Dales Pony
12. Dartmoor
13. Exmoor
14. Fell
15. Highland
16. Shetland
17. New Forest

Ice/Tundra

Mountains/Uplands

Tropical forest

Forest/Woodland

Grassland

Savanna

Scrub

Desert

● Towns/Cities

□ Studs

Light Horse

Pony

Heavy Horse

Shetland Isles

LERWICK

Orkneys

Outer
Hebrides

NW Highlands

HIGHLANDS

Barra

SCOTLAND

GLASGOW

R. Clyde

EDINBURGH

GALLOWAY

N IRELAND

BELFAST

Lake District

Pennines

York Moors

YORK

NORTH
SEA

Lough Conn

Lough Corrib

CLIFDEN
CONNEMARA

Isle of
Man

IRISH
SEA

LIVERPOOL

MANCHESTER

R. Humber

R. Shannon

DUBLIN

KILDARE

LIMERICK

EIRE

Wicklow Mtns

ENGLAND

Cambrian Mtns

WALES

BIRMINGHAM

NEWMARKET

CORK

CARDIFF

R. Thames

BRISTOL

LONDON

ATLANTIC
OCEAN

Exmoor

Dartmoor

NEW FOREST

SOUTHAMPTON

ENGLISH CHANNEL

Great Britain

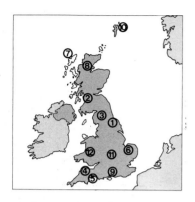

1. *North-east Yorkshire is the home of the Cleveland Bay.*
2. *The Clydesdale horse came originally from the lowland region of Lanarkshire, south of Glasgow.*
3. *Dales ponies come from east of the Pennines, Fell ponies from the west.*
4 & 5. *The two moorland areas of the West Country with their respective breeds of pony are Exmoor (4) and Dartmoor (5).*
6. *East Anglia is known for two breeds in particular, the Hackney from Norfolk, and the Suffolk Punch in Suffolk.*
7 & 8. *The Highland pony is divided into three types, the Barra and Western Isles ponies from the Outer Hebrides (7) and the Garron from the mainland (8).*
9. *New Forest ponies have their home in the woodlands of Hampshire.*
10. *The Shetlands lie halfway between Scotland and Norway.*
11. *The Midland shires formed the central farming area of England employing the haulage power of the Shire horse.*
12. *Welsh ponies have become world-wide favourites.*

Cleveland Bay
The Cleveland Bay is recognized as one of the oldest breeds in Britain, having been bred in the Cleveland district of north-east Yorkshire for more than two hundred years. This light, active working and riding horse has, despite the injection of thoroughbred blood at the end of the eighteenth century, remained almost unchanged.

The ideal Cleveland Bay stands 16–16.2hh (163–168cm) with some 22–25cm (8½–10in) of bone just below the knee, supporting a deep, short, compact body. In action it is powerful and more fluent than many other dual-purpose breeds and also cleaner legged (not hairy or feathered). Clevelands are normally bay with black points, the only acceptable white in their markings being a very small white star on the forehead. They have a strong aptitude for jumping and some of the early 'showjumpers' at agricultural shows were locally-bred Cleveland Bays.

The breed has known periods in its history when it seemed certain to disappear, but it has been saved by dedicated breeders, the demand for more 'sporting' horses, and its own fertility and ability to cross successfully with other strains of light horse. In 1884 the Cleveland Bay Horse Society was formed and in order to protect the strain and type, the society decreed that animals with thoroughbred or heavy draught blood would be excluded from its stud book.

In the 1950s, however, the popularity of the breed for hunting and showjumping, when thoroughbred blood had been added, brought about a change of policy. It was appreciated that the Cleveland's role in a sport-orientated equestrian world was for use in cross-breeding. Its influence can now be seen in show hunters, showjumpers and three-day eventers although the carriage horses of the Royal Mews are still pure Cleveland Bays. The breed has its own society in the United States and many good stallions and brood mares have been exported successfully to Canada, South Africa, Japan, Pakistan, Czechoslovakia and Australia.

Clydesdale
The northern regions of Great Britain have, over the centuries, produced a long and flexible list of agricultural livestock. Few breeds of working horse could have been better value in the days of non-mechanized economies than the Clydesdale.

This big, high-actioned horse with long feathered legs is a native of the Clyde Valley in the county of Lanarkshire, Scotland. It was originally bred by local farmers as a portage animal but in the middle of the eighteenth century, local mares were crossed with Flemish stallions ultimately to produce the type known today, a good-looking, weighty and strong animal with great soundness of limb, and by nature, docile and easy to handle.

The ideal specimen of the breed has open, round feet, broad clearly defined hocks, big knees, an intelligent eye, big ears and a long well-arched neck. The Clydesdale stands around 16.2hh (168cm) and the breed association is the Clydesdale Society. The breed has been exported around the world and in 1911 the Clydesdale stallion Baron of Buchlyvie was sold at public auction for £9,500, a vast sum in those days.

Right: *HRH Prince Philip, Duke of Edinburgh, is an enthusiastic and successful competitor in international driving grands prix. The Duke often drives a team of Cleveland Bays.*

Dales/Fell Pony

The handsome and versatile Dales Pony is the largest of the British Mountain and Moorland ponies. It stands between 14–14.2hh (142–147cm) with 20–22cm (8–8½in) of bone, and can carry a man of 100kg (16 stone) on the Fell or pull a ton weight between the shafts.

At about the end of the nineteenth century, a Welsh Cob stallion called Comet arrived in the county of Westmorland in northern England to compete in local trotting races. Trotting at that time was a very popular sport in Wales and north and east England. Comet, with a man of 77kg (12 stone) on his back, could trot ten miles (16km) in 33 minutes. When he returned to Wales he left behind him many good colts, as today every Dales Pony traces back to Comet. The ponies are native to the east of the Pennine range and have been bred by farmers in Northumberland, County Durham and the North Yorkshire Dales for many generations.

The Dales Pony with his active gait, great bone, open feet and powerful shoulders has worked on the farm, down the mines and in northern towns pulling tradesmen's vehicles. A victim of modern mechanization, by the early 1950s it had almost disappeared. But thanks to a few dedicated breeders and the recent popularity of pony trekking, the breed is now as popular as ever. The Dales Pony is ideal for trekking or trail-riding, being strong, sure-footed and easy to handle.

In the past, Dales have been crossed with Clydesdales and more recently with Thoroughbreds. But the generally accepted standard today is an active pony, about 14.2hh (147cm) with lightly feathered heels and a flowing mane and tail. Colours should be black, dark brown, sometimes grey but never chesnut, skewbald or piebald. The Dales Pony Society was formed in 1964 to ensure these standards.

The Fell Pony is a close relative of the Dales and almost identical in looks. The original ponies came from the western side of the Pennines in northern England. Before the days of mechanization, the Fell Pony was a 'Jack-of-all-trades', shepherding on the fells of the English Lake District, and pulling the family trap on a variety of domestic chores, besides being a great racing-trotter. For many years the Fell was used as a pannier pony to carry lead from the mines to the sea, travelling some 240 miles (386km) in a week and carrying up to 100kg (16 stone).

The Fell Pony Society was founded in 1927 to promote the breeding of pure-bred Fell Ponies which are registered in the National Pony Stud Book. The standard height can be up to 14hh (142cm) although the average is 13.2hh (137cm) and accepted colours are black, dark brown, dark bay and occasionally grey. The pony should have a high head carriage set on good sloping shoulders with a compact body very deep around the girth. The breed has been kept almost pure for over 70 years now and Fell Pony stallions have been exported to Canada, Spain, Libya, Germany, Pakistan and many other countries to improve local stock.

Above: *A Clydesdale enjoys some time off work gambolling in a field. These powerful horses have worked in agriculture for generations before the advent of mechanized transport. Thanks to enthusiastic breeders around the world they still thrive and are very popular with show ring spectators.*

Dartmoor Pony

In the south-west of England is a windswept area of rugged granite upland known as Dartmoor lying between 250 and 600m (750–2,000ft) above sea level. A kind, intelligent breed of small pony has lived there since earliest times. They roamed the moors in a semi-wild state, as many still do today, with little or no control exerted over their breeding until 1899, when the Polo Pony Society, which later became the National Pony Society, began a Dartmoor section in its Stud Book.

In earlier years Shetland stallions were turned out on the moors in order to produce a smaller, tougher cross-bred pony suitable for work down the mines. Since 1945 the Dartmoor Pony Society has selectively built up the breed after the deleterious effects of World War II, when Dartmoor became a battle-training area. In 1961 it opened an up-grading Supplementary Register to the Stud Book with strict terms of entry. This first grade Supplementary Register was closed in 1966 with 280 entries but the Society's second grade Supplementary Register remains open. All Supplementary Registered ponies carry the Dartmoor Pony Society's triangle brand on the neck.

The ideal Dartmoor Pony stands at 12hh (122cm); it is very rare for a true Dartmoor to exceed 12.2hh (127cm). The accepted colours are usually bay, black and brown although some greys and chesnut, can be seen on the moors. The Stud Book accepts every colour but skewbald.

Dartmoor ponies make ideal first ponies for children, for they are kind and sensible by nature with good conformation and a good head-carriage. They are hardy and sure-footed, but with plenty of elegance and charm. They are very popular in Canada, the United States, Denmark, Holland, Belgium, Germany, France and Australia.

Exmoor Pony

To the north of Dartmoor lies another sweeping expanse of moorland, Exmoor. The Exmoor pony is one of the hardiest and purest of the British native breeds and its toughness and honesty is recognized by breeders throughout the world.

The Exmoor has changed very little over the years. The mares do not exceed 12.2hh (127cm) and the stallions and geldings 12.3hh (129·5cm). They are usually bay-brown or dun, a typical shade being a mousy-brown with mealy-coloured areas under the belly and inside the forearms and legs. Their muzzles are also mealy-coloured as are the upper and lower lids of their very prominent wide set eyes, known locally as 'toad-eyes'.

The Exmoor Pony Society was founded in 1921 to improve and encourage breeding; ponies are registered in the National Pony Stud Book.

Hackney Horse and Pony

These high-stepping horses and ponies are very popular in the show rings of Great Britain, Australia and the United States. Derived from a practical strain of light working horse that travelled the roads of England long before the days of rail and motor transport, the Hackney Horse is a direct descendant of the world-famous Norfolk Trotter. This powerful, well-built carriage horse, later known as the Norfolk Roadster, was bred by England's East Anglian farmers for its great stamina. Many of these horses had more than a sprinkling of thoroughbred blood and the name Hackney (from the Norman *haquenée* meaning ambling nag or ungainly woman) was used in England for many centuries to describe a riding horse as distinct from a war-horse.

By the middle of the nineteenth century Hackney stallions were in great demand as 'getters' of military and carriage horses and in 1883 a society, formed in Norwich to compile a stud book for English Trotting Horses, first named them Hackneys.

The Hackney's trot must be spectacular with free shoulder movement and high ground-covering action, and a moment of suspension to mark each step. Its head should be small and convex in profile with a small muzzle, the neck strong with a good crest, and the shoulders powerful with a compact body set on short legs supported by well-shaped feet. The Hackney horse varies from 14.3hh–15.3hh (150–160cm) but can sometimes be as tall as 16.2hh (168cm).

The Hackney Pony, a smaller version of the horse, is now recognized as a separate breed, one which used to be a great favourite with tradesmen. It usually stands around 14hh (142cm) and is bred in great numbers in North America, Australia and South Africa.

Highland Pony

Experts claim that after the North Sea had finally separated Britain from Europe, the larger type of pony stayed in Scotland while the smaller types went south. The breed originates in the Highlands of Scotland where they were bred and used by crofters; they are still used to cart stags. Its main characteristics are sure-footedness and a tough constitution.

The breed consists of three types: the smallest standing 12.2hh–13.2hh (127–137cm) and found on Barra and other outer islands; the riding pony standing 13.2hh–14.2hh (137–147cm) and the strongest, the Mainland pony, standing 14.2hh (147cm). Colours range from dun through black, brown, grey to a fox-colour with a silver mane and tail. Most pure-bred Highland ponies, except blacks, browns and dark greys, have a dorsal stripe running down the spine. The Highland Pony Society was founded in 1923.

Above: *Dartmoor Ponies.*

Right: *An Exmoor pony mare and foal. Many of these herds of pony live in a semi-wild state on the moorlands of south-west England.*

Far right: *A Highland Pony brood mare.*

Above: *Two New Forest ponies enjoy some mutual preening by a pond. The ponies are rounded up each year for the annual Pony Sales held at Beaulieu Road on the edge of the forest.*

New Forest Pony

Herds of wild ponies living in an area of forest and moorland in southern England are mentioned in the pages of the Domesday Book of 1085. Around 1071 William Rufus, son of William the Conqueror, declared part of the county of Hampshire a royal hunting forest and it has been known ever since as the New Forest. Those herds of wild ponies seem to have been the ancestors of the hardy New Forest Pony.

The ponies live as near to the natural state as any domesticated creature can, roaming the 60,000 acres (25,000 hectares) of the New Forest, a heavily wooded region with open spaces covered with grass and heather. Some of the grazing in the area is not very good and in many ways this has improved the breed by ensuring that only the fittest survive.

Many of the British Mountain and Moorland pony breeds have benefited from time to time from the injection of eastern blood. In 1852 Queen Victoria lent her Arab stallion, Zora, so that he could be left to breed naturally with the ponies. He lived in the forest for eight years, and his influence and that of other foreign bloodlines introduced over the years has given the New Forest the concave profile which is a feature of many eastern horses.

The New Forest Pony Breeding and Cattle Society was formed in 1938 by amalgamating the two original societies which dated back to 1906. The first New Forest Pony Stud Book was published in 1910 but since 1959 the Society has published its own stud book each year. Since 1938 no foreign blood has been introduced to the breed.

The number of ponies wandering in the New Forest is somewhere between 2,000 and 2,500 of which about 150 are stallions. Only registered stallions are permitted to run in the Forest. These are inspected each spring and any that do not come up to the required standard are not allowed to run in the Forest again. The New Forest Pony is so popular today that many highly successful pure-strain studs have been established in Sweden, Canada, France, the United States, Holland and Denmark. The latter two publish their own stud book.

The New Forest should not exceed 14·2hh (147cm) and any colour is acceptable except piebald and skewbald. They are superb riding ponies with good temperaments, showing plenty of quality with nice heads, good shoulders, short backs, strong loins and quarters, good feet and plenty of bone. There are two types, Type A which stands 13.2hh–14.2hh (137–147cm), and is capable of carrying an adult yet still narrow enough for a child, and Type B which is basically the same but measures a maximum of 13.1hh (135cm).

Shetland Pony

One of the most popular, best loved but smallest of the pony breeds of Britain is the Shetland which varies in size from 26 inches (66cm) to the stud book limit of 42 inches (107cm). (Shetlands are traditionally measured in inches not hands.) The austere Shetland Islands 120 miles (190km) off the coast of northern Scotland are the home of these tough, long-lived little ponies. Their lack of height is often thought to be the result of the poor grazing conditions on the Islands and the severe climate. But these hairy little ponies could be animals of great antiquity, for remains have been found on the Islands that seem to support the theory that they were domesticated as far back as the Bronze Age, 3,000 years ago. The original ponies are thought to have been of Tundra origin, standing around 13.2hh (137cm.) With the passing of time, and changes in demand and fashion, they became smaller, and apart from the influence of stallions brought to the Islands by the first Norse settlers a thousand years ago, the breed has changed very little.

Black and brown are the most common colours, although chesnut and grey have become very popular in recent times. Roan, dun and cream are now quite rare but skewbald and piebald can still be seen on the Islands.

Until the mid-1800s there were no roads in the Shetlands so ponies and boats provided the only means of transport. The Shetland Pony acquired a reputation as a dual-purpose animal, capable of carrying heavy loads or people over rough and difficult ground. Around 1860 there was a big demand for ponies to work underground in the expanding mines of north-east England, so a thick, heavy type of Shetland was developed for draught work. With the advent of mechanization, this type of Shetland practically disappeared.

The Shetland is gentle and easy to train, although it possesses strength, courage and versatility out of all proportion to its size. The ideal Shetland (or 'Sheltie') has a small head and muzzle, neat short ears and large kind eyes; its compact body is supported by short legs. The mane is generous and the tail thick and carried high. Height limits are 42 inches (107cm) for four years old and over and 40 inches (102cm) for three years old and under. The Shetland Pony Stud Book Society was founded in 1891.

Shetland Ponies are now bred in many countries of the world, such as the United States (where the ponies are more slender than the native Scots pony), Canada and the Falkland Islands. They can adapt easily to strange climates without deviating from their true type and size. The leading importers are now Holland, Sweden, Denmark, Belgium and France all of whom have their own stud books for the breed. The Shetland is very popular as a child's pony.

Above: *The popular Shetland Pony, a British native breed that many experts believe dates back to the Bronze Age.*

Above: *A Welsh Cob (Section D) stallion.*

Top: *Spring work for Shires in the fields of southern England. These gentle giants get their name from the 'Shires' district of the Midlands of Britain.*

Shire horse

The Shire, the gentle giant among British breeds, is as well known and respected throughout the world as the English Thoroughbred. These tall, massive horses are the greatest of Britain's agricultural and working horses and can still be seen today working in the fields or pulling brewers' wagons in the streets of London.

In the early part of the fourteenth century, several horses were brought to England from Lombardy to be crossed with the native stock with the aim of producing a weight-carrying war-horse. This battle horse became known as the Great Horse of Europe and many support the theory that the Shire is a direct descendant of this Great Horse and was himself bred as a war-horse. A fully-armed knight weighed around 190kg (30 stone) so his mount certainly had to be a strong horse. But 'great' need not imply size, for much of the armour used by those demanding horsemen does not fit the smallest of Shire horses. It is more likely that the Shire was developed for its pulling power than its ability to carry heavy weights, and that it joined the agricultural industry much later than is often realized. The name of the breed would suggest this as it comes from one of the first 'big field' farming regions of England, the Midland Shires, made up of the counties of Leicestershire, Warwickshire, Northamptonshire and parts of Lincolnshire.

The Shire has great docility, strength and stamina and although a slow-moving animal, is capable of pulling immense weights. It ranges from 16.2hh to 17.2hh (168–178cm) and has a compact body with deep powerful shoulders, wide chest and round well-muscled hindquarters. Shires often have a considerable amount of white on their feet and legs and the lower leg is feathered with fine silky hair. Bays and browns are the most common colours but there are also blacks and greys.

The Shire Horse Society was established in 1878 and is now under the patronage of Her Majesty Queen Elizabeth II. The Society publishes a stud book, promotes the breed, organizes sales and stages the annual Shire Horse Show.

The popularity of the breed seems to be stronger than ever. Many farmers and commercial organizations have found that the heavy horse is still an economical proposition on certain agricultural units and for short-haul transportation. Visitors to the Courage Shire Horse Centre near Maidenhead, Berkshire topped half a million in September 1978. Shires are now exported all over the world to countries like the United States, Australia and Russia.

Suffolk Punch

The Suffolk Punch, which gets its name from the county of Suffolk in eastern England, dates back,

it is claimed, to 1506. These gentle chesnut horses that are mainly seen today in the show ring can be traced back in an unbroken male line to a horse foaled in 1760. The breed is always chesnut in colour, and along with the Percheron, is the only clean-legged heavy draught horse bred in England. The breed has been infused with foreign blood from time to time, producing a finer forehand and a more active gait, and in spite of its massive body, it is able to trot quite freely and fast. It has tremendous pulling power, does well on little food and usually stands at around 16hh (163cm).

One fascinating aspect of the Suffolk Punch is its longevity. It is not unusual for mares to breed regularly well into their twenties and one famous Suffolk gelding was shown at the London Cart Horse Parade seventeen years in succession until he was 21 years old. Much of the credit for the continued purity of the breed must go to the enthusiastic East Anglian breeders and the strict rules adopted by the Suffolk Horse Society, founded in 1878. No animal can be shown at leading agricultural shows or sold at the Society's sales without a veterinary surgeon's certificate of soundness.

The Suffolk is exported to all parts of the world including the USSR, Australia and the United States, and demand is increasing each year for these practical big-girthed animals.

Welsh Pony and Cob

The Welsh Pony is one of the most beautiful of the British native breeds, with its neat, intelligent head, bold eye and agile body. There are still many herds living in the Welsh hills although many highly successful studs are now established outside Wales and beyond the shores of Great Britain.

The Welsh Stud Book, first published in 1902, divides the breed into four sections, Section A denotes the Welsh Mountain Pony standing up to 12hh (122cm); Section B denotes the Welsh Pony standing 12.2–13.2hh (127–137cm); Section C denotes the Welsh Pony Cob Type which should not exceed 13.2hh (137cm) and Section D denotes the Welsh Cob which has a deep, strong body set on short legs with powerful hocks and stands between 14–15hh (142–152cm). They are all well known for their agility, natural aptitude for jumping, intelligence, soundness of limb and tough constitution. These qualities have brought them a world-wide reputation as foundation stock from which to breed larger ponies and horses. Many of the childrens' riding ponies and show ponies today have a high percentage of Welsh blood in their veins.

The dished-face profile of the Welsh strains suggests the influence of eastern blood during its development and many experts believe that this influence dates back to Roman times.

Above: *Three Welsh Mountain Ponies (Section A) roaming the hills of South Wales.*

Ireland

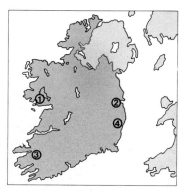

1. The Connemara pony has evolved in the bleak climate of the western moorlands.
2. The Dublin Horse Show has become internationally famous.
3 & 4. Most popular areas for pony-trekking are Kerry (3) and Wicklow (4).

Right: The Connemara Pony, Ashfield Bobby Sparrow, in full flight. One of Ireland's top international showjumpers of the late 1950s and early 1960s, Dundrum, was part Connemara.

Connemara Pony

The Connemara Pony is Ireland's only native breed. It is a sturdy, general-purpose pony standing between 13–14.2hh (132–147cm). Its colouring is grey, black, bay, brown, or dun (a yellow-brown or greyish-black coat, and black mane and tail), with occasional roans (those with white hair running through their natural colour) and chesnuts.

The Connemara has a deep, compact body standing on short legs with clean, hard, flat bone about 18–20cm (7–8in) below the knee. It has a well-balanced head and neck, sloping shoulders and a free and easy movement.

It is named after the part of Ireland from which it comes, a wild area of barren mountains, lakes, bogs and rocky ground offering meagre subsistence for man or pony. To the east are Lakes Corrib and Mask, to the south, Galway Bay, and on the west, the Atlantic Ocean. Living naturally in these conditions, the Connemara has survived and developed into a pony known for its stamina, soundness, staying power and versatility. It is also notably free from hereditary disease and as it is gentle, intelligent and adaptable, it makes a suitable children's pony. It can carry a lightweight adult out hunting, prove a fearless and natural show jumper and make a steady, reliable driving pony.

The origins of the Connemara are uncertain. It is thought to be the descendant of the Celtic pony which drew war chariots and raced in Ireland from 500 BC. There is evidence of the introduction of Andalusian, Spanish, Barb and Arabian blood over the years. Towards the end of the last century, Welsh stallions and some hackneys were introduced too.

In 1923, the Connemara Pony Breeders' Society was formed to preserve and improve the breed. The best ponies were selected and registered and some stallions of the highest quality were purchased. Some 75 mares and six stallions were registered initially, and the first volume of the Stud Book appeared in 1926.

Since then, limited Thoroughbred and Arab blood has helped to develop and refine the breed and in the future, further non-Connemara sires may be used to this end.

Connemara ponies are exported to many countries around the world and there are breeders' societies throughout Europe and in America and Australia. In August, over 400 ponies are exhibited at their annual show at Clifden in the heart of Connemara.

Irish Draught

On a rare occasion deep in the countryside of Ireland, you can still see a farmer walking behind his Irish Draught Horse as they plough the land.

The Irish Draught is a deep-chested, flat-boned

horse with an oval rib cage and sloping shoulders. It stands 15.3–16.3hh (160–170cm) and is bay, grey, brown or chesnut. It has a high-set tail and a short, smooth coat with little or no feather (hair) on its legs, and is docile, with great courage, stamina and soundness.

The Irish Draught was best known as Ireland's working horse until farm mechanization and industrialization threatened its existence. Although farmers are reluctant for financial reasons to continue breeding these horses, their value to the light horse industry is acknowledged and efforts are made continually to preserve and develop the breed.

An Irish Draught Horse Book was started by the Department of Agriculture in 1917 and published three years later, but no breed society was formed until January 1976. This Society intends to open its own herd book in the hope that the Irish Draught may be recognized as an international breed by the EEC. The Irish Horse Board, a government body responsible for the non-thoroughbred industry in Ireland, runs a register and offers various incentive schemes. It has also started progeny testing.

However, some equestrian authorities, in contrast, consider the horse to be a type, not a breed. As there was no early stud book, no foundation sires can be identified and policy was often changed regarding the suitability and even recognition, of mares or colts as Irish Draught. The introduction of Clydesdale and Shire blood earlier this century also divided opinion. Indeed, the very origin of the Irish Draught is obscure, although it may have evolved from the Connemara Pony.

Irish Half-Bred Hunter

Ireland contains some of the best hunting country in the world and hunting provides basic schooling for young horses. They have to learn to jump ditches, walls, hedges and banks often 1–2m (1–2yd) high with ditches on either side.

The Irish Half-Bred Hunter is more of a type than a breed. It is often the progeny of an Irish Draught mare and a Thoroughbred sire and has courage, speed and stamina. Many such horses in the past went on to be showjumpers or eventers, their training in the field making them fearless jumpers, but there is a tendency now to use three-quarters, seven-eighths or even Thoroughbreds for these sports.

Hunters are categorized on weight-carrying ability with a small hunter not exceeding 15.2hh (157cm) proving a valuable young rider's mount. The lightweight hunter carries up to 79kg (12 stone 7lb) and the heavyweight more than 89kg (14 stone). Most top Irish show horses and jumpers come from the middleweight bracket, 79–89kg (12½–14 stone).

Below: *The Irish Draught mare Pink Carnation, owned by Patrick Duane of Co Galway and winner of the National Irish Draught Mare Championship in 1977.*

Above: *The brown mare Sky Line, a classic example of an Irish half-bred type. She was bred by Mrs J. W. Nicholson of Balrath Bury Stud, Co Meath, and ridden here by Mrs Mary McCann.*

Scandinavia

Recorded in Sweden as early as the twentieth century BC, on a Bronze Age burial carving at Kivik, horses also featured in Scandinavian mythology in the shape of a yellow-maned horse ridden by Heimdal, and Sleipnir the grey horse of Odin, chief of the gods. Sleipnir had eight legs and could travel both on land and sea.

Many of the pony breeds discussed in this section bear a physical resemblance to those of the British Isles, and it is assumed that all are descended from the early 'Northern Dun'. The only breed still truly representative of that bloodline is Przewalski's Wild Horse from Mongolia. The main characteristics of the type are the big, heavy head set on a solid, stocky body with a thick neck and short, strong legs. The most common colour is dun, frequently with a dark dorsal stripe.

World War II had a dramatic effect on the horse population of most European countries. Denmark was no exception; numbers there dropped drastically but have since recovered to around 35,000. Riding as a recreation has gained tremendous popularity, particularly among the younger generation whose favourite pony seems to be the Norwegian Fjord.

Finland has about 2,500 horses and ponies, about 80 per cent of which are imported geldings. Riding horses are mainly imported from Poland, Denmark and the Soviet Union, and the pony stock generally originates from Sweden and Denmark.

In 1978 the Finnish Warmblood Horse Breeders' Association was given a special grant to lease Danish stallions and so improve warm-blooded riding horses. About 20,000 people ride in Finland, where the Equestrian Federation and the Riding Institute are both granted government support.

Sweden has also seen an enormous increase in riding interest over the last 20 years and to satisfy the demand, huge numbers of New Forest, Welsh, Shetland, Connemara, Icelandic and Norwegian ponies have been imported and used for breeding. Whereas the Russ Gotland was once the only children's riding pony it now has some healthy competition, bred under the auspices of the Swedish Pony Society.

Iceland is the most northerly area other than Siberia to have an indigenous breed of ponies. There are still as many ponies as there are people on the island. Only one-sixth of the land is habitable and a mere one per cent cultivated; although road and air transport have expanded, much of the island is still negotiable only with the aid of horse-power. To cater for the tourist industry there are several trekking and trail-riding centres and there is also a resurgence of interest in recreational riding among the inhabitants.

This map of the basic physical divisions of the region locates the areas where major horse breeds originated. Present-day important breeding areas and studs are also indicated.

Heavy Horse
1. Finnish (Draught)
2. Jutland
3. North Swedish

Light Horse
4. Finnish (Ridden)
5. Frederiksborg
6. Knabstrup
7. Swedish Warmblood

Pony
8. Døle Gudbrandsal
9. Fjordhest
10. Icelandic Pony
11. Lyngen
12. Russ/Gotland

Left: *Iceland Ponies. These tough, hardy little animals were brought to the region by the Norwegians in the 9th century.*

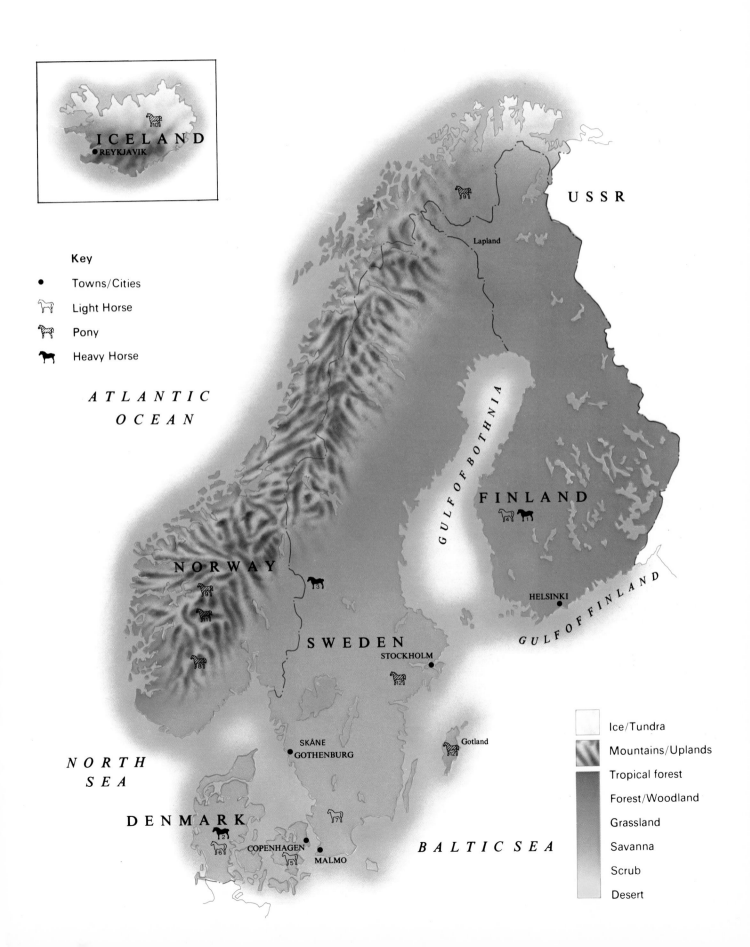

ICELAND

REYKJAVIK

Key

- Towns/Cities
- Light Horse
- Pony
- Heavy Horse

ATLANTIC
OCEAN

USSR

Lapland

GULF OF BOTHNIA

FINLAND

NORWAY

SWEDEN

HELSINKI

GULF OF FINLAND

STOCKHOLM

Gotland

NORTH
SEA

SKÅNE
GOTHENBURG

DENMARK

BALTIC SEA

COPENHAGEN

MALMO

Ice/Tundra

Mountains/Uplands

Tropical forest

Forest/Woodland

Grassland

Savanna

Scrub

Desert

Denmark

1. The royal stud at Frederiksborg, from which the Frederiksborg breed derived its name, was dissolved in 1839 after 300 years.
2. The most popular breed of Danish heavy horse comes from Jutland.

Above: *The Knabstrup, a distinctive spotted horse dating back to the Napoleonic wars.*

Top: *The Frederiksborg, one of the most versatile of the three Danish breeds. Originally bred from Andalusian stock, British, Dutch, Neapolitan and Turkish bloodlines have been added.*

Frederiksborg

Perhaps the most utilitarian of the three Danish breeds is the Frederiksborg, which takes its name from a famous royal stud established by King Frederik II, near Copenhagen in 1562. In those days Denmark was the leading breeder and supplier of good riding horses in Europe. The royal stud's foundation stock was Spanish Andalusian, specially imported by the King and later infused with British, Dutch, Neapolitan and Turkish bloodlines.

The Frederiksborg horse developed into a powerful, active breed standing 15–16hh (152–163cm). It became established as an all-round working horse used under saddle, in agriculture and in military service. It was employed in all the great European riding schools of the eighteenth and nineteenth centuries and as 'improver' stock in most principal studs.

Frederiksborgs are noted for their deep bodies, short, strong legs, and powerful shoulders, and have 'plenty of bone' – a general term indicating the circumference of the bone below the animal's knee or hock. They usually have a Roman nose, inherited from their Spanish or Arabian ancestors. The colouring is predominantly a rich chesnut, and the character is good. The breed's action may be described as 'strong, sweeping and high'. The modern-day Frederiksborg bears little resemblance to its heavier ancestor, though it is still considered ideal for riding, competition harness or light draught work.

Jutland

From the region of Jutland comes a breed of heavy horse said to have existed for more than 1,000 years. It was once the most popular Danish breed and was used extensively during the Middle Ages as a charger, having the strong, powerful conformation necessary to carry the considerable weight of knights in armour. More recently its qualities have been better suited to agriculture and other heavy draught work but the Jutland has been one of many breeds to suffer a dramatic decline during the twentieth century.

The ancient history of the Jutland is not well known but the horse is closely related to the German Schleswig. The province of Schleswig was once part of Denmark. In the late nineteenth century an association was formed to develop the Schleswig into a more adaptable animal for modern-day purposes and until World War II there was much cross-breeding. The Jutland's foundation sire is Oppenheim LXII, a Suffolk Punch shipped from Britain in 1860.

The Jutland stands a solid 15.2–16.2hh (157·5–168cm), has a wide body, deep chest and girth, short legs covered with fine, silky hair, an intelligent head and kind eye. Ninety-five per cent of registered Jutlands are chesnuts.

Knabstrup

The origin of the distinctive spotted Knabstrup horse dates back to the Napoleonic wars when an officer of the Spanish troops stationed in Denmark left behind his spotted chesnut mare called Flaebehoppen. Despite her reputation for extraordinary speed and endurance, and for her distinctive blanket markings with white mane and tail, she nevertheless found herself working the delivery rounds of a local butcher. But it was not long before she caught the eye of one Major Villars Lunn who took her home to Knabstrup.

The Major was already an established horse breeder, with stock originating from the Royal Frederiksborg Stud. The Spanish mare (whose conformation was apparently more akin to an English hunter than anything Spanish) was put to a palomino Frederiksborg stallion about 1808. The resultant colt, Flaebehingsten, had similar colouring to his mother, and became the foundation stallion of the Knabstrup Horse.

In its home country, interest in the Knabstrup runs high; there is more than one society and a number of representative studs. In recent years more importance seems to have been placed on the actual markings, described as either 'blanket', 'leopard' or 'snow flake', than on the animal's conformation. Flaebehingsten, though like his dam, was of a somewhat lighter, almost metallic, shade and displayed more than 20 colours!

Being of a good medium weight and height, averaging 15.3hh (160cm), noted for strength, speed, endurance and appearance, the Knabstrup horse is particularly popular in the circus trade.

Finland

Right: *The Finnish Horse is a close relation of the cold-blooded breeds of Britain and northern Europe.*

Finnish Horse

The Finnish Horse belongs to the 'Scandinavian' group of breeds from Norway, Sweden and the Baltic States, all closely related to the cold-blooded breeds of the British Isles and north Europe.

This is the only officially recognized breed in Finland and is a relatively recent result of the amalgamation of the old Finnish Draught and Universal horses, closely related breeds, with imported warm blood.

The modern Finnish Horse is an attractive, cobby all-rounder for riding or draught purposes. In fact, two exercises the Finnish excels at are timber hauling and trotting.

The Finnish Horse has a fine temperament and constitution: physical strength, activity, staying power and a desire to please. The horse is not more than 15.2hh (157·5cm), has a strong, muscular body, clean legs, hard feet and plenty of bone. The colouring is predominantly chesnut, brown and bay or, less often, black.

1. The Gotland pony is a popular breed from the Baltic island of Gotland.
2. Flyinge in Skåne is now the most important breeding centre in Sweden.

Sweden

Russ/Gotland

From the island of Gotland in the Baltic Sea originates Scandinavia's oldest and smallest breed – the Russ or Gotland pony.

This pony is believed to have existed since the Stone Age, though its actual ancestry is open to speculation. It probably descended from the eastern-European Tarpan, with the more recent addition of Arab and English blood. During the latter half of the last century some oriental blood was also introduced, but this failed to have much noticeable effect and the Russ Gotland still retains a certain 'primitive' air. It also bears a strong resemblance to Poland's Konik pony breed.

Herds of the Russ Gotland still run wild in Sweden, particularly through the Lojsta forests. At the turn of the century their numbers dwindled – at the same time as their quality improved – but now selective breeding and strict judging has resulted in stabilizing this elegant, light pony.

The Gotland is a versatile breed suitable for most types of work, but as the trot is its easiest natural gait, it has earned a solid reputation as a good trotting pony. It is quick, agile, and a keen jumper, and is therefore a popular child's pony.

The Russ Gotland averages 12hh (122cm) and is a narrow, delicate pony, easily managed but sometimes a little obstinate – as are many small pony breeds. The head should be small with a broad forehead, small ears, large eyes and nostrils; the neck short, shoulders long and sloping, with a long back leading to a short, round croup. The legs, though light, should be strong and muscular and the hooves small and hard. The breed society allows all colours, including palomino. A dark dorsal stripe is often seen, though socks or stockings are rare.

North Swedish

In 1900 an association was formed with the sole aim of creating a special draught horse – the North Swedish, until then a type rather than a uniform breed. In 1924 the breed society became nationally recognized with its own registry and stud book.

The breed was established by way of steadily upgrading local stock with Døle Gudbrandsdals imported from Norway until the mid-1940s, when there were about 15,000 North Swedish mares being covered by some 8,000 home-bred stallions each year. Since then Oldenburg blood has also been introduced.

The stallions stand 15.1–15.3hh (155–160cm) and tend to be taller than the mares. The breed possesses an especially good temperament and is renowned for its longevity and good resistance to contagious equine diseases. It is easy to handle and economic to feed, so it has been a valuable worker on the farms and forestry reserves of north Sweden. In the past it was also employed by the army as a harness horse and cavalry remount.

Its movement is lively and long-striding, more akin to a riding horse than a draught, but its trotting ability has made it suited to the tracks. The general appearance of the North Swedish denotes a powerful working animal: large head, short neck, broad deep body and short legs with plenty of bone. It can be black, brown, bay, chesnut or dun.

Swedish Ardennais

Sweden's most popular draught horse is the Swedish Ardennais, originally imported from Belgium during the 1830s. Mechanization has affected all breeds of heavy horse and this is no exception. Yet there are still farms and crofts relying on horse-power, while some already automated establishments are finding it more economical to return to the way of the horse, the latter sometimes being cheaper and more reliable than its mechanical counterparts. Nevertheless, most Swedish Ardennais have been used in the forests for transporting timber until recently.

The Belgian-imported stock was originally crossed with the North Swedish horse and soon produced a consistent type standing between 15.2–16hh (157·5–163cm) with a thick, crested neck and a deep, muscular body set on short, strong legs showing little feather. Black, bay, chesnut and brown are the most common colours. The breed is good-natured and quiet to handle, yet surprisingly energetic and alert.

In 1901 a stud book was opened and for more than 50 years the Breeding Association for the Swedish Ardennais has registered all foals and kept papers on all pedigree stock.

Swedish Warmblood

The most suitable riding horse of the four Swedish breeds, and the one which has received international acclaim – particularly in the dressage arena – is the half-bred Swedish Warmblood. This is a general utility horse resulting from the union between local cold-blooded and imported warm-blooded stock. During the seventeenth century, stallions were imported from Spain and the orient and put to the tough little Swedish natives. This resulted in a larger, more adaptable type ideal for army use. Later the strain was crossed again with English Thoroughbred, Trakehner, Holstein and Arab.

The famous Swedish Army Riding School at Strömsholm (1868–1968) was used as a stallion depot for rigorously examining breeding stallions. Since the Strömsholm school's closure the depot at Flyinge, in southern Sweden, alone exports large numbers of Warmbloods to Switzerland, Britain and the United States, mostly for dressage purposes.

The Warmblood is ideal for driving and riding, has a particular aptitude for high school work and, to a lesser extent, showjumping. It is a strong, sound, genuine breed with a good temperament and good conformation. It is an attractive mount, capable of carrying a fair riding weight and standing no taller than 16.2hh (168cm). The horse should show plenty of depth through the girth and have short, 'clean' legs. All solid colours are permitted, chestnut probably being the most common.

Left: *The Russ/Gotland pony, Scandinavia's oldest and smallest breed.*

Below: *A group of North Swedish Horses, renowned for their longevity and resistance to contagious equine diseases.*

1. The trade and pack route through the Gudbrandsdal valley has been used since early times to link the Atlantic seaboard with the Oslo region.
2. The Fjord pony comes from the western fjord area.
3. Lofoten ponies from the north were taken by the Vikings to the Shetlands.

Norway

Døle Gudbrandsdal

Displaying a remarkable similarity to the English Dales and Fell breeds, the Døle Gudbrandsdal takes its name from the central valley linking the Atlantic coastlands with the district of Oslo. Horse-drawn wagons travelled the flat valley floors, but where the narrow tracks climbed steeply over rough terrain the horses were required to become pack animals, and in this role the Gudbrandsdal excelled.

The sturdy little horse was used in agriculture on the steep terrain even now inaccessible to motorized transport. Norway was the first European country to record the use of a horse-drawn plough.

The English Dales and Fell show many similarities to the Døle for they probably descend from the same ancestor, widespread in prehistoric times when Britian was physically joined to the rest of Europe. Commerce and migration furthered contact in later days, and between AD 400 and 800 Friesian merchants conducted considerable sea trade between Britain and Norway – indeed, the Dutch Friesian is of a similar stamp to those mentioned above.

In the 1830s an English Thoroughbred called Odin was exported to Norway. His influence on

the Døle Gudbrandsdal soon resulted in a lighter, finer strain which is today used for riding, fast harness and trotting – the most popular form of horse racing in Norway. But the utility type still thrives and has the mark of a true draught horse: strength with great pulling power in relation to its height, 14.2–15.2hh (147–157·5cm). It has a wide chest, long back, deep girth, powerful quarters with short legs and plenty of feather. The predominant colours are black, brown and bay.

Because of their versatility Gudbrandsdals were widely requisitioned by the Germans during World War II. Horse-breeding was compulsorily expanded so that by 1945 Norway was in the relatively unique position of claiming a high equine population. Since then numbers have declined, although recently riding for pleasure has experienced a boom.

Fjordhest

The distinctive little Fjord or Westlands ponies come from western Norway and are said to have been the mounts of the Vikings – as well as the contestants in their fearful sport of horse fighting.

Since their distant beginnings, the ponies have spread themselves throughout northern Europe and are particularly popular in Denmark where they are used for light agricultural work.

The Fjord has the look of a 'primitive' pony, which is accentuated by its dun colouring and the dark dorsal stripe running the length of its backbone, dark legs and frequent zebra markings. The average height is 14 hands (142cm). The

Right: *The mount of the Vikings, the attractive Fjord Pony of Norway with its neat head, distinctive dun colouring and alert ears.*

head is neat with small, pert ears and widely spaced eyes. The mane generally shows silver or cream hairs running the length of the crest and on either side of the dorsal stripe, a trait repeated in the tail. The back should be long, well developed and muscular; the legs short, strong and clean with hard feet.

The breed is by nature thrifty and easily fed; in temperament it is quiet and friendly and it loves company – either animal or human. The short-strided action of the pony makes it less popular for riding than for light draught or passenger harness, the most suitable trap for it being a two-wheeled dog-cart.

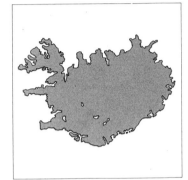

Iceland

Icelandic Pony

It was during the ninth century that the Vikings first landed in Iceland. Along with their household goods and farming stock they took their ponies: short, stocky little mounts, hardy, sure-footed and dependable. These were the ponies ridden by Burnt Njal and Gissur White.

Other early settlers on Iceland came from Orkney, Shetland and the Western Isles, thus introducing mixed blood into the 'native' stock. However, despite its rather indefinite ancestry, the Icelandic – or Viking – Pony is now a pure-bred line, no horse or pony having been allowed into Iceland for the past 800 years. Moreover, exported ponies are not allowed re-entry.

Bred on such rough open land touching the Arctic Circle, only the strongest strains have survived the climate over the centuries. The breed

is distinguished by its large head, short, thick neck, a heavy mane, forelock and tail, and coarse grey or dun-coloured coat. The average height is 13hh (140cm). Major characteristics are the Icelandic's five distinct gaits: walk, trot, canter, pace and tolt (running walk), the last two being most comfortable for the rider over long distances.

The temperament of the pony is friendly and docile, though decidedly independent. Conventional horse training methods seldom have much effect on the Viking Pony, most accepting orders by voice alone. The breed is also renowned for its keen eyesight and an amazing homing instinct.

Until comparatively recently, there was no alternative method of transport on Iceland and the stock was therefore put to work. Some ponies were exported to Britain for use underground in the mines and others were bred for local consumption, island conditions not being favourable for cattle. Numbers of the native Icelandic Pony have declined, though a few are still employed on the land and, of course, for the ever-increasing tourist trade.

Below: *A herd of Iceland Ponies graze peacefully with their young.*

Central Europe

Central Europe includes two of the most famous horse-breeding countries in the world, France and Germany. The latter is particularly renowned for the Hanoverian, Trakehner and Holstein riding horses. German horses have won 48 Olympic medals at just ten Equestrian Games and they took the dressage and showjumping individual world titles in both 1974 and 1978.

France earns her reputation from having the largest equine population in western Europe, nearly twice that of Germany. French horses have shone in every sphere: the Percheron is the most popular heavy horse in the world, French Trotters and Thoroughbreds have won most of the major international races and French riding horses have won Olympic gold medals. Although French ponies might not rival the native British breeds, the horses of the Camargue which roam wild in the Rhône delta are one of the world's most popular equine tourist attractions.

Much of the success of the French and German horses in international competition is due to the financial and administrative aid given by their respective governments. In Germany the state runs regional studs, gives considerable assistance to individual breeders and ensures that all stallions are of the highest quality.

In France, the Pari-Mutuel of racing provides huge funds for the Ministry of Agriculture's department, the Service des Haras. Its activities

include running 23 regional studs, organizing and financing competitions, distributing premiums and aiding racing and equitation. In all, it spends about £25 million a year. This does help to ensure that the French horses remain some of the best in the world.

Austria, the Netherlands and Belgium on the other hand are all countries where breeding and horse numbers have recently declined. All three can still boast ancient breeds which flourish today – the Noriker in Austria, the Friesian in the Netherlands and the Brabant in Belgium. But modern demands have resulted in greater specialization in the type of horse bred and the functions it is expected to perform. The Netherlands for example, has witnessed an upsurge in the popularity of trotting races and this has contributed to the creation of a versatile utility horse, the Dutch Warmblood. Likewise in Switzerland, multi-purpose warmblood horses have been specially bred in order to produce a horse with good jumping ability and stamina.

But these countries can still boast their own national curiosities from the spectacular feats of the Austrian Lipizzaners, trained exclusively at the Spanish Riding School in Vienna, to the winter racing on the frozen lake of St. Moritz and other Swiss 'racecourses'. It is this variety of types and functions which make the breeds of Central Europe so interesting.

This map of the basic physical divisions of the region locates the areas where major horse breeds originated. Present-day important breeding areas and studs are also indicated.

Heavy Horse
1. Ardennais
2. Ariège
3. Boulonnais
4. Brabant
5. Breton
6. Comtois
7. Dutch Draught
8. East Friesian
9. Einsiedler (Draught)
10. Franch-Montagnes (also known as Freiburger or Jura)
11. Friesian (Draught)
12. Gelderland
13. Noric (also known as South German Coldblood)
14. Oldenburg (Draught)
15. Percheron
16. Poitevin
17. Rhenish-German Coldblood
18. Rhineland Heavy Draught
19. Schleswiger
20. Württemberg
21. Zweibrücker

Light Horse
22. Arab
23. Bavarian Warmblood
24. Camarguais
25. Dutch Warmblood
26. Einsiedler (Ridden)
27. East Friesian (Ridden)
28. East Prussian (also known as Trakehner)
29. French Anglo-Arab
30. French Thoroughbred
31. French Trotter
32. Friesian (Ridden)
33. Groningen (off shoot of Oldenburger)

Left: *A winter scene in Austria, a land perhaps better known as the home of the Spanish Riding School, where classical riding and training are still carried out according to the teachings of the great riding masters of the past.*

34. Hanoverian
35. Hessen and Rhinelander
36. Holstein
37. Lipizzaner
38. Mecklenburg
39. Oldenburg
40. Selle Français
41. Württemberg
42. Zweibrüker

Pony
43. Haflinger
44. Landais
45. Pottock

Key

- Towns/Cities
- ▫ Studs
- Light Horse
- Pony
- Heavy Horse

Ice/Tundra
Mountains/Uplands
Tropical forest
Forest/Woodland
Grassland
Savanna
Scrub
Desert

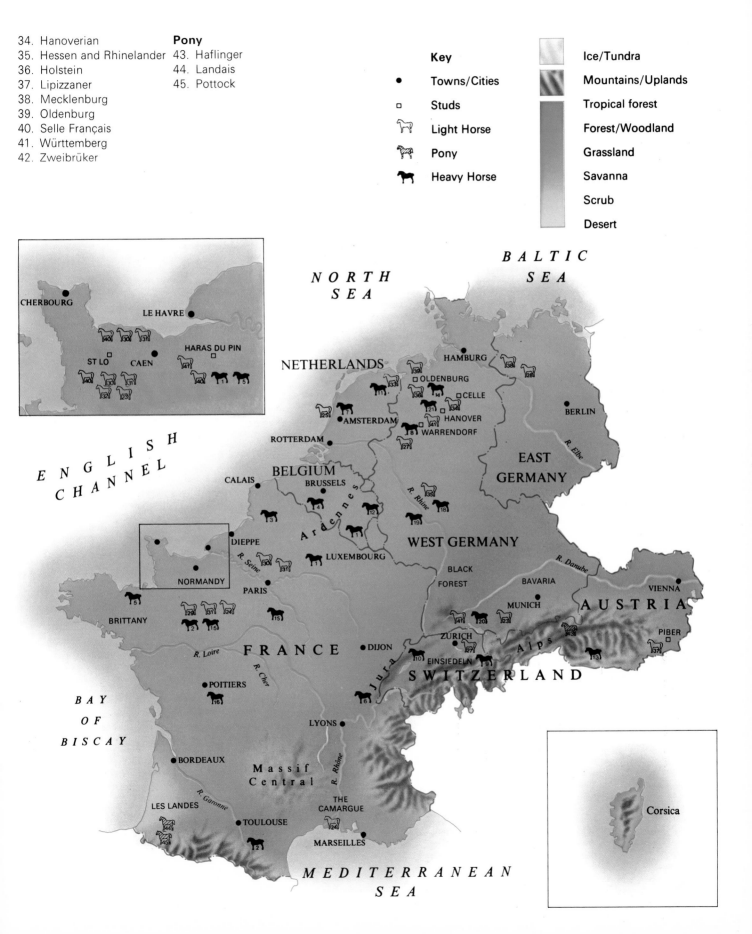

Netherlands

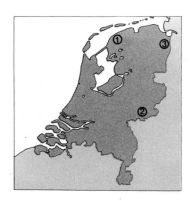

1. *Friesland's native horse, the Friesian, is one of the oldest European breeds.*
2. *& 3. The breeds from Gelderland (2) and Groningen (3) have been combined in the Dutch Warmblood.*

Above right: *The Dutch Draught Horse is one of the most heavily built and muscled of all the European Heavy Horse breeds.*

Dutch Draught
The weighty Dutch Draught horse is thought to be the largest and most solid of all European heavy horses and dates back about 100 years. Its ancestry can be traced through the national stud books of the Royal Netherlands Draught Horse Society.

Only the progeny of officially registered stock is eligible and as no horse of unknown origin has been registered since 1925, the Dutch Draught can claim to be the purest of all Dutch breeds. A preferential stud book exists of all examined, registered stock over two-and-a-half years old.

The Dutch Draught is bred to work on all types of soil found in the Netherlands – sand, heavy silt and peat. The horse possesses intelligence, stamina and docility and it can also boast a long working life. It stands up to 16.3hh (170cm), has a notably short thick neck, rather light withers, heavy shoulders and immensely strong quarters. The predominant colours are chestnut, bay, roan and grey.

Friesian
From the north-western province of Friesland comes the heavy Friesian horse. The Friesian is entirely indigenous to the Netherlands and is one of the oldest European breeds; indeed a heavy horse is known to have existed in the province since about 1000 BC. It was particularly popular during the Middle Ages because of its ability to cope with the rigours of medieval warfare.

During the seventeenth century, the Friesian was used as a weight-carrying riding horse but some two hundred years later, the popularity of trotting races brought about a change of role and Friesians were harnessed to 'chaises', light open carriages which could carry one or two passengers. The Friesian's trotting prowess led to an emphasis on the lighter, finer types which in turn led to an overall decline in numbers through its over-specialized role. However, with the founding of the Friesian Stud Book in 1879, the breed was improved and numbers were soon restored. Nowadays, the horse is recognized for its good temperament and amazingly economical feeding habits. Two of its most noticeable features are its finely shaped head and small pricked ears. The mane and tail carry a thatch of hair and both have been known to touch the ground as neither pulling nor docking are tolerated. The Friesian averages 15hh (152cm), its legs are heavily feathered and the only colour is black.

Gelderland
The warm-blooded Gelderland horse has its beginnings in the sandy, mid-eastern province of the same name. Although not officially bred since the late 1960s, the Gelderland Stud Book accounted for the horse of central, southern and western Holland and the breed was strongly influenced by Hackney, Arab, Hanoverian, Holstein, Westphalia and French blood.

As well as being a first-class carriage horse with beautiful conformation and stylish action, the Gelderland was also a good saddle horse with successes in the showjumping arena. The height of the Gelderland ranged between 15.2hh and 16hh (157·5–163cm). It had high head carriage, well-set and sloping shoulders, powerful quarters and a highly carried tail. Gelderlands were usually chestnut, grey and occasionally skewbald.

Groningen
From the north-western province of Groningen came the other Dutch breed which is almost extinct today, the draught Groningen horse. The breed came into being by crossing Friesians and Oldenburgs. The attractive carriage horse which resulted has a quick stylish action and also shows endurance, docility and obedience. Its conformation is also good with strength in the back and legs, a refined head and neck and high head carriage. The height range is the same as the Gelderland and the breed's principal colours are black, dark brown and bay.

Dutch Warmblood
The almost total mechanization of agriculture imposed a limit on the roles of working horses.

Where once the horse was required to assist in the daily running of the community, it was suddenly only of recreational use. Because of this change and the desire to produce a more up-to-date horse, the modern day Dutch utility horse was evolved.

In 1968 the Warmbloed Paardenstamboek Nederland (the Dutch Warmblood Stud Book or WPN for short) was formed. Its aim was to develop a light harness-cum-riding horse by crossing Gelderlands and Groningens with imported bloodstock. Thoroughbred stallions from Britain, France and Germany were imported and the operation, so far successful, has brought about the breeding of a wide, supple-gaited horse with a suitable disposition for all horse sports.

To ensure that high standards are maintained, a rigid selection system has been enforced in order to breed only the most reliable, willing, honest and intelligent progeny. Stud Book stewards record the progress of all young stock.

The WPN, being dual-purpose bred, has gained an impressive reputation for its performance between the traces, and is frequently seen competing at world class level in driving events. There are Dutch Warmbloods in the top echelons of all riding disciplines – showjumping, combined training and dressage. The breed is also suitable for riding clubs and hunting.

Dutch riding horses are now exported all over the world but principally to Germany, Switzerland and Austria. Many mares have been exported to Belgium to improve the warm-blooded stock in that country, and the first WPN stallion to stand at stud in Hanover was Jasper Z in 1978.

The most important gait of the Dutch Warmblood is the trot. Conformation is not standardized and the WPN could almost be described as a type rather than a breed. The height should be over 15.2hh (157·5cm) to 16hh (163cm).

Below: *A team of Friesian horses taking part in a driving event. The breed has developed into a strong tractable carriage horse but is still very much in use in agriculture.*

Switzerland

1. Avenches, on the edge of the Freiberg canton, is now the centre of Swiss horse breeding.
2. Einsiedlers, first bred at the Einsiedeln monastery, were once in great demand all over Europe.

Below: *The Anglo-Norman, one of the most successful saddle horses in Europe. Bred mainly in the Normandy area and at the National Stud (Haras du Pin) these good-looking horses have a brilliant record in international showjumping and eventing.*

Below: *Einsiedler brood mare and foal at stud. An operational stud farm was in existence at the Benedictine monastery of Einsiedeln as far back as AD 1064.*

Switzerland has slightly more than 40,000 horses, some of them imported. Two hundred stallions form the basis of a small but carefully-guarded breeding industry. Half the stallions are Freiberger, Switzerland's own particular breed, eighty are Warmblood, a dozen Haflingers, and the remaining handful are Thoroughbreds, Standardbreds and Arabs.

Today's figures, however, do little justice to the long history of horse-breeding in Switzerland. There were periods during which Swiss-bred horses were famous all over Europe, especially in the eighteenth century and for a short period around 1850.

Horse-breeding in Switzerland was first mentioned in 1064 and confirms the existence of a stud in the Benedictine Monastery of Einsiedeln. The rough, poor grazing of the high Sihl valley created a breed with stamina and speed, extraordinarily surefooted on the mountain paths.

Soon the Einsiedlers were in great demand as riding, pack and cart-horses. Italians were especially keen to buy the 'Cavalli della Madonna'. For centuries the stallions of Einsiedeln were Schwyzers, but it is known that the monks experimented with Friesians, Turkish and Spanish horses in the eighteenth century, but with little success. In 1866 the Yorkshire stallion Bracken was imported; in 1883 two Anglo-Normans finally replaced the Schwyzers as breeding stock.

Einsiedeln, however, never produced large numbers of horses. Breeding on a large scale began in the second part of the fifteenth century, when fifteen to twenty thousand horses were captured from Charles of Burgundy. The mares went to the farms; the stallions were kept by the monasteries, landowners or the rural clergy.

Swiss horse-breeding at this time was commercially successful, the horses being less famed for their looks than for their frugality and sturdiness. In 1714 the French Army bought ten thousand of them for remounts, and in 1784 twelve thousand. Swiss horses were used as barge-horses on the waterways of the Rhône and the Saône; the better ones worked as coach-horses down to the Pyrenees. The first period of Swiss breeding was ended by the French whose invasion forces requisitioned nearly all the Swiss horses in 1798.

Restocking began twenty years later, this time under the guidance of regional breeding associations. But developing industrialization soon stunted this new prosperity. Within a few years the Emmental coach-horse had died out and the once flourishing breeding industry of the Erlenbacher had disappeared. The one remaining centre of any importance was in the mountains of the Jura. Around 1880 efforts there were directed at producing a heavier draught-horse, and by importing the British Thoroughbred Leo and the British Halfbred Vaillant II this was achieved. The Jura horses came to be known as Freibergers.

After some prosperous years during World War II, when the total number of horses in Switzerland rose to a record 152,000, agricultural mechanization reduced demand for the Freiberger, although they are still important as pack-horses in the army.

The reduction in the number of Freibergers was partly offset by an increase in Warmblood breeding, mainly using imported Holsteins, Anglo–Normans and Swedish Halfbreds.

Warmblood breeding was started with the aim of producing a multi-purpose horse, but now tends towards the production of a horse with jumping ability and stamina.

Thoroughbreds have only been bred on a national basis for the past seven years, although formerly some private studs had produced horses that raced successfully in Switzerland, Austria and Germany. In 1973 the newly formed Swiss Arabian Breed Association registered its first Arabians and around the same time a Standardbred register was established in Switzerland.

Belgium

1. The Brabant region around Brussels has produced the majority of Belgium's heavy horses.
2. Ardennes, the region crossed by the French border, is also well known for its heavy breed.

Brabant

Also known as the Brabançon, Belgian Heavy Draught, or Flanders horse, the Brabant originates from the low-lying areas of Belgium. These fertile regions with their succulent herbage produced a large, heavy and very powerful horse, standing 16–17hh (163–173cm).

This mighty animal is the result of centuries of selective breeding and in the era of the heavy working horse it found a ready market both at home and abroad. The Brabant was also considered invaluable for crossing with other breeds and was used extensively in producing the German Rhineland, or Rhenish, horse now, sadly, almost extinct. It is said to have influenced the Shire and the Ardennais breeds. The Brabant is extensively bred in Gorki in the USSR.

About 90 per cent of Belgium's equine population once consisted of heavy horses, the majority being the Brabant. The rich diluvial soil tended to cause lymphatic joints in working horses, but this trait has now been bred out. The resulting modern Belgian horse is a strong, short-backed animal, heavily muscled with short, thick legs and a great deal of feather. The head is square and small in relation to the rest of the body, while the breed's character is kind and affable. The most predominant colours are chestnut and red roan, though all others occur.

Right: *The powerful Brabant or Belgian horse, bred in Flanders, Brabant, Hainaut, Liège, Namur and Luxembourg. The Brabant bloodline has improved many other continental breeds and Belgian stallions contributed to the British Clydesdale and Shire breeds some centuries ago.*

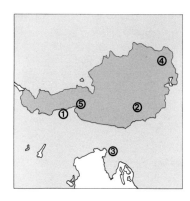

1. *The Haflinger originates from South Tyrol in the area ceded to Italy after World War I.*
2. *The famous stud farm at Piber still breeds Lipizzaners for the Spanish School.*
3. *The original Lipizzaner stud was close to Trieste, in the area now in Yugoslavia.*
4. *The Spanish Riding School in Vienna is famous for its haute école performances.*
5. *The modern Noriker has descended from the Pinzgau district, hence its alternative name Pinzgauer.*

Austria

Haflinger

The Haflinger, with its brand of an edelweiss (the Austrian national flower) with an H in the centre, is a Tyrolean breed originating from Hafling near Merano. Generally considered to have early origins, it has been suggested that the Haflinger is a descendant of the Alpine Heavy Horse. An alternative suggestion gives its ancestry as selective crosses of wild pony blood. As well as Noriker blood, there is undoubtedly a good deal of Oriental blood in the breed and the foundation sire is claimed to be an Arab called El Bedavi II.

The Haflinger stands about 14hh (142cm) and is chestnut with an eye-catching flaxen mane and tail. It has been described as 'a prince in front, a peasant behind' for a pretty head topped with smallish ears and tapering to the muzzle is supported by a workmanlike sturdy body. The chest is broad and deep, the back long, the hindquarters powerful and the legs short with plenty of bone. This makes the pony strong and sure-footed and therefore ideal for mountain work. In addition it has a kind temperament, is frugal by nature and has a tendency to live to a great age, all of which makes it exceptionally popular with farmers and pack carriers in the Austrian mountains. Although they are not generally put to work until they are four years old, it is claimed by some that there are horses over forty years old still working. A new use has also been found for it this century as the ideal breed for carrying the increasing number of tourists through Austria's beautiful country on trekking holidays.

The excellence of the Haflinger has resulted in a strong export market, and so many have gone to Italy that a closely related but slightly larger breed known as the Avelignese has been developed there. The demand for the Haflinger from the rest of the world is steadily increasing, for as well as for trekking it has proved especially suitable for the fast expanding sport of driving.

Lipizzaner

The Lipizzaner is Austria's most famous horse, yet out of the country's total equine population of 60,000 there are only 300 of this breed. The reason is that their great intelligence and particular brand of athleticism makes them specialists in one sphere only – collected dressage work known as High School. They are the mounts of the most well known horsemen in this art, the members of Vienna's Spanish Riding School. From the start, Lipizzaners have been rather too clever, and are lacking in the extended paces necessary to make popular general riding horses.

They are beautiful horses, the majority being silver grey, although there is an occasional bay or brown. All foals are, however, born a dark colour and may not turn grey until they are seven years of age. The head has a straight profile with rather narrow nostrils and large eyes. The neck is elegant and crested, the body deep and the hindquarters exceptionally powerful, enabling them to perform the 'airs above the ground'. The legs are strong with plenty of bone and the feet small. The coat is sleek and there is an abundance of mane and tail hair. They move with high knee action and elastic steps. Although normally ranging from 15hh to only 15.2hh (152–157·5cm), and sometimes as little as 14.2hh (147cm), the Lipizzaner gives the appearance of being much larger than its actual height.

Another feature of the Lipizzaners is their longevity; they live for twenty-four to twenty-six years and many remain in work until their late teens. They are, however, slow to mature and benefit from not being worked too hard until they are five or six years old.

The foundation stock for the Lipizzaner was imported from Spain, hence the name Spanish Riding School. In the years of the Muslim emirate in Spain, the Moors brought with them Arabs and Barbs which were crossed with the heavier horses found in southern Spain. The result was the Andalusian and its relations which proved to be extremely popular in the courts of Europe by virtue of their high intelligence and athleticism.

When in the mid-sixteenth century the fashion for High School riding started to spread in Europe, the Imperial Court in Vienna was determined not to be outdone. In 1562 Emperor Maximilian II imported Spanish horses which were bred at the Kladrub stud (now in Czechoslovakia) and in 1580 his brother Archduke Charles enlarged his stock, bringing in nine stallions and twenty-four mares. Archduke Charles chose a stud where the bare stony lands had been proven by the Romans and Venetians to be first class breeding grounds. Its name was Lipizza and it was close to Trieste. All the stock born at this stud were named Lipizzaners.

Over the years many Lipizzaners were used to cross with native central European horses to produce draught and riding horses of better temperament and intelligence than the local breeds. In more modern times the Lipizzaner has been bred in several countries of Eastern Europe for use in agriculture, and in Czechoslovakia they have often been used as circus mounts.

Above left: *Three flaxen maned and tailed Haflingers ponies play in the snow in their native Austria.*

Bottom left: *A Lipizzaner at the Piber Stud. These horses originated from Spanish bloodlines and were first intensively bred in Yugoslavia.*

Archduke Charles's horses from Lipizza were a success at the court of Vienna and more were imported from Spain. Later, in the eighteenth century, Italian, German and Danish horses were imported and cross-bred with them, as were Arabs from Syria and Palestine in the nineteenth century. Today the Austrians are satisfied with their Lipizzaners; there is little cross-breeding, in fact some inbreeding is practised. The primary consideration is performance ability; only the outstanding stallions from the Spanish Riding School are used as sires. Even the mares are selected on the basis of their performance ability. They are broken both to saddle and harness, tested and sold if not satisfactory.

Largely as a result of the turbulent history of their breeding grounds, Lipizzaners are found in other central European countries, in Czechoslovakia, Italy and Yugoslavia where their original stud of Lipizza now lies.

The area of Lipizza has always been plagued by conflicts; during the Napoleonic wars the stock had to be evacuated four times. World War I led to another evacuation when in 1915 the stock was taken to Vienna. The peace settlement brought more permanent disruptions as Lipizza was declared Italian territory and after much wrangling the Italians claimed over half the Lipizzaners.

The Austrians had to choose a new home for their depleted but prized stock and selected an old military stud in the south at Piber where there were 143 acres of rugged lands and a seventeenth-century castle to house the offices.

Even Piber was not a safe residence when war struck again, and in 1941 and 1942 stock from there and Lipizza was moved to Hostau in the Bohemian Forest. Then in April 1945 came the Allied advance and horse lovers among the American army persuaded General Patton to put a priority on capturing this unusual prize from the enemy. The Americans' valued war booty was then quickly driven to Schwarzenburg to avoid disputes with the Russians. Today's generation of Austrian Lipizzaners now graze peacefully at the Piber Stud.

Noriker

The Noriker is a small cold-blooded (heavy) horse standing a little over 16hh (163cm). It is usually bay, brown, chestnut (often with flaxen mane and tail) skewbald or spotted. About 200 years ago spotted Norikers were more common.

The Noriker is not a pretty horse for it has a rather large head, with small ears. But its short crested neck, straight shoulder, broad chest, compact body, muscular hindquarters and short strong legs make it very powerful; and its full fine mane and tail and lack of feather make it rather eye catching.

It is a sure-footed horse with good action, and this, together with its strength, makes it a popular horse for agricultural work especially in the mountains. The Noriker is popular with farmers all over southern Europe but the highest concentration of the breed is around Salzburg in Austria and in Upper and Lower Bavaria. Its numbers are said to be increasing.

In Germany the Noriker is known as the South German Coldblood and although used mainly for agricultural work some have been subjected to outcrossing with Norfolk, Norman, Cleveland, Holstein, Oldenburg, Thoroughbred and Arab blood to make the South German Coldblood into a suitable horse for the army.

The Noriker has ancient origins for it is generally accepted to have been bred by the Romans in their kingdom of Noricum, which covers much of modern Austria. Today's descendants are mainly in Austria's Pinzgau district, hence the name, Pinzgauer Noriker which it is sometimes given.

It was in this area that Andalusian and Neapolitan blood was injected into the breed during the Renaissance and a large number of spotted horses was one of the results. Selective breeding of the Pinzgauer Noriker was started in 1903 when a stud book was opened with 450 stallions and 1,000 mares. The South German Coldblood has been selectively bred for some time.

Far left (top): *'The Dancing White Stallions of Vienna' – The Spanish Riding School in performance. The brilliant chandeliered riding hall, open to visitors, is one of the few places where the classical art of equitation dating back to the 16th and 17th centuries can be seen.*

Far left (bottom): *A Lipizzaner of the Spanish School performs the dramatic 'Capriole'. In this high school movement 'above the ground' the horse is encouraged to jump forward while kicking his hindlegs out with great energy and then land balanced on all four legs.*

Below: *A group of Noriker horses, a strain of small agricultural horses originally bred in the Roman province of Noricum. There are two types, Oberlander and Pinzgauer.*

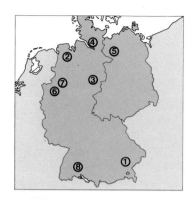

1. *The southern German state of Bavaria has produced both the Bavarian Warmblood and the Rottaler, named after a valley of that name.*
2. *The East Friesian and the similar Oldenburg come from the north-western region.*
3. *Hanoverian horses were developed by the Electors of Hanover for carriage and cavalry use.*
4. *Schleswig-Holstein is noted for several breeds. The Holstein has been raised in the lowlands around the Elbe for centuries, and the Schleswig Heavy horse is one of the two main cold-blooded German breeds. More recently the Trakehner found a new home there.*
5. *The Mecklenburg in East Germany is closely related to the Hanoverian.*
6. *The Rhineland Heavy Draught used to be Germany's most popular working horse.*
7. *Westphalia is an important breeding and riding centre.*
8. *The Württemberg stud was established in 1573.*

Germany

Bavarian Warmblood

The Bavarian Warmblood is one of Germany's regional breeds of riding horse. It is a little heavier than most of the others with a deep broad powerful body and plenty of bone. It has a kind temperament and generally stands between 15.3hh and 16.2hh (160–168cm).

Bred in South Germany, its origins lie in the Rott valley in Lower Bavaria. This area produced the Rottaler, originally famous as a breed of battle charger, which later became popular for agriculture and draught work. More recently Thoroughbred, Cleveland Bay and Norman blood has been introduced to refine it into the Bavarian Warmblood.

Dülmen

The Dülmen which stands about 12.3hh (129·5cm) is usually dark in colour but varies in shape. Mentioned as a breed as far back as 1315, it has been subjected to a great deal of outcrossing with British and Polish stock.

Dülmen roam wild on the Duke of Croy's estate on the Meerfelder Bruch in Westphalia. There are about 100 mares and an annual round-up is made of the yearlings which are then sold at a local festival. Numbers of this rather heterogeneous breed are diminishing and it is to be hoped that they will not share the fate of the only other native German pony, the Senner, which used to run wild in the Teutoburg Forest of Hanover, but is now virtually extinct.

East Friesian

The East Friesian stands between 16hh and 16.2hh (163–168cm) and is a slightly smaller and more refined version of the Oldenburg. It is found in all solid colours and has a kind temperament which makes it an excellent riding horse like the Oldenburg.

The East Friesian was in fact identical to the Oldenburg before the division of Germany. But thirty years of isolation from Oldenburg blood and infusions of Arabian blood in its place has tended to produce a more elegant horse.

German Trotter

The German Trotter is a smallish horse of about 15.3hh (160cm). It has a rather straight shoulder, prominent withers, a deep strong chest, and lean hindquarters. The legs are hard and fine, and it moves with long easy strides.

The Trotters are used for racing and the sport is more popular than flat-racing in Germany. The fashion started about 100 years ago when Orlov Trotters were imported from Russia as foundation stock. Since then a good deal of American Standardbred and French Trotter blood has been added.

Hanoverian

The Hanoverian is a powerful athlete renowned as a showjumper and a dressage horse. In 1974 the breed was the world champion in both these sports.

Hanoverians vary a good deal in shape and size ranging from 15.2hh to 17hh (158–173cm) and from light to heavyweight; but they all possess the ability to move spectacularly and have a temperament which enables them to accept discipline from their riders willingly. Most have heads that are a little on the plain side with straightish profiles, but their shoulders are strong, their bodies deep and their hindquarters very powerful. The tail is often set a little high. The legs are strong with substantial bone, and the cannon bones are short. The feet tend to be narrow.

The Hanoverian is probably the most famous breed of competition horse in the world today but previously it had been equally well-known as a carriage-horse and before that as a battle-horse.

Its origins can be traced back to the Great War Horse of the Middle Ages, but when gunpowder led to the demand for a more mobile cavalry the Hanoverian was turned into a cavalry mount.

When the demand for carriage-horses grew it was Electress Sophia of Hanover who instigated the breeding of small, cream coach-horses with café-au-lait manes and tails at the royal residence of Herrenhausen. Then in 1714 when England acquired its first Hanoverian king, George I, he took with him those cream horses which were then used in all Britain's royal processions until replaced by Windsor Greys in George V's time.

Horses were also sent from Britain to Germany, for Thoroughbreds and Yorkshire Coach Horses were used in Germany to lighten and refine the Hanoverians. The Hanoverian electors maintained an interest in their home country and in 1735 George II founded the Landgestut at Celle, north of Hanover, which remains the state stud of the breed today.

For 200 years until World War II the Hanoverian was one of Europe's most successful carriage-horse and cavalry horse. Then the breed society took steps to meet the new need of horses for sport competitors and leisure riding. They brought in Thoroughbred, Arab and Trakehner blood to refine their rather hefty steed into a more distinguished-looking horse, which still retained the movement and temperament of the old carriage-horse.

Above: *Dülmen wild ponies search for grazing in the snow.*

Right: *The Hanoverian, one of Germany's most popular and successful sporting horses, has been made famous by many top German riders. These include Alwin Schockemöhle who on Warwick Rex took the individual gold medal at the 1976 Olympic Games in Montreal and the late Hartwig Steenken whose mare Simona III carried him to the 1974 Men's World Showjumping Championship title.*

Above: *A team of Oldenburger carriage horses. These are the heaviest of the German warm-blooded breeds. They mature very early and often stand some 17hh. Today the breed has thoroughbred blood in the strain.*

Hessen and Rhineland
The Hessen and Rhineland, bred in the central states of Germany around the Rhine, are less famous regional breeds of German Warmbloods. They are similar in shape, temperament, size and movement to the Hanoverian, have much Hanoverian blood in their pedigree, and are used for riding and competitions.

Holstein
The Holstein is a handsome big docile horse with an intelligent head and is usually of a heavier type than the Hanoverian. It is normally a dark colour, although greys are found, and stands between 15.3hh and 17hh (160–173cm). It has a strong shoulder, broad chest, compact and deep body and strong but rather flat hindquarters. Its legs are short with plenty of bone and its action is extravagant but a little higher than the Hanoverian.

The Holstein has been bred in the marshlands along the river Elbe in Schleswig-Holstein for

centuries. It can be traced back to the Marsh Horse which was one of the Great Horses used by heavily armoured knights of the Middle Ages to ride into battle.

Imported Neapolitan and Andalusian blood was used to refine the breed as far back as the thirteenth century when there is reference to a stud at the Uetersen monastery near Hamburg. A royal stud was later set up at Esserom and in 1680 regulations for breeding were issued. The Holstein rapidly became one of the most popular breeds in Europe. In 1876 another important stud was started at Traventhal, but this was closed in 1960, and today Elmshorn is the centre for Holstein breeding activities like auctions and stallion selections.

British blood has also played a part in the development of the Holstein as Thoroughbred, Cleveland Bay and Yorkshire Coach Horse stallions were used during the nineteenth and twentieth centuries. The Thoroughbred influence has been particularly strong in the last twenty years, as breeders have tried to breed horses that are less hefty, with more speed and elegance than the old-fashioned Holstein.

Mecklenburg

The Mecklenburg, standing between 15.2hh and 16.3hh (157·5–170cm) is very similar to, but usually a little smaller than, the Hanoverian. It is also used as a general riding and competition horse.

Before the political separation of East and West Germany, there were frequent exchanges between these breeds which accounts for their similarity, and these related bloodlines can be traced back to the fourteenth century. Nearly three-quarters of the Mecklenburg breed was lost during World War II, but after the war a new stud was started in Schwerin in East Germany.

Oldenburg

The Oldenburg is the tallest and heaviest of the German warmbloods, standing between 16.1hh and 17.1hh (165–175cm). It has a rather large head with a straight profile. The neck is thick, the shoulders muscular, the chest broad, the hindquarters strong and the legs short with plenty of bone. It is much closer to the coldbloods than the other German riding horses and tends to mature early and lack stamina. It makes an excellent all-round horse for use in agriculture and carriage work as well as for riding.

The breed has flourished since the seventeenth century and over the last 300 years has been subjected to a great deal of outcrossing. The foundation stock was of Friesian type and to this were added Andalusians, Neapolitans, Barbs, Thoroughbreds, Hanoverians, Cleveland Bays and Anglo-Normans to produce one of the best coach horses in the world.

With today's demand for a lighter type of horse there have been further injections of Thoroughbred, Anglo-Norman and Hanoverian blood, but although it is used for riding competitions, it is in driving competitions that the Oldenburg excels.

Rhineland Heavy Draught

The Rhineland Heavy Draught is a massive, rather square cold-blood standing between 16hh and 17hh (163–173cm). It is usually light in colour – sorrel, chestnut, red roan with a flaxen mane and tail, red roan with a black mane and tail being most common. The head is relatively small and well proportioned, with a kind eye. The neck is large and crested, the shoulder exceptionally strong, the chest deep and broad, and the back round and powerful. The legs are short with good bone and a little feather.

The Rhineland Heavy Draught is a powerful horse, and as it also has a docile temperament it is ideal for agricultural and heavy draught work. It resembles the Belgian and both have ancestors which came from the Ardennes and are thought to trace back to the diluvial or Forest horse of prehistoric times.

This breed became very popular in agriculture and industry at the end of the last century. In 1876 a stud book was started and by the beginning of this century the Rhineland was the most numerous of all the German breeds. Other German states used it to establish their local breed of coldblood. Nowadays of course most of its work is done by machines and numbers are dwindling fast.

Schleswig Heavy Draught

The Schleswig Heavy Draught is Germany's other main breed of coldblood but it is smaller than the Rhineland, standing between 15.2hh and 16hh (157·5–163cm). It is a cob type with short legs. The head is rather large and plain, the neck well crested, the wither flat, the chest broad, the girth deep and the back long. There is a little feather on the legs and the feet may be flat. It is usually a chestnut colour and normally has a flaxen mane and tail.

It has a willing disposition and good movement which makes it a popular worker both with farmers and in industry, and it was in great demand in the late nineteenth and early twentieth century. It was developed as a breed in the mid-nineteenth century in the north of Germany and much Jutland blood was used, a breed to which it is very similar. Suffolk Punch, Breton, Boulonnais and even Thoroughbred and Yorkshire Coach Horse blood was added.

Below: The Schleswig horse bred on the lush grass of the Schleswig province. This old breed dates back to the Middle Ages when a stronger horse was needed to carry the heavily armoured knights into battle. The province was at one time Danish so the Schleswig is a close relation of the Danish heavy horse.

Trakehner

The Trakehner (formerly known as the East Prussian) is generally considered to be the most elegant of the German warmbloods. It has a head like a Thoroughbred with attentive intelligent eyes. It has a long neck, a good shoulder and a longish but strong back with flattish hindquarters. It has less bone than the other German riding horses but it is good strong bone. Its action is light and extravagant and its temperament is intelligent and kind. It stands between 15.3hh and 16.2hh (160–168cm).

The Trakehner is popular for riding and is one of the more successful breeds in dressage, showjumping and eventing. Before the last war it was considered to be Germany's most successful riding horse, but with the loss of its breeding grounds (now in Poland) and the splitting of its stock between East and West, the Hanoverian has taken over.

The Trakehner is one of the older German breeds as its stud was founded in 1732 by Frederick William I. Thoroughbred and Oriental horses were crossed with the local work horse, the Schweiken, to provide horses and revenue for the royal stable.

Frederick the Great took much interest in the stud his father had founded and helped to modify the Trakehner into an agile horse for his troops.

The Trakehner has another famous patron, for the Kaiser introduced more Arab blood to turn it into one of the first breeds to be light enough to have the characteristics of today's warmbloods. The Kaiser also wanted a uniform bodyguard, so by selective breeding black was made the predominant colour of the breed.

The breeding grounds of the Trakehner lie close to what is now Olsztyn in Poland and are run by the Polish Ministry of Agriculture. They have however deteriorated since their hey-day in the late nineteenth and early twentieth century. The royal stud of Trakehnen was surrounded by 34,000 acres of marshy ground, rich in the phosphorous and lime so suitable for the rearing of horses. By 1939 there were 25,000 registered brood mares in the hands of 15,000 breeders.

Unhappily, it was a disputed area and like the Lipizzaners, the Trakehners have been forced to evacuate their home during times of war. In the winter of 1944–45 the most permanent disruptions occurred when, in anticipation of the arrival of the Russians, some of the local breeders

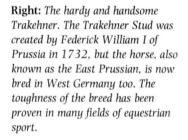

Right: *The hardy and handsome Trakehner. The Trakehner Stud was created by Federick William I of Prussia in 1732, but the horse, also known as the East Prussian, is now bred in West Germany too. The toughness of the breed has been proven in many fields of equestrian sport.*

decided to head west. They harnessed stock to wagons to pull their belongings, rode the stallions and herded the mares and youngstock and set off on a trek through the cold winter.

The horses that arrived in West Germany formed the nucleus of today's Trakehner breed. Mares and stallions were sold all over Germany, and the Trakehner became the only German warmblood with a national as opposed to a regional organization. The Trakehner Society set up its stud at Rantzau in Schleswig-Holstein and the surrounding area contains the largest concentration of Trakehners.

In Poland the horses left behind by the former inhabitants were reconstituted by the authorities into a breed identical to the Trakehner known as the Masuren. This has now been amalgamated with another warmblood, the Poznan, to establish the Wielkopolski.

Westphalian

All German warm-blooded breeds (except the Trakehner) are named according to the areas in which they are born and not according to the breed of their parents. This makes the Westphalian breed numerically very important.

The large equine population there is largely due to the siting of important equestrian centres such as the Olympic and National Riding Schools. The Westphalian breed is however indistinguishable from its neighbour the Hanoverian, which supplied the original stock for the stallion depot

set up in Warrendorf, Westphalia, in 1826. Since then there have been continuous injections of Hanoverian blood, so that apart from their place of birth they are practically identical.

Württemberg

The Württemberg is a cobby type of warm-blooded horse standing about 16hh (163cm). The head usually has a straight profile, the shoulders are strong, the chest is deep and broad, the back straight and the hindquarters powerful. The legs are strong with substantial bone and good hard feet.

The Württemberg is usually bay, brown, chesnut or black and has a docile co-operative temperament. It has been bred in the south-west of Germany for centuries and used as an all-round animal on the farm. Its central stud of Marbach was founded as far back as 1573 but it was not until 1895 that a stud book was started.

Left: *The warm-blooded Württemberg, bred mainly at Marbach. The breed developed through the mixture of several strains including Arab, Oldenburg, Nonius and Anglo-Norman, producing a strong but well-made capable horse.*

France

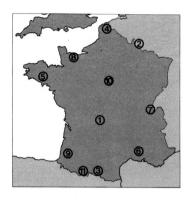

1. The Limousin region in central France produces its own strain of Anglo-Arab.

2. Ardennes, a cross-border region of France and Belgium, is famous for its heavy horses which have influenced heavy horse breeding around the world.

3. Ariègeois ponies, from Ariège in the south, were first mentioned by Julius Caesar.

4. Boulonnais horses come from the Calais region.

5. Brittany has several related breeds of horses of various weights and crosses.

6. The wild horses in the Camargue marshlands have become a tourist attraction.

7. The Jura mountains on the Swiss border are the home of the Comtois breed.

8. Normandy has the best breeding grounds in France and many famous studs. Norman, Anglo-Norman and French Trotters are raised there.

9. Landais ponies are found in south-western France around the Adour River.

10. The popular Percheron heavy breed originated from the valleys of the Perche region south west of Paris.

11. The Pottock or Basque Pony lives wild in the Pyrenees among the sheep.

Above right: The Ardennais, a breed of heavy horse from France and Belgium, which is also popular in Sweden and Poland.

Anglo-Arab

The Anglo-Arab has an elegant head with a broad forehead, alert bold eyes, a straightish profile and well opened nostrils. Its neck is long and crested, its withers prominent, and the shoulders strong and sloping. Its back is muscular, and its tail is set on high and carried proudly like that of the Arab. The legs are fine and on the long side but the bone is very dense and hard, and the feet are well shaped.

Before the last war, Anglo-Arabs were rarely more than 15.3hh (160cm) but following the trend to produce larger horses they have been bred up to about 16.1hh (165cm).

The Anglo-Arab moves lightly, with great agility and suppleness. It is an excellent athlete that jumps well in arenas and across country, and performs dressage. It is an elegant, alert, sensitive animal which was very popular with the troops but is now used by French riders for all forms of equestrian competitions. Its sensitivity however implies a need for more skilful handling than the riding horse bred in the north of France, the Selle Français.

In the south-west of France where the Anglo-Arabs are usually lighter and closer to the Thoroughbred than they are elsewhere, they have run in races confined to their breed since 1874. The major race of the year is for three-year

olds, the Grand Prix of Anglo-Arabs run at Tarbes prior to the famous annual auction of Anglo-Arab stallions.

The Anglo-Arabs bred further north in the Limousin tend to be larger and usually find their vocation in showjumping or dressage arenas rather than on the racetrack.

Both types of Anglo-Arab have been used along with the Thoroughbred to add sensitivity, quality and stamina to the other breeds of French riding horses. Large numbers of the Selle Français are sired by Anglo-Arabs.

French Anglo-Arabs are bred in the Pyrenees and the Massif Central, and are derived from crossing the Thoroughbred with either Arabs or the native mares of south-west France. These native mares had distinctive Oriental features, and were said to be descendants of horses left by the Muslim invaders in the eighth century AD. Since then wars and a good deal of trading kept up the numbers of this Oriental stock and a continual injection of their quality and stamina into native French animals has been maintained.

These horses in the south-west were successively known as Iberian, Navarrine (used by the cavalry during the Revolution and the Napoleonic era), Bigourdan (Navarrines made taller mainly through Thoroughbred blood) and Tarbenian (direct forbears of today's Anglo-Arabs,

Left: *The French Anglo-Arab, a sporting horse that is quickly establishing a reputation to rival the Anglo-Norman and the Irish Hunter.*

and the result of alternate crossing between the Thoroughbred, native mares and the Arab). A stable homogeneousness was established and today Anglo-Arabs are bred to Anglo-Arabs so that crossing is no longer essential.

It was at the Pompadour stud, founded by Louis XV in 1761, that systematic breeding of the Anglo-Arab first began. Monsieur de Lespinats, who was director from 1834 to 1843 and was succeeded by Monsieur Gayot, carried out systematic crossing which led to the pure breed of Anglo-Arab. Oriental stallions Massoud and Aslam were imported from Syria, Thoroughbred mares were imported from Britain, and native Oriental mares from the south west were used. Cross-breeding between this foundation stock ultimately provided France with the Anglo-Arab of today.

Ardennais

The Ardennais (like the region it is named after) has Belgian and French families. The French Ardennais is divided further into three types, each with its own stud book. There is the Ardennais which is the smallest of the three and is closest to the original type; the Northern Ardennais (or Trait du Nord) which is very large and has Belgian Brabant blood in it, and the Auxois which was developed at the beginning of this century in an attempt to enlarge the Ardennais.

There is little distinction between these varieties other than height; all have a rectangular-shaped head with a broad face, large expressive eyes, pointed ears and large well opened nostrils. The neck is crested, the chest wide and deep, the body compact and massive, the hindquarters powerful, the legs short but broad and muscular with abundant feather.

The coat is usually roan, iron grey or chestnut but it can be bay. Ardennais range from 15–16hh (152–162cm), the stallions and geldings a little larger.

The Ardennais is still used in agriculture, a sphere in which it was very popular until the tractor took over, but its most extensive use in France is for meat.

The Ardennais can perhaps be linked to the 'robust, hard and untiring' horse observed during Caesar's Gaul campaign, and more certainly to the Great Horse of the Middle Ages. Then during the late eighteenth and early nineteenth centuries, Oriental blood was added to modify it into a horse to be ridden by the troops and to pull artillery during the time of Napoleon. Some were further lightened and used as carriage horses, but by the beginning of this century the trend was to re-establish the breed as a small powerful horse suitable for agriculture and portage.

Above: *Camargue horses are a breed of ancient origin thought to descend from the Solutrean 'ram-headed horse, the forefather of the modern Barb.*

Ariègeois

The Ariègeois is a small dark-coloured pony which in its native country – the high valley of the Ariège in south-west France – does not grow to more than 13.3hh (140cm) but when reared in milder regions can grow to 14.3hh (150cm). The head is fine and expressive with a flat face, short ears and alert eyes. The neck and back are long, the shoulder rather straight, the croup round, and the legs quite fine but tough. For 2,000 years this breed has remained remarkably free from outcrossing because of the inaccessibility of the Ariège valley.

The Ariègeois is very tough, robust and sure footed; it is well adapted to living rough in high altitudes and to traversing the mountains of its homelands. It is used on farms for pack work, and for carriage work. Its role has not changed for centuries.

Boulonnais

The Boulonnais has an elegant head for such a heavy horse, with a flat face, large lively eyes, small ears, open nostrils and a small mouth. The neck is thick, the girth deep, the back slightly dipped, the hindquarters rounded and powerful. The legs are strong, shortish and have little feather. The mane is thick and the coat silky. The general effect is of a well made, elegant, powerful horse standing 15.1–16.3hh (155–170cm). Most Boulonnais are a shade of grey but some are chestnut or bay. Sadly its numbers are dwindling fast. Today it is mainly reared for meat.

The homelands of the Boulonnais are in the north-west of France around Calais. It was from this area that Caesar's troops invaded Britain bringing with them Oriental horses that cross-bred with the local Gaulish horses. Returning Crusaders brought more Oriental horses to cross with the local breed. These Oriental blood infusions added great elegance to this heavy horse which was not actually named a breed until the seventeenth century. A stud book for the Boulonnais was started in 1886.

Breton

The Breton has a well-proportioned head with a broad face and small ears, set on a shortish neck but one which is strong and crested. Its wither is flat, its shoulder long and sloping, its back short and strong, and its hindquarters powerful. Its legs are short with very little feather. It is usually red or blue roan, chesnut or bay; black is very rarely found.

The Breton stands 15–16.1hh (152–166cm), but varies enough to be divided into two types. The Draught Breton is the larger, more powerful version that is used for heavier haulage and farm work. Today it is also popular for meat.

The Postier Breton is strong and tough but smaller, and its showy action makes it popular for coach work as well as on the farm. The Breton's adaptability, energy and toughness has enabled it to retain its popularity as a work horse where one is still needed in the French vineyards, and in underdeveloped countries to which it is regularly exported. It is used particularly for improving other heavy horse breeds.

The Breton is the indigenous horse of north-west France but has been the subject of much outcrossing. The Draught Breton resulted from crosses with the Percheron, Ardennais and Boulonnais, and it was importations of the Norfolk Trotter and the Hackney from Britain last century that led to the more active and finer Postier Breton.

These outcrosses were stopped in 1920 eleven years after stud books were started for the Draught and the Postier. Since the 1920s selection has been confined to the Bretons, and the stud book was closed in 1951.

Camarguais

The Camarguais is a robust horse with a large rectangular-shaped head, and a flat face. The ears are short and broad at the base, the eyes are large and bold, with a good width between them, and the neck is short, as is the shoulder which is also rather upright. The back is short, with powerful hindquarters that tend to slope sharply to the tail; the legs are fine but strong, and the mane and tail are thick.

It stands 13.1–14.1hh (135–145cm) and is normally grey. It is a slow maturer but lives to a very old age, is agile, lively, frugal and tough.

The Camarguais run wild in the marshlands of the Rhône Delta in herds consisting of one stallion, his mares and progeny. The fillies are caught and branded as yearlings and the colts thought unsuitable for breeding are gelded at three years old.

Some Camarguais are broken-in. As they have rather wild natures this can be difficult, but once broken in they are strong and agile enough to make excellent mounts for the *guardiens* of the area who tend herds of bulls. The Camarguais can also make a good riding horse for the large number of tourists who want to see the spectacularly bleak scenery of this part of France.

The Camarguais is an ancient breed of obscure origins. It is certain that wild horses have roamed the delta for many hundreds of years. It is also likely that some of the blood was indigenous and that Asiatic, Arabian and African blood played a part, but to an unknown extent. There has however been little outcrossing except in the nineteenth century. A stud book was started only in 1968.

Left: *The Breton from Brittany is a heavy breed with a fine reputation for hardiness and endurance.*

Comtois

The Comtois is a small and relatively light horse standing between 14.3 and 15.3hh (150–160cm). It has a large head, with alert eyes and small ears. Its neck is well muscled but rather straight, its girth deep and its back long. Its legs are strong with substantial bone. There is little feather but the mane and tail are thick.

The Comtois is usually bay or chestnut and is exceptionally robust, active, sure-footed and kind in temperament. These characteristics serve it well in its homelands, the Jura mountains on the Swiss-French border. There it is used on farms, for transportation and even at ski resorts. In these areas mechanization has not been total so it is still in demand, as it is in North Africa where it is regularly exported. The butchers like the meat of the Comtois, and as one of the lighter draught animals, breeders use it for cross-breeding to add size and substance to riding horses. It has not dwindled in number to the same extent as other breeds of heavy horse, because of the continuing demand for its services.

French Trotter

The French Trotter (or Demi-Sang Français) varies in height and conformation a great deal but tends to be larger than other countries' breeds of trotters. It is a lightweight horse which can be very like the Thoroughbred with a refined head, long neck, sloping shoulder, straight back and sloping hindquarters; or it can resemble its other ancestor, the Anglo-Norman, with a plainer head, straight shoulder and more substantial body. All Trotters tend to have very powerful hindquarters, to be quite long in the leg, and to have a rounded action; they are able to trot at phenomenal speeds of nearly 30mph (48·3kph).

Chesnuts, bays and browns are the most common colours. Grey is very rare.

They are mainly used in trotting, a sport in France which with 5,000 to 6,000 races a year is as popular as flat-racing. Some are used for show-jumping, eventing and general riding and a large number for breeding the Selle Français (see below). They are one of the most numerous breeds, there being more Trotters than Thoroughbreds in France.

Trotting races were first held in France at Cherbourg in 1836. The French were following the example of the British who already raced Norfolk Trotters, the Russians who raced the Orlov Trotter and the Americans who raced the Standardbreds. The French chose to use their all-purpose riding-cum-carriage-horse, the Norman, to cross with the Norfolk Trotter and the Thoroughbred to produce their own breed of Trotter. This cross-breeding was centred at the government studs in Normandy, the Haras du Pin where the most influential sire for the Trotter was Norfolk Phenomenon, and the Haras de Saint Lô where the Thoroughbred, The Heir of Linne played an important role as a foundation sire.

In 1922 a French Trotter stud book was officially opened to include any Anglo-Norman that could trot one kilometre in 1 minute 42 seconds or less. In 1941 it was closed so that only progeny of registered stock was eligible; thus the French Trotter was established as a pure breed.

Landais Pony

The Landais (or Barthais) ponies are not very homogeneous, but are all fine intelligent and robust animals. They stand less than 13.1hh (135cm) and are usually bay or brown. They usually have an Arab-like head with large eyes and small pointed ears, set on a long neck and sloping shoulders. They have short straight backs, and sloping croup; the mane and tail are long, and the coat is fine.

The Landais lives semi-wild in the forests of Les Landes around the Adour river. As it lives out all the year round, this pony has developed a robust constitution. It is an excellent riding or driving pony.

The breed has existed for a long time and the strong Arab influence in it was thought to come from the Oriental horses left behind by the Moors after the French defeated them at the battle of Poitiers in AD 732.

A stud book was started in 1951, and care is being taken to preserve the diminishing numbers of this breed.

Below: The Comtois, a breed thought to have been brought to France by the Burgundians. These robust horses were popular as troop horses during the Middle Ages. They were favourites of Louis XIV, who used them for his cavalry as did Napoleon, particularly in his Russian campaign.

Right: The French, or Norman, Trotter. In modern times the French Trotter has become a more protected strain through its own breed society and is accepted throughout the world as one of the best clean-bred trotting strains. It is a larger breed than most trotting horses, capable of racing under saddle.

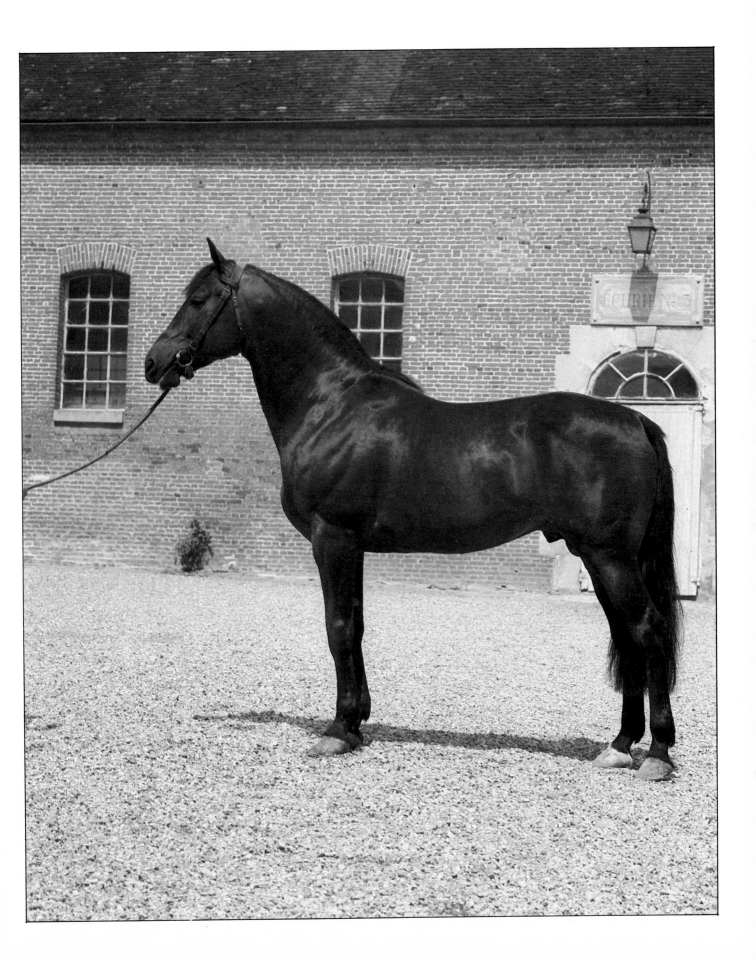

Above: *A successful competition horse, the Cheval de Selle, Anglo-Norman or French Saddle Horse. These are all strains of the same breed, not precisely or readily distinguished from one another.*

Percheron

The Percheron has an elegant head with a flat face, long fine ears, and intelligent eyes with good width between them. It has a long crested neck, sloping shoulders, broad deep chest, short back, and powerful rounded hindquarters. Its legs are strong, well made and with very little feather.

It is usually grey or black and stands between 15.2 and 17hh (158–172cm).

It is a very active heavy horse moving well, with great presence and a kindly temperament. Its strength, elegance and good looks have made it one of the most popular heavy horses in the world, and it is still used on some farms, for transportation and for cross-breeding to increase size and substance. It is also reared for meat production.

It developed in the temperate climate of Perche, a region of small valleys where the grass is rich in phosphate. These are conditions conducive to the breeding of good horses.

The most influential blood has been Arabian which was probably first used after the victory of Poitiers in the eighth century. More Arabs were brought to France and Perche by the returning Crusaders, and in 1769 at the Haras du Pin Arab stallions were made available to Percheron breeders.

These Arabs were crossed with the breeds indigenous to the Perche region to produce a horse that was used in war, agriculture and, in its hey-day from 1880 to 1920, to improve other heavy horses all over the world. As its role in urban settings diminished however, its use in predominantly rural areas encouraged a general increase in weight.

The stud book was started in 1883, and closed soon afterwards, but was re-opened in 1966.

Above: *The Percheron, here engaged in its time-honoured occupation on the farm, has influenced breeds throughout the world. It is known under several different local names in France, such as Loire and Augeron.*

Poitevin

The Poitevin has a large long head with big ears, a long neck, upright shoulder and a long back with sloping hindquarters, thick legs and heavy feather. It is an undistinguished heavy horse which has a quiet, rather lazy temperament. It stands 15.1–16.3hh (155–170cm) and is to be found in most colours.

It performs the usual functions of the heavy horse being used on the farm, for transportation and meat; but in addition has the unusual function of being used to produce mules.

The Poitevin was derived from horses imported from Holland to help in the drainage of the marshes around Poitiers. A stud book was started in 1885 but today has very few entries, and it seems likely that this unusual breed, whose strength and large feet enable it to work in the marshlands, is in danger of extinction.

Pottok (or Basque) Pony

The Pottok has a primitive appearance with a rectangular head, short ears and small eyes. Its neck is short, its back long and its legs strong. It stands between 11.1 and 13hh (115–132cm).

It has bred wild in the Pyrenees and has therefore developed great powers of endurance, being frugal with a robust nature. When caught it has been used as a pit pony, and for meat. Today it is popular as a children's riding pony, especially when crossed with Arabs or Welsh ponies.

Its origins are obscure.

Selle Français (French Saddle Horse)

The Selle Français is a heterogeneous breed varying in height from 15.3–16.3hh (160–170cm). The head is usually fine with wide-set eyes and long ears set on a long neck. The shoulder is sloping, the chest deep and the back a little long. The hindquarters are powerful and the legs long with plenty of bone. It is a lively mover and has a spirited but kind temperament.

It is found in all colours, but chesnut and bay are most common.

The Selle Français was named in 1958, and a stud book started to include all the various French regional breeds of riding horses: Angevin, Vendée, Charolais, Limousin and Anglo-Norman. All the included breeds of riding horses were descendants of the work horses of France, differing in type according to the area, soil, climate and foundation stock. These heavy horses were crossed with finer breeds (Thoroughbred, Arab, Anglo-Arab and Trotter) to produce the horses that are now so much in demand. These cross-bred but pedigree horses were named the Selle Français.

Of the constituents of the Selle Français by far the largest and most successful original breed was the Anglo-Norman. This breed's homelands are in Normandy which contains France's best horse-breeding grounds. Horses bred in this area have long been famous.

William the Conqueror brought some war horses from Normandy to England and these are the likely ancestors of the British breeds of heavy horse. In Normandy these great beasts were crossed with Arabs, Danish and German horses in the seventeenth and eighteenth century. Then in the nineteenth century, further refining took place with the injection of British Thoroughbred, half-bred and Norfolk Trotter blood. The result was the Anglo-Norman of which two branches developed. One was used for trotting and became the French Trotter; the other was used for carriage work, then as a cavalry remount and eventually, after amalgamation with similar breeds, as the riding horse now known as the Selle Français.

Southern Europe

The horse population in southern Europe, and the Iberian peninsula in particular, has decreased drastically since World War II. This is due mainly to the mechanization of the military, for horse-breeding, particularly in Spain and Italy, was for many centuries geared to supplying the requirements of the armed forces. Although horses are now used very little by the army in Spain and Italy they are still required by both the cavalry and the police in Turkey where the horse population is still fairly large and of very mixed quality. The best animals are used by the police and cavalry. The 'country-breds' are still used by the peasant population both in agriculture and for transport.

Agriculture also formed the second main area of work for horses in other southern European countries but here too they have largely been replaced by the tractor, especially in the lowland areas. In the mountainous regions and on remote farmsteads, however, the horse still holds its own as a versatile farm animal.

Italy's Neapolitan horse was famous throughout Europe as a riding horse in the Renaissance period but with the decline of *haute école* the breed lost its popularity, and its descendant, the Lipizzaner, was left to carry on the tradition of this equestrian art. The Greek cavalry officer Xenophon (430 BC), provided the first land-mark in classical equitation with his two books *Hippike* and *Hipparchikos*. These laid the foundations of riding as they are still taught today, but Greece has produced little since then in the form of either horses or horsemasters.

But if the horse has declined as a work animal in southern Europe it has become popular for use in sport. Showjumping is popular throughout Italy, and it was an Italian, Federico Caprilli, who completely revolutionized showjumping with the use of the forward seat in the early 1900s. The first Italian International horse show was held in Turin in 1902 and the second in Rome six years later. Racing in harness and on the flat are also popular Italian sports. The first trotting track was established in 1808 at about the same time as flat-racing became popular in Naples and Florence. To cater for these interests many Thoroughbred and Trotter studs have been founded with stock imported from Britain, America and France, the most famous of which is Federico Tesio's Dormello Stud which produced such horses as Nearco, Donatello and Ribot.

Racing is also popular in Spain, the main centres being Madrid, Seville and San Sebastian, and recently hurdle racing and steeplechasing have been introduced. Trotting is popular in the Balearic Islands, and polo has a small but enthusiastic following around Madrid, Barcelona and Jerez de la Frontera. This last is also the centre of Andalusian and Arab breeding.

This map of the basic physical divisions of the region locates the areas where major horse breeds originated. Present-day important breeding areas are also indicated.

Heavy Horse
1. Avelignese (Draught)
2. Italian Heavy Draught
3. Maremma
4. Murgese (Draught)
5. Sorraia Draught)

Light Horse
6. Altér-Real
7. Andalusian, Carthusian and Zapateros
8. Anglo-Arab
9. Avelignese (Ridden)
10. Calabrese and Salerno
11. Hispano Anglo-Arab
12. Jaf
13. Karacabey
14. Lusitano
15. Murgese (Ridden)
16. Sorraia (Ridden)
17. Thessalian
18. Thoroughbred

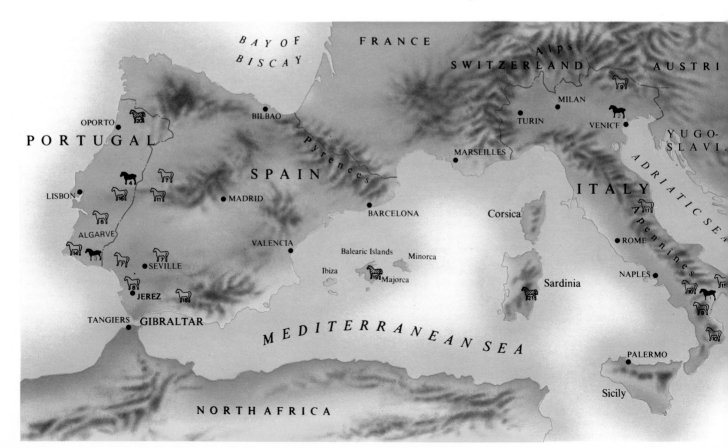

Below: *A pair of horses working in the corn fields of central Spain.*

Pony
19. Balearic Island Ponies
20. Garrano
21. Sardinian Pony
22. Skyros

Key

●	Towns/Cities
▢	Studs
🐎	Light Horse
🦓	Pony
🐴	Heavy Horse

Ice/Tundra

Mountains/Uplands

Tropical forest

Forest/Woodland

Grassland

Savanna

Scrub

Desert

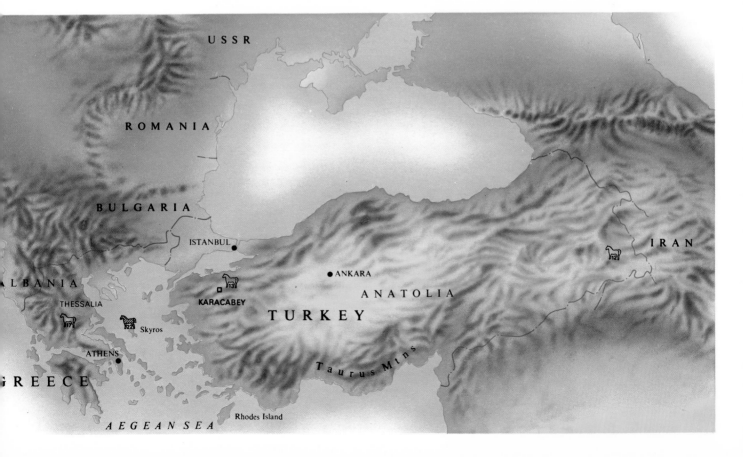

1. Garranos or Minhos take their name from the Garrano do Minho area.
2. The Sorraia comes from eastern Portugal.

Below: *The Altér Real, a strong, compact, quality horse based on Andalusian blood.*

Portugal

Altér Real
The Altér Real is based on Andalusian stock. The original stud at Vila de Portel, in the Alentejo Province, was founded in the mid-1700s by the House of Braganza, with 300 Andalusian mares imported from the Jerez de la Frontera region of Spain.

A strong, compact horse of quality, the Altér Real stands 15–16hh (152–163cm), and is usually bay or brown, although chesnuts and greys are also found. The Altér has a short, arched neck and a small head with a straight or slightly Roman profile. It is deep through the girth with a wide chest and well-muscled quarters. Its action is elevated and showy with a deal of knee action, but as a result it lacks extension. Despite its often difficult temperament however, this horse is good under saddle and is particularly suitable for *haute école* riding.

The breed thrived under royal patronage until French invaders in the Napoleonic Wars stole the best animals, and the royal stables were abolished. The subsequent introduction of outside blood, particularly Arab, resulted in a general degeneration of the breed, which was further threatened by the eventual confiscation of its pasture lands. However, in the 1930s Andalusian blood was reintroduced and only the best animals were retained, thus ensuring a future for the breed.

Lusitano
The Lusitano also owes its origin to the Andalusian, which it resembles. It is a good-looking and very active horse standing 15–16hh (152–163cm), almost always grey in colour. The head is small and the neck tends to be short and fairly thick, and there is an abundance of wavy mane and tail hair. The action again tends to be high and showy.

Originally bred for the cavalry, and later used for light agricultural jobs, the Lusitano is now in demand in the Portuguese bullrings. Being highly courageous and very agile, the Lusitano will face a charging bull with equanimity and is therefore much sought after by the *cavaleiro*.

In Portuguese bullfighting the horse is unpadded and must never be touched by the bull even when meeting the latter's charge at a headlong gallop. Only at the very last moment should the horse swerve and it must therefore respond immediately to the *rejoneador's* demands. Bullfighting is much more artistic in Portugal than in Spain and it takes many years to train these horses, which have to be taught the *piaffe*, *passage* and *pirouette* as well as the usual reining movements.

Garrano
The luxuriant green mountain valleys in the Garrano do Minho and Reaz dos Montes regions of Portugal are the home of the Garrano or Minho pony. It is almost always dark chesnut in colour with a wealth of mane and tail hair and it stands 10–12hh (102–122cm).

It is a very hardy pony, strong and sure-footed with generally good conformation. It owes its undoubted quality to its Arab ancestors, for the best of the Garranos were crossed with Arab stallions which were imported by the army in an attempt to upgrade them for their own use, principally as pack ponies.

At one time very popular trotting races were

Left: *A grey Lusitano and his cavaleiro in training for the bullring. These courageous and agile Portuguese horses will face a charging bull with equanimity.*

Below: *The Sorraia is a native of both Portugal and Spain.*

held for these ponies, and they were bred and trained for this purpose. Garranos are traded at horse fairs at Vila Real and Famalicao, and although no longer used for trotting, they are still used for light agricultural work and are still popular with the army.

Sorraia

The Sorraia is a native of both Portugal and neighbouring Spain, from the areas surrounding the Sorraia, Sor and Raia rivers which drain from the mountainous Alto Alentejo regions on the borders of Spain. The breed is noted for its ability to withstand extremes of climate and to survive on very little food, and this toughness once made it valued by the local stockmen.

The Sorraia stands 12.2–13hh (127–132cm). Its ancient origins can be seen in its colouring, which is usually dun with a black eel stripe down the centre of the back and with striped zebra markings round the legs. It can also be palomino or grey, has a long mane and tail, the latter set rather low, and black tips to its ears.

It has a large head, with high-set eyes and a straight or Roman profile. Its limbs are long and lacking in bone, and the neck and quarters are weak and unmuscled.

At one time the breed was used extensively for agricultural purposes but it has tended to degenerate and decrease in number.

1. Balearic Island ponies are found mainly in the Palma region of Majorca.
2. Andulusian and Carthusian horses were bred at the southern monasteries of Cadiz and Seville (Andulusians) and Jerez de la Frontera (Carthusians).
3 & 4. Named after their regional homes Galician and Asturian ponies are found in north-western Spain (3); Basque Navarre ponies come from the north east (4).

Right: Spanish thoroughbred Cartuga horses. The name Cartuga is used as a synonym of Carthusian horses.

Far right: The Andalusian horse of Spain still has an international reputation as a dressage and haute école horse as it did in the 16th and 17th centuries.

Spain

Andalusian

The Andalusian owes its ancestry to the eastern horses, probably Barbs, brought over initially by the Moors and later by the Syrians. The crossing of these with the native stock resulted in a strong, active riding horse of quality, whose fame spread across Europe as the riding horse *par excellence*.

It had no equal as a mount for high school riding in the sixteenth and seventeenth centuries, and its great presence, its agility, showy action and good looks made it the obvious choice of the aristocracy.

The monasteries at Cordoba and Seville were the early centres of selective Andalusian breeding, the monks following a planned breeding programme and refusing to allow any outcrosses of 'foreign' blood. The Andalusian stands about 15.2hh (157·5cm) and is usually grey with a wealth of mane and tail hair.

Carthusian

An offshoot of the Andalusian, and frequently known as the Andalusian-Carthusian, this breed originated at the Carthusian monastery in Jerez where stallions of North African descent continued to be used in bringing about greater refinement.

A few Carthusians are still bred in Spain and they are very similar to the Andalusian in appearance usually being grey and standing 15.2hh (157·5cm). Following the Napoleonic invasions, however, the majority were stolen, and another related breed, the Zapateros, has largely taken their place.

Balearic Island ponies

The Balearic Islands in general, and Majorca in particular, have a large number of native, rather scrubby ponies. Mainly small and of generally poor conformation, these country-breds are widely used on the small farmsteads as work ponies and as pack animals. They are also used by the largely peasant population as saddle horses and, in harness, as a means of transport. The ponies are frequently bay, chestnut or grey in colour; their usual height is about 14hh (142cm).

Italy

Avelignese

The Avelignese is very similar in appearance to the Haflinger from Austria and both are believed to be descendants of the now extinct Avellinum-Haflinger. In addition the Avelignese can claim a little Arab ancestry through an imported Arabian stallion, El Bedavi.

The breed comes from the mountainous regions throughout Italy but particularly around Tuscany and in the Veneto where it is used extensively for light agricultural work. Being very hardy and sure-footed it is also a splendid pack pony.

The Avelignese is a very muscular pony with short legs and good depth through the girth. It averages 13.3–14.3hh (140–150cm) and is nearly always chestnut in colour, frequently with a flaxen mane and tail, although palominos are occasionally found. It is noted for its equable temperament, and like other ponies, for its longevity.

Italian Heavy Draught

The Italian Heavy Draught is derived from the French Breton and is bred throughout northern and central Italy, the principal breeding area being around Venice. A compact, active horse standing 15–16hh (152–163cm), it is deep through the girth with a short neck, well-muscled quarters and short legs. It is usually chestnut, frequently with a flaxen mane and tail, but it may also be roan in colour.

This breed is extremely powerful and surprisingly fast, and was used extensively throughout the whole of Italy for all agricultural purposes, its tireless efforts and docile temperament making it very popular with farmers. Because of increasing mechanization this horse is now bred almost exclusively for meat.

Salerno

One of Italy's two national Warmbloods, the Salerno, is bred in the Salerno and Maremma areas, although it was evolved at the state stud of Persano, a hunting reserve of Charles III of Bourbon.

It can be traced back to the Neapolitan horse which was famous throughout Europe and which also numbers among its descendants the Lipizzaner and the Kladruber. It is a good all-round riding horse possessing considerable jumping ability. It can be any colour, stands about 16hh (163cm), and was once used extensively by the Italian cavalry. Now, however, its popularity as a riding horse has been usurped by the imported Thoroughbred.

Murgese

The present Murgese horse is a relatively new breed, not having been established until the 1920s, and it shows a degree of imported eastern blood. It takes its name from the Murgese area near Puglia where horses of top quality were bred for many centuries until about 200 years ago when the horse suddenly lost favour.

The old Murgese horse came from the mountainous regions around Gravina and can be traced back as far as the fifteenth century when the governor of the Venetian republic owned several hundred as cavalry mounts.

The Murgese is used principally as a light

agricultural horse, but it is also occasionally ridden, and when put to a Thoroughbred or Arabian stallion produces a very much better riding horse. It stands between 15–16hh (152–163cm) and is usually chestnut in colour.

Maremma

A rather common, cobby type of horse used both on the land and under saddle, the Maremma originates from Tuscany where it was first bred at the state stud of Grossetto. It is a tough, hardy horse that does well on the minimum of feed. It is used by the Italian mounted police as well as by Italian cattle herdsmen, and it is also a useful horse for light agricultural and haulage work. It stands 15.2–16hh (157·5–163cm) and can be any colour.

Calabrese

The other of Italy's national Warmbloods, the Calabrese, comes from southern Italy and is bred principally in Calabria. It too was used extensively by the Italian cavalry, and declined in popularity as the army became mechanized.

It is, however, still bred at a few of the state studs and has a certain talent for showjumping, as well as being a good all-round riding horse. It is frequently crossed with Thoroughbred stock to improve its quality. The Calabrese stands around 16hh (163cm) and can be any colour.

Sardinian Pony

The Sardinian Pony, a native of Sardinia, is a wild, country-bred animal standing 13–14hh (132–142cm). It is very hardy and sure-footed and does well on the minimum of feed. It is used both under saddle and on the land. Almost always bay in colour, it is a tireless worker but of generally poor conformation.

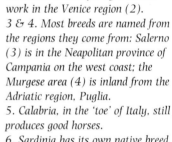

1 & 2. Basically a mountain pony, the Avelignese is used extensively in Tuscany (1), as is the Maremma, but it is also used for agricultural work in the Venice region (2).
3 & 4. Most breeds are named from the regions they come from: Salerno (3) is in the Neapolitan province of Campania on the west coast; the Murgese area (4) is inland from the Adriatic region, Puglia.
5. Calabria, in the 'toe' of Italy, still produces good horses.
6. Sardinia has its own native breed.

Below left: *The Salerno is one of Italy's two national warm-blood breeds, and a quality all-round riding horse with an aptitude for jumping.*

Below: *The strong, deep-bodied Avelignese is bred throughout the mountainous regions of north, south and central Italy.*

1. Ponies bred today in the Pindus mountains are probably related to the breeds of the ancient Greeks.
2. Skyros, in the Aegean, has its own hardy ponies.

Greece

Thessalian

Greece is not noted for its equine breeds. The number of horses and ponies on the mainland and the islands is small and they are generally uninspiring. As far back as AD 211, however, the Greek poet Oppian mentioned three breeds of which the Thessalian was 'the most noted for beauty, courage and endurance'.

Records of pony breeding in Thessaly can be traced back to ancient times; the present ponies, bred in the Pindus Mountains between Thessaly and Epirus, are known as Pindos. Standing 12–13hh (122–132cm), they are principally bay or grey in colour and are extremely hardy, sure-footed and strong.

They are used as a means of transport and for light agricultural work as well as for riding, and the mares are frequently used for breeding mules. Other breeds mentioned in ancient times, but which no longer exist, are Thracian, Peloponnese, Argive, Arcadian, Epidaurian and Acarnanian.

Skyros

On the island of Skyros in the Aegean a small breed of pony has existed since ancient times. Although its history is somewhat obscure, the Skyros pony does bear a strong resemblance to the horses depicted on the Parthenon in Athens, and on Greek statues and friezes.

For most of the year the Skyros ponies live wild on the island where they eke out an existence in the mountainous areas. Shortly before harvest time the islanders keep a close watch on them and round them up for work on the farms. The islanders use them particularly for threshing the corn, when three or four ponies are tied together and required to walk round and round in circles over the unthreshed wheat and barley. During this time the ponies are well-fed by the islanders and in order to preserve them for work the following winter the islanders feed them during the winter months too when they are turned out on the mountains.

The original Skyros pony stands no more than 11hh (112cm) and, although it can be any colour, grey predominates. The feet, however, must be composed of good, hard black horn, for white horn is frowned upon. They are extremely hardy, sure-footed ponies and very tough and strong. The heads should be small as should the ears, but the neck tends to be weak and the quarters under-developed.

Attempts to cross-breed the Skyros to produce larger ponies have been largely unsuccessful, since the resulting animals were unable to stand up to the hard winter conditions. Now with the increased mechanization of the farmsteads the pony's use is waning and the islanders are being encouraged to find other uses for the Skyros. To this end racing is organized in a small way and the tourist trade is keeping other animals occupied. In spite of these efforts to keep the breed going, however, there are not very many pure-bred ponies living on Skyros nowadays.

Right: *The little Skyros Pony lives in the wild for most of the year on the island of Skyros in the Aegean Sea.*

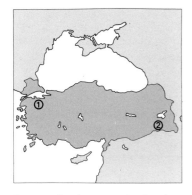

1. Karacabey horses are bred at the government studs at Karacabey near the Sea of Marmara.
2. The Jaf is a typical desert breed from Kurdistan in eastern Turkey.

Turkey

Karacabey

Although Turkey produced some very good horses for many centuries, there is now only one native Turkish breed remaining. This is the Karacabey, which, although derived from native stock, has been greatly influenced by the Nonius from Hungary.

The Karacabey is bred principally at the stud of the same name, for which the Turkish government is responsible, and it is a very popular mount in the Turkish army. The Karacabey is an animal of good quality, and is also used for light agricultural work. In addition, it makes a sure-footed packhorse in the mountainous regions. Karacabeys are also used in harness and under saddle, although imported Thoroughbreds, Arabians and Anglo-Arabs prove to be more popular riding horses. The Karacabey stands about 16hh (163cm), and is noted for its calm temperament. It can be any whole colour.

As well as the stud at Karacabey, the Turkish government is also responsible for several Thoroughbred, Arabian and Anglo-Arab studs, while in Kurdistan, the Jaf, a quality saddle-horse of 15.2–16hh (157·5–163cm) is bred. This breed is particularly noted for its toughness, stamina and gentle disposition, which make it a typical desert horse.

The most famous horse to come out of Turkey was the Byerley Turk. Along with two other Oriental stallions, the Darley Arabian and Godolphin Arabian, these three horses were exported to England and were the founders of the present-day Thoroughbred.

Right: *Horses are frequently used in Turkey as a means of transport.*

Eastern Europe

One of the reasons for the many political and territorial changes which have occurred in this region is its vulnerable position between Germany and Russia; another is its great natural, mineral, agricultural and industrial wealth. All these factors have contributed to the enormous depth, variety and quality of the horse population and the breeding industries which flourish in these countries today.

Poland has been a nation of horse breeders and horse masters for over a thousand years, and today, with its register of some $2\frac{1}{2}$ million horses, it boasts the largest horse population in Europe. The Poles have been breeding Arabians for many centuries, since the first Arabian and Syrian stallions were brought back to Poland by returning crusaders. They have also bred English Thoroughbreds for over two centuries, and the subsequent interbreeding of the two types to produce the Polish Anglo-Arab has resulted in a competition horse of superb quality.

Climate and conquest have combined to produce native ponies of extraordinary resilience and quality, like the Hucul and the Konik which trace back to the celebrated tarpan of the Mongol emperors and beyond, and sound, free-moving, dual-purpose horses like the Malopolski and the Wielkopolski.

Czechoslovakia, too, has a long tradition of breeding good horses. The famous stud at

Kladruby near Pardubice, scene of the longest steeplechase in continental Europe, was founded with Spanish stock by the Hapsburg Emperor Rudolph II in 1572, to produce the famous Kladruber carriage-horses. It was controlled by the Imperial Court until 1918, since when the Czechoslovak State has encouraged the production of young stallions with the aim of improving working horses for agricultural purposes. The same emperor was responsible for the foundation of the second imperial stud farm in 1580 at Lipizza, source of the now world-famous Lipizzaner breed.

Landlocked Hungary, to the south of Czechoslovakia and Poland, was once the grain-store of central Europe, thanks to its favourable climate and rich soil which also helped to produce the splendid horses for which the country has been famous for centuries. During the century-and-a-half-long occupation by the forces of the Ottoman empire, the horse population was greatly influenced by the Arabian and Syrian stallions of the Turkish Cavalry.

Two Arab strains, the Shagya and the Gidran, have proved themselves both prolific and powerful when crossed with good local mares, while the English Thoroughbred and half-bred have also played an important part in improving many local breeds. Lipizzaners (called Lipizzans in Hungary) are also bred in several regions.

This map of the basic physical divisions of the region locates the areas where major horse breeds originated. Present-day important breeding areas and studs are also indicated.

Heavy Horse
1. East Bulgarian
2. Hucul (Draught)
3. Konik
4. Malopolski (Draught)
5. Nonius
6. Nonius (Clean-bred)
7. Slaski
8. Wielkopolski (Draught)

Light Horse
9. Anglo-Arab, Polish
10. Arab
11. Arab, Polish
12. Bábolna
13. East Bulgarian
14. Furioso
15. Kisbér
16. Kladruber
17. Lipizzaner (Lipizzan)
18. Malopolski (Ridden)
19. Murakosi
20. Shagya Arab
21. Thoroughbred Trotter
22. Thoroughbred, English
23. Thoroughbred, Polish
24. Wielkopolski (Ridden)

Pony
25. Bosnian Pony
26. Hucul

Left: *Lipizzaner carriage horses at exercise in Hungary.*

BALTIC SEA

● OLSZTYN

● POZNAN

● WARSAW

POLAND

□ JANOW PODLASKI

🐎 24

R. Labe

● BRESLAU

🐎 18 🐎 24 🐎 21

🐎 22 🐎 17 🐎 23

🐎 11 🐎 9 🐎 10

🐴 8 🐴 5

🐴 4

🐎 16 🐎 17 🐎 20

KLADRUBY □

🐎 7

PRAGUE ●

□ PARDUBICE

Bohemia

CZECHO-
SLOVAKIA

🐎 16

🐎 17

🐎 25 🐎 17

🐴 3

🐎 22 🐎 20

Carpathian

Buke
Mts

🐎 20

🐴 5 🐴 2

🐎 12 🐎 17

KISBÉR

🐴 5

🐎 5

🐎 14

BUDAPEST ● □ □ MEZÖNGYES

🐎 19

🐎 15

HUNGARY

🐎 21

🐴 6

R. Mura

🐎 24

SZEGED ●

🐎 12

ROMANIA

□ BORIME

ZAGREB ●

Bosnia

● NOVI SAD

🐴 25

● BELGRADE

Mountains

● BUCHAREST

R. Danube

ADRIATIC

🐴 25

🐴 25

BLACK
SEA

YUGOSLAVIA

🐎 13

🐴 11

SEA

SOPHIA ●

BULGARIA

🐴 25

ALBANIA

Key

● Towns/Cities

□ Studs

🐎 Light Horse

🐴 Pony

🐴 Heavy Horse

Ice/Tundra

Mountains/Uplands

Tropical forest

Forest/Woodland

Grassland

Savanna

Scrub

Desert

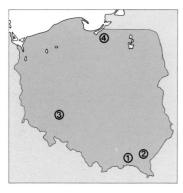

1. *The Hucul, used widely throughout southern Poland as well as in the other countries of Eastern Europe, is also known as the Carpathian Pony after the mountain range where it is extensively bred.*
2. *The Malopolski in the south east is a useful dual-purpose horse.*
3. *Many local breeds in central Poland have been merged and upgraded recently and are now often known as Wielkopolski.*
4. *The original stud of the Trakehener is at Olsztyn in the north, once East Prussia.*

Poland

Below: *The Wielkopolski, which is bred in central and western Poland. The Masuren and Poznan horses are now merged in the Wielkopolski horse.*

The nomads who pastured their herds of animals, horses, cattle and goats over the steppes of central Asia counted their wealth in livestock. Their horses, which became a central part of their lives, were medium-sized with neat heads, good shoulders, straight backs and hard legs – the distinguishing features of the tarpan. The name derives from the Mongol word meaning stallion. This was the original primitive wild horse of Europe which disappeared from western Europe altogether during the sixteenth century, surviving only in some regions of Poland, Prussia and Lithuania until the end of the eighteenth century.

The powerful, though primitive Hucul and Konik ('small horse') pony breeds of Poland are probably direct descendants of the tarpan. The immediate ancestors of the Hucul have been bred in the Carpathian mountains for thousands of years, and there is evidence that injections of eastern blood have helped to produce the modern type which is a strong, elegant pony, bay or dun though sometimes piebald, with a medium-sized head, short back and sloping quarters. Originally used as a pack animal in the mountains, today the Hucul is used mainly in harness, and is the standard work-horse for thousands of highland farms in southern Poland and throughout the Carpathian range.

The name Konik is given to several native Polish breeds of working pony which, although standing only about 13hh (132cm), is more of a horse than a pony. Robust but docile, the Konik

has retained many of the characteristics of the original tarpan, including the ability to thrive and work hard on a poor diet, making it popular with many small farmers in Poland and throughout eastern Europe.

Since World War II, Polish breeders, with considerable backing from the state, have been very successful in their efforts to produce a good quality all-purpose breed. The Malopolski, the dual-purpose horse of south-eastern Poland, was produced by mating native mares with Arabians and Anglo-Arabian stallions. Lighter than the Wielkopolski – its equivalent in central Poland – the Malopolski is noted for its calm and willing temperament, its soundness and straightness of movement, and its remarkable stamina. Like most recently developed breeds, the type varies in different regions, the better quality making first-class riding stock. The largest and most powerful of all the local strains is the Sadecki, used primarily as a draught horse. It contains Hungarian Furioso blood and the Polish government is now seeking to establish it as a riding horse by selective upgrading of the lighter specimens, at the government stud at Stubno. The Dabrowsko-Tarnowski is another important local type which shows the influence of Gidran blood.

The dual-purpose horses of central and western Poland are now grouped under one breed, the Wielkopolski, produced by crossing native mares with eastern, and to a lesser extent, with Trakehner stallions. Strongly built with excellent temperaments, the Wielkopolski are equally suitable for riding or driving, and are also capable of most agricultural work. Under this label are now grouped the much older Poznan horse, which no longer officially exists as a breed, and the Masuren, which has a large proportion of Trakehner blood.

By far the most popular horse in the south-western district of Silesia is a heavy draught horse of enormous strength, the Slaski, stemming from the powerful Oldenburg breed. The Slaski, which is in the process of gaining official recognition as a breed, is divided into two types, the larger cart-horse type capable of the heaviest draught work and the smaller, sharper type which makes an excellent harness horse.

The Polish Arab
Christian knights brought back Arabian and Syrian stallions from the Crusades to improve their stock of native horses and Polish breeders have looked to the Arab to ensure continuity of the quality and purity of their famous riding horses. Pure-bred Arabians were produced in Poland at least as long ago as 1508, and the spoils of many wars with the Turks provided the Poles with a steady supply of both Arab mares

and stallions through the centuries.

During World War I, much of Poland's best Arab stock was destroyed. However, fine studs of both Arabians and Thoroughbreds were built up again between the wars, only to be destroyed in the bitter fighting of World War II.

One of the most famous Arabian stallions of all time, Lady Wentworth's Skowronek, bred by Count Potocki at the celebrated Antoniny Stud in 1909, was exported to Britain in 1912 and eventually purchased by the Crabbet Stud in 1920 where he founded one of the most successful of all modern Arab bloodlines.

In the past twenty-five years, the Poles have set up new Arabian studs and the measure of their success is that today Polish-bred Arab stallions are regularly exported to Britain, Canada, Czechoslovakia, East Germany, Hungary, Italy, Romania, Russia and the United States. The high quality of Polish Arabs is maintained by a policy of strict selection and the best specimens are tested in races run over special courses at Levow, Lublin and Piotrkow, at all distances from 1,000 to 2,250 metres. In addition, new blood is introduced from time to time by importing true, desert-bred Arabian horses from the Middle East.

Above: *The Konik, a small horse native to Poland and closely resembling the wild horse of the steppe.*

Left: *The Hucul, a close relative of the Konik.*

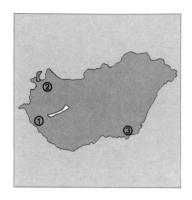

1. The Mura River region on the borders of Hungary and Yugoslavia produced the once-numerous Muraköz and Mur Island breeds.
2. Halfbreds and Thoroughbreds are raised at the famous stud at Kisbér in western Hungary.
3. Mezöhegyes, founded in 1785, is Hungary's oldest and most important stud farm. Furioso-North Star horses are also called Mezöhegyes Halfbred.

Below right: *The handsome Shagya Arab of Hungary is the purest half-bred strain of Oriental horse.*

Below: *The Nonius originated from the Anglo-Norman strain and is now bred in Yugoslavia, Romania and Czechoslovakia.*

Hungary

Furioso/North Star
The original Furioso was imported from Britain in about 1840 and between 1841 and 1851 he produced 95 stallions which were distributed to studs throughout the old Austrian Empire. The breed thus established was later strengthened by further injections of British blood, the most famous stallion used being North Star, a grandson of Touchstone out of a grand-daughter of Wasy, which was believed to have Norfolk Roadster blood. North Star was said to be a well-set, dark brown horse with a beautiful head. The Furioso and North Star families were consistently interbred over the years and are now generally regarded as one breed.

Now found throughout Austria, Hungary, Czechoslovakia and Romania, these handsome animals make excellent riding horses and have been winners in almost every area of equestrian competition. A few of the heavier types are used for light draught work.

Gidran
Hungary has long been noted for her Arabian horses and one of the best known strains is the Gidran, descended from the superb chesnut Arabian stallion Siglavy-Gidran, which was imported from Arabia in 1816. The modern Gidran, which usually stands around 16hh

(163cm), has been developed by crossing native mares with English Thoroughbred and half-bred stallions, and is now found throughout eastern Europe. The middle European type is heavier and more substantial while the southern and eastern type is more reminiscent of its Arabian origin. Usually chesnut in colour, although occasionally bay, Gidrans make splendid riding and competition horses with their lovely heads and good conformation. Heavier specimens are also driven.

Muraköz
The Muraköz has been developed in the past sixty years in the southern area of Hungary around the river Mura. The foundation stock consisted of native mares of a type sometimes known as Mur-Insulan, mated to imported Percheron and Belgian Ardennais stallions, or good quality Hungarian stallions and occasionally even Noriker horses from Austria. Now it is the Ardennais stallions whose blood links with the eastern horses used earlier gives the present-day Muraköz a stamp of quality which distinguishes it from other central European draught breeds.

Noted for its strong constitution and calm temperament, the Muraköz now falls into two types, the heavier at around 16hh (163cm) and the lighter which is smaller but more active. The most usual colours are chesnut, bay and black.

Nonius
This Hungarian breed is named after its foundation stallion, the Anglo-Norman Nonius Senior, foaled in the Calvados region of France in 1810. During the Napoleonic wars, he was

captured from the Rosières Stud by Hungarian cavalrymen and taken back to stand at Hungary's Mezöhegyes stud. Put to high-quality Hungarian mares of Anglo-Norman, Arabian, Holstein, Lipizzan, Spanish and Turkish blood, he produced fifteen great stallions, the most potent of which was Nonius IX.

Today there are two main types of Nonius: the 'Large Nonius', which is big-boned, strongly-built and stands at around 17hh (173cm), and the 'Small Nonius' often bay in colour which stands at around 15hh (152cm).

Shagya

The best of all the Hungarian breeds is the Shagya, a special strain of Hungarian Arab whose name derives from its founding stallion, a desert-bred Arabian bought in Syria in 1836. The Shagya of today is a very tough little horse, 14–15hh (142–152cm) in height, and usually grey in colour. A fine mover, he thrives on a poor diet and displays most of the best qualities of the Arab. The Shagya breed has spread widely throughout eastern Europe and is still thriving in Hungary and the neighbouring countries.

Czechoslovakia

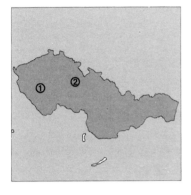

1. The famous Kladruby stud is situated near Plzen.
2. Both men and women take part in the tough Pardubice steeplechases.

Kladruber horses (below) *have been very successful in international combined driving events. The Kladruby State Stud* (below right) *is thought to be the oldest operating stud in the world.*

Kladruber

The Kladruber breed takes its name from the famous Kladruby Stud in Bohemia and traces back to foundation stock originally imported from Spain. Since the beginning of the nineteenth century only white and black horses have been bred.

The imperial stables never had less than eighteen stallions of each colour and these superb creatures, standing all of 17 or 18hh (173–183cm), drew the imperial coaches in teams of six or eight until the end of the Austro-Hungarian Empire in 1918. In 1916 black Kladruber stallions from the royal mews in Vienna drew the funeral coach of the Emperor Franz Josef.

The Kladruby Stud and stud book were destroyed in 1759, but the Kladruber retains all the characteristics of the original stock from which it has inherited its conformation: high action, roman nose and long, heavy-crested neck.

Black and white Kladrubers were interbred over the years to a considerable extent, and for centuries no blood other than Spanish or Neapolitan was introduced. But in the early 1900s crossing Kladrubers with a Shagya Arabian proved successful and since 1918 the size of the Kladruber has been reduced; the finest specimens now stand at between 16.2–17hh (168–178cm). These smaller stallions are being used to improve agricultural horses and also to produce successful cross-breds for riding.

1 & 2. Bosnian ponies are bred from Bosnia (1) in the north to Macedonia (2) in the south.
3. Posavina Draught horses come from the Posavina valley south east of Zagreb.

Yugoslavia

The Bosnian Pony

Pack-horses have been the main form of transport in the mountainous Balkan States for centuries and one of the most important of the tough, compact mountain pony breeds in the area is the Bosnian Pony. Bred originally in Bosnia, Herzegovina, Montenegro, Macedonia and parts of Serbia, and similar to the Polish Hucul, these ponies are usually brown or chesnut, black or grey in colour.

The Bosnian Pony is believed to trace back to the ancient tarpan, crossed with steppe-bred ponies similar to the Przewalski. When the Turkish cavalry of the Ottoman emperors swept

Below: *The Yugoslavian team competing in the dressage phase of the World Driving Championships in Poland.*

over the area, eastern blood was injected into the strain, eventually weakening it until breeders reverted to the original breeding-pattern with much improved results.

In 1933, three stallions were selected as foundation stock for the present day Bosnian Pony and these produced first-class stock. These stallions, which remained at stud until the end of the last war, were the highly influential Misko, a small, compact pony of the tarpan stamp, and Barut and Agan which were both heavier and bigger than Misko. Nowadays, Agan's blood is only found in the pedigree female lines of the breed.

Today all stallions are still tested as pack-horses, being made to carry a weight of about 100 kilos (220lb) over 16 kilometres. This has often been achieved in just over one hour.

Right: *The horse and pony are still an important means of transport in many parts of the world. Here countrywomen are driving into Zadar in Yugoslavia.*

Bulgaria

1–3. Bulgaria's modern breeds are based on three localized breeds, the Danube (1), the Pleven (2) and the East Bulgarian (3).
4. Bulgarian Native ponies are to be found in the southern mountain region.

In 1864, the Turkish overlords set up the Kabuik stud to provide horses for their armies. This was taken over by the Bulgars when the country was liberated in 1878. The foundation stock, mainly of Arabian strains, was strengthened and developed with the importation of other pure-bred stallions from Austria, Hungary and Russia.

Today the state studs produce English Thoroughbreds, Gidrans and Nonius, while a successful policy of cross-breeding has produced the East Bulgarian, an excellent dual-purpose horse. The Pleven, of Hungarian origin, is also found in Bulgaria and there is also a Bulgarian type of Arab with its own stud book.

Right: *Bulgarian horsemen. Pack animals are still in use in countries such as Bulgaria particularly in mountainous and rugged regions.*

The Soviet Union

This map of the basic physical divisions of the region indicates the areas where major horse breeds originated.

Heavy Horse
1. Karabair (Draught)
2. Kazakh (Draught)
3. Lithuanian Heavy Draught
4. Lokai (Draught)
5. Russian Heavy Draught
6. Soviet Heavy Horse
7. Toric

8. Vladimir Heavy Draught
9. Yakut

Light Horse
10. Akhal-Teke
11. Budyonny
12. Don Horse
13. Kabardin

14. Karabair (Ridden)
15. Karabakh
16. Kazakh (Ridden)
17. Lokai (Ridden)
18. Novokirgiz
19. Orlov Trotter
20. Russian Trotter
21. Tersk

Key

- Towns/Cities
□ Studs
Light Horse
Pony
Heavy Horse

Ice/Tundra
Mountains/Uplands
Tropical forest
Forest/Woodland
Grassland
Savanna
Scrub
Desert

In spite of the relentless spread of mechanization, modern Russia still supports a population of eight million horses, half of them at work on farms, in the forests, or as general draught animals. This huge area of differing types of terrain, has been a land of horsemen, and the vast plains have supported nomads and their herds of horses for thousands of years.

The central role played by horsemanship in the lives of the early nomads was revealed during the excavations between 1929–1954 in southern Siberia when archaeologists examined some 2,500-year-old tombs in the Altai Mountains. These nomads of the Altai were buried together with all the things it was believed they would need in the after-life. Normally organic materials such as leather, fabric, wood, and human and animal bodies rot when buried. But at Pazyryk, where many of the most remarkable finds were made, the weather conditions had combined with the design of the burial chambers to create conditions in which the contents of the tomb were deep-frozen. When the tombs were opened archaeologists found, as well as human remains, the bodies of riding and draught horses together with wonderfully well-preserved equipment, such as ornately carved bridles and richly embroidered felt saddle-cloths. These finds are now on display at the Hermitage Museum, Leningrad.

The knowledge of these early horsemen was handed down to successive generations and even today there remain areas such as Kirgizia, Kazakhstan and Bashkiria, where horses are reared in herds much as they were thousands of years ago.

Horse sports and activities in the Soviet Union are many and varied. There are some sixty racecourses and also several harness racetracks where trotting takes place. Despite mechanization driving is one skill which has never died out. Russia is also a great stronghold of the circus where many skilful equestrian acts can be seen. Then there are the remarkable traditional horseback games, such as *kok-par*, which involves two mounted teams vying with each other for the possession of a goat's carcass; archery, done at the gallop; a type of mounted tennis; and a game where the object is to catch a girl who pretends to run away.

In international competitive sports Russian riders and horses are particularly successful in dressage and did very well at Olympic level during the 1960s.

Horse breeding is in the charge of the national studs, and state and collective farms. Riding is becoming increasingly popular and the number of riding centres continues to increase. Schools and clubs are run by such bodies as agricultural schools and stud farms under the Equestrian Federation of the USSR.

Right: *The Karabair, found mainly in Soviet Central Asia, is used both for riding and harness work.*

1–3. The Caucasus (1) and Soviet Central Asia from Turkmenistan (2) to Kazakhstan (3) and Kirgizia have long been areas renowned for their horses and horsemen.
4. Soviet and Vladimir Heavy Draught horses are bred in the districts east and south of Moscow.
5. Yakuts manage to survive in the appalling climate of the Lena valley in the Arctic Circle.

*The USSR is rich in light, heavy and dual purpose breeds. The Budyonny (**below**) was developed in the Rostov region some fifty years ago by crossing Don mares with Thoroughbred stallions. In contrast the Akhal-Teke (**above right**) is an ancient breed which is bred in the Caucasus and parts of Soviet Central Asia. One of Russia's most famous horses, the Don (**bottom right**), has had English thoroughbred blood introduced into the breed by Russian Army stud farms to create the Anglo Don. In 1951, a Don horse called Zenith covered a record 311·6 km in twenty-four hours (being ridden for twenty hours and rested for four). As well as being a useful all-round mount, the Don is strong enough to be used as a draught horse when required.*

Akhal-Teke

The Akhal-Teke is one of the most ancient breeds of horse. Archaeologists have unearthed skeletons which prove that horses of a type and conformation closely comparable with the modern Akhal-Teke existed in the Turkmenistan region at least 2,500 years ago. The breed has always been associated with the Turkmenian people, who have raised horses in the central Asian deserts for many centuries. Instead of running their horses in herds, as most Russian horsemen did, these people tethered their animals and fed them concentrated feedstuffs such as barley and alfalfa. The harsh climate has produced an immensely hardy animal capable of withstanding very hot weather and able to travel long distances in desert conditions on a minimum of food and water.

Although other colours, such as bay, chesnut and cream occur, the Akhal-Teke's predominant colour is a golden shade with a metallic sheen. Standing up to about 15.2hh (157·5cm), the Akhal-Teke has all the usual characteristics of desert-bred horses: a light, rather racy build, longish, slender legs and small, very hard feet. The neck is long and the head slender, while the hindquarters tend to be rather sloping. The tail is set low and is usually fine and rather sparse, as is the mane.

The Akhal-Teke makes an excellent all-round riding horse and has achieved a good deal of success in sports from dressage to racing. Because of their hardiness Akhal-Tekes are also ideal mounts for long-distance rides and several representatives of the breed were among the horses which successfully carried a group of Turkmenians in 1935 on the now-famous journey from Ashkhabad to Moscow, a distance of 4,300km. To achieve this they had to cross the Kara-Kum desert – over 600km of it – and it is a great testimony to their toughness and courage that the horses completed this phase of the journey in three days on an almost non-existent supply of water. The whole journey was completed in 84 days.

Another famous representative of the breed was the dressage horse Absent who in 1960, ridden by Serge Filatov, won the individual gold medal in the Grand Prix de Dressage at the Olympic Games in Rome.

Going back much further in history, Marco Polo suggested that Alexander the Great's horse Bucephalus was the foundation sire of the Akhal-Teke breed.

Today Akhal-Tekes are bred over a wide area ranging from the Caspian Sea to the Chinese border. The most important stud farms are Makhmut Kuli, near Ashkhabad, Lugovsk in Kazakhstan, Tersk in northern Caucasus and Alma-Ata.

Budyonny

The Budyonny is a breed which originated in the twentieth century. Between the years 1920 and 1950 a programme of cross-breeding was carried out in the Rostov region, Don mares being mated with Thoroughbred stallions and the best of their progeny being interbred. The breed which evolved became known as the Budyonny after Marshall Budyonny, a hero of the 1917 Revolution, who was responsible for its development.

The horses he produced were intended for military use, and the result of his policy of careful selection was a well-built, good-tempered horse of excellent conformation with particularly strong limbs. The average height is 15.2–16hh (157·5–163cm) and the predominant colours are bay and chestnut.

Now that the army is mechanized, the Budyonny is used as a sports horse and is particularly successful in the fields of showjumping and steeplechasing. It races on the flat, and makes a good mount for long-distance rides. One notable Budyonny stallion showed the breed's toughness by completing a journey of over 300km in twenty-four hours during which he rested for only four hours.

Don

This breed owes its origins to the famous Don Cossacks who took their name from the river Don, the valley of which they inhabited, and from the Turkish word *quzzaq*, meaning 'bandit' or 'light-armed horseman'. The horses which roamed the steppes of these regions were small, wiry creatures known as Kalmuks. Using these as their basic stock, the Cossacks were able to produce bigger and stronger animals by introducing into the herds Karabakh, Turkmene and Persian horses – many, no doubt, captured from their enemies. The horses thus produced carried the Don Cossacks when they harried Napoleon's army in 1812.

Further crossings during the nineteenth century, this time with Thoroughbreds, gave the breed still more substance. However, the policy of introducing outside blood was stopped at the beginning of the twentieth century and the breed now stands at around 15.3hh (160cm). The chief colours are bay and chestnut, although some Dons have the same metallic golden sheen as the Akhal-Teke. The body is long but deep and strong, the neck powerful and the legs well made.

Raised in the tough environment of the steppes where winter food is scarce and augmented only minimally by man, the Don has developed into a horse capable of enduring harsh conditions. It is thus an ideal long-distance riding horse.

Dons are still bred in the Kirgiz Republic and in Kazakhstan, chiefly at the Zimovnikov and Budyonny stud farms.

Right: *The Lokai, a general purpose breed often used in the mountains of Tadzhikstan for hawking.*

Below: *A pair of Orlov Trotters at exercise in the USSR. The Orlov Trotter has been bred for over 200 years in Russia where the sport of trotting racing is very popular.*

Kabardin

Originating in the Caucasus, the Kabardin is a mountain breed of quite extraordinary sure-footedness, capable of carrying a rider safely along narrow mountain tracks and up and down precipitous slopes over the roughest terrain. It is known to have existed for some 400 years and was developed into its present form by the introduction of Arab, Turkmene and Karabakh blood which increased its height and quality.

Today the Kabardin stands up to about 15hh (152cm). It is a stocky little horse with shortish legs which are extremely strong and sound. The usual colours are bay and dark brown or black. Its docile temperament, which helps to make it such a safe horse to ride in the mountains of its homeland, also ensures its popularity as an all-round riding horse. It is still much used for long rides in the mountain ranges as well as in local equestrian sports which include the type of informal racing which takes place throughout the horse-raising regions of Russia.

Karabair

The Karabair comes from Uzbekistan and is respected as one of the most useful dual-purpose harness and riding horses in Central Asia. The breed is normally bay, chestnut and grey in colour with a strong constitution, sound legs and considerable endurance. Karabairs usually stand around 15.1–15.2hh (1.53–1.54m) and are bred at the Dzhizak Stud near Samarkand.

Karabakh

Although they are only pony-size, Karabakhs are classed as horses and are so strong, agile and good-natured that they are in great demand as mounts for the rather wild equestrian games played in the Caucasus. The breed comes from Azerbaijan, the area between the rivers Araks

Left: *The Kabardin, a mountain breed originating in the Caucasus.*

and Kura in Trans-Caucasia. Karabakhs have oriental blood in their veins, particularly Arabian, and have also been influenced by the Akhal-Teke. The metallic golden coat colouring of the latter often occurs in the Karabakh, though not to the exclusion of other colours. Chesnuts, bays and duns are equally common. The average height is around 14hh (142cm), but this active little horse can produce a really good gallop and for this reason is much used in the game of Chavgan, a sport not unlike polo.

Kazakh
The Kazakh is a small Russian pony some 13hh (1.43m) which can cope with extreme changes in climate. It is used for milk and meat production as well as under saddle and in herding cattle. The mares are now crossed with Thoroughbreds, Dons and Heavy Draughts on the state farms of Kazakhstan.

Orlov Trotter
The Orlov Trotter has been bred in Russia for more than 200 years and was for a long time the best trotting racehorse in the world. The breed was established towards the end of the eighteenth century by Count Alexis Grigorievich Orlov, a gentleman who enjoyed several claims to fame. He was one of the assassins of Peter III in 1762. A gifted and courageous man, he was made an admiral in 1768 and in 1770 led the Russian fleet to vicory over the Turks at the Naval battle of Cheshme in the Aegean. When the war ended he turned his attentions to breeding horses and became just as successful at this activiy as he had been as a naval commander. His Khrenov stud became the cradle of the trotting horse which bears his name.

He began by purchasing a pure-bredArabian stallion, Smetanka, which he mated with a Dutch-bred mare. Her pedigree is uncertain but she was probably a Friesian or a Frederiksborg. The colt produced by this mating, called Polkan, was in turn put to another mare of Dutch extraction and another colt, Barss, was produced. Among Barss's offspring were three particularly fine stallions: Dobroy, Lebed and Lubesnoy. The dam of Dobroy was an English Thoroughbred; that of Lebed a Thoroughbred/Arab/Mecklenburg cross; and that of Lubesnoy an Arab/Mecklenburg cross. These stallions, all with a good deal of Arabian blood in their veins, were to become the foundation sires of the Orlov breed.

Until the development of the American Standardbred, Orlovs were the fastest trotters in the world, though they were never thought of exclusively as racehorses. Many were expected to perform the usual duties of a light harness horse for which they were well suited. Trotting became a popular sport in Moscow, where races were held as early as 1799.

After Count Orlov died his widow sold the stud farm to the government which decided, during the nineteenth century, to introduce more Thoroughbred blood in an endeavour to improve performances on the racecourse. Such improvements as were made, however, were not sufficient to prevent the Orlov being outstripped by the American Standardbred and it was only a matter of time before Standardbreds began to be imported for stud purposes. The Standardbred/Orlov cross-breed, known as the Russian Trotter, is faster than the Orlov, though resembling it in appearance.

The Orlov is a strong horse, standing about 16hh (163cm), with a deep body and good, sound legs. The most common colours are grey, bay, black and chesnut. The Orlov is a long-lived animal and is still used as a general purpose harness horse.

Soviet Heavy Draught

The Soviet Heavy Draught horse is the most popular of all the heavy horses in Russia. It is one of the youngest Russian breeds, having been developed during the first half of this century. In order to produce a really top quality working horse a policy was adopted of importing stallions from Belgium and crossing them with native draught mares. Carefully-controlled breeding on these lines was begun after the revolution in 1917 and by 1940 a distinct type had evolved.

It is a rather less massive horse than the other Russian heavy-weights and is exceptionally tough, being able to withstand the worst excesses of the Russian climate. It stands up to 16hh (163cm), weighs around 800kg, has a kind temperament and is a willing, energetic worker, frequently winning prizes in weight-pulling contests. The breed is widely distributed throughout the country. The chief breeding centres are the Pochinkov and Mordovian studs, but it is also bred on collective farms, particularly in the Vladimir district.

Tersk

The Tersk horse comes from the Caucasus and was evolved during the first half of this century. It is based on the Strelets Arabian, a breed which flourished during the nineteenth century. Strelets Arabians were produced by crossing pure-bred Arab horses with Anglo-Arabs (that is horses that are half Arab and half Thoroughbred) from the Orlov and Rostopchin studs, and were highly thought of in the international Arab horse market. They were awarded gold medals at the 1900 World Exhibition in Paris.

During World War I the Strelets Arabian nearly died out and when peace returned only two stallions could be found, Cylinder and Tsenitel. Both were excellent examples of the Strelets Arabian who, many people believed, possessed all the best characteristics of the Arabian horse. In an effort to preserve something of these qualities, the two stallions were mated with a variety of pure-bred and part-bred Arab mares at the studs of Tersk and Stavropol. Much emphasis was given to good conformation and only those horses which most resembled the old Strelets strain, with its distinctive light-grey colouring, were retaind at the studs.

Between 1921 and 1950 this breeding policy was to lead to the evolution of a new type of horse, the Tersk. In appearance it resembles the Arabian, though it is taller, standing up to 15.2hh (157·5cm). The majority of Tersk horses have retained the light-grey colouring of the Strelets Arabian and some have a very pale, almost white coat. It is a handsome horse whose eye-catching appearance makes it popular for work in the circus ring. Its excellent temperament also makes it an ideal dressage horse, another quality which is exploited by circus riders. In addition it is fast enough to race successfully and can be seen competing against Arabian horses on the racecourse at Pyatigorsk.

The Tersk stud now only breeds Arabians while the Stavropol stud is the chief breeding centre of the Tersk horse.

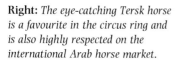

Right: *The eye-catching Tersk horse is a favourite in the circus ring and is also highly respected on the international Arab horse market.*

Bottom: *Although the Russian Heavy Draught is the smallest of the heavy draught breeds it is still a powerful animal. This stallion called Satyr pulled a record weight of 15 tons (453kg).*

Below: *The Yakut lives within the Arctic Circle, probably the most inhospitable region known to the horse.*

Vladimir Heavy Draught

A great many heavy horse breeds have been used in the development of the Vladimir Heavy Draught horse, among them Suffolks and Shires from England, Clydesdales from Scotland and Percherons and Ardennais from France. In addition some Cleveland Bay and Trotter blood was used. Stallions of all these breeds were crossed with the local mares of the Vladimir district, which lies to the east of Moscow, during the years after the Revolution.

The heavy horse that evolved from this policy of inter-breeding became recognized as a distinct breed in 1946. It stands about 16hh (163cm) and has a rather long, but strong body, set on sturdy limbs. The usual colour is bay.

In spite of its massive build it is particularly noted for its active paces. This quality, together with its great pulling power, makes the Vladimir an excellent work horse and it is, in addition, blessed with great soundness of limb.

The chief breeding centres are the state-run stud farms at Ivanovo, Tambov, Vladimir and Yaroslavel.

Yakut

The pale grey, or mouse-coloured Yakut horses, named after the Yakut tribesmen of the Lena valley who used them as summer mounts, are remarkable in that they inhabit what is probably the most inhospitable region known to the equine race. Much of their range is within the Arctic Circle, but they have learned to dig through the snow and ice in search of food. The winters are very long and harsh with an average temperature of minus 40°C.

The Yakut has adapted to its surroundings most efficiently. Its coat is thick and can be 10cm long. With the accumulation of outside dirt and natural grease from the horse's body, such a coat will give protection from the coldest and wettest of weather.

Two types of Yakut horse are seen, one somewhat larger than the other. The southern strain is related to the wild Mongolian Horse, the Przewalski, which it resembles and is smaller than the type found in the north, averaging about 13.2hh (137cm). No one knows for sure the history of the bigger northern type which may be upwards of 14.2hh (147cm). Remains of an extinct breed of horse have been found in the tundra regions and the Yakut may be descended from this, but as yet not enough is known about it.

Yakuts are sturdy little horses, with large bodies and particularly deep chests. Despite their comparatively small size they often weigh as much as half a tonne. They are real all-round work-horses, being ridden, driven and used as pack-horses.

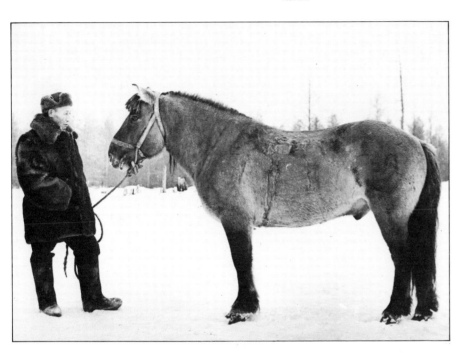

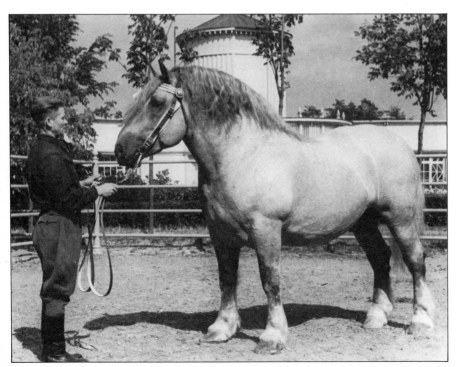

Africa & the Middle East

Two members of the family of wild *Equidae* are restricted to Africa and two to Asia. Africa is the home of the asses and zebras, and Asia of the horses and half-asses. True wild horses never appeared on the African continent.

The first people to introduce the domesticated horse into Africa were the Hyksos who came from Anatolia in the seventeenth century BC and conquered Syria, Palestine and Egypt. The earliest reference to the horse in Egypt dates from the sixteenth century BC when a general of the Pharaoh Aahmes is recorded as accompanying his master in a horse-drawn chariot in pursuit of fleeing Hyksos chariots. A skeleton of a horse from the seventeenth century BC was found in the debris of the fortress at Buhen.

Egypt has always depended on equine stock imported from Asia. Thus, Solomon, King of Israel, supplied the Egyptians with horses imported from Cilicia, and the profitable transit trade helped to finance a large stud for himself. Greater numbers of horses were introduced into Africa from Asia during the Arab invasions in the seventh and eleventh centuries AD. These horses were all of the so-called Oriental type, the typical representative of which is the Arabian horse.

Slightly later than the introduction of horses to Egypt by the Hyksos, a very different type of horse was introduced into North Africa from Spain and the islands of the Aegean Sea. From Spain they reached Morocco, Algeria and Tunisia, while from the Aegean islands they were taken in boats to Libya by the 'Sea Peoples', who tried to conquer Egypt from the west.

This Occidental type of horse differs from the Oriental type in the conformation of head and body. Its presence in Africa was first recorded by the Egyptians in about 1230 BC among the booty taken by Merneptah from the western invaders and a few decades later when Rameses III captured 180 horses and asses from a Libyan tribe.

No horses at all existed in Arabia at the time of the Hyksos invasion of Egypt. During the first millennium BC, when nearly all the peoples of western Asia and northern Africa possessed horses, the Arabs were invariably portrayed as camel-riders. It was only shortly before the rise of Mohammed that the Arabs began to breed horses. When Mohammed attacked the Koreish, he had only two horses in his army, and there is no mention of horses in the booty. Owing to the unfavourable environment the number of horses in Arabia remained small.

Domesticated horses were introduced into Asia Minor, northern Syria and Mesopotamia shortly after 2000 BC by intruders from the north. Before this the Syrians and the Mesopotamians relied on the onager to pull their solid-wheeled wagons and carts.

Left: *The far-reaching influence of the Arabian horse's breeding qualities can be seen in the mounts of these African tribal leaders.*

This map of the basic physical
divisions of the region indicates
the areas where major horse
breeds originated.

Light Horse
1. Arabians
2. Barb
3. Dongola

4. Oriental Horse
5. Thoroughbred, Saddle Horse
   Arabs and Anglo-Arabs
6. Turkoman

Pony
7. African Ponies
8. Basuto

MEDITERRANEAN SEA

TANGIERS ALGIERS TUNIS
TUNISIA
MOROCCO Atlas Mts TRIPOLI
Canary Islands
WESTERN SAHARA
ALGERIA LIBYA EGYPT CAIRO
MAURITANIA R. Niger
SENEGAL MALI NIGER CHAD KHARTOUM
GAMBIA
GUINEA
BISSAU UPPER
VOLTA NIGERIA SUDAN ETHIOPIA
GUINEA
SIERRE
LEONE IVORY
COAST CENTRAL
AFRICAN
REPUBLIC
LIBERIA GHANA TOGO BENIN CAMEROON
EQUATORIAL GUINEA GABON R. Congo UGANDA SOMALIA
CONGO RWANDA KENYA
ZAIRE BURUNDI
Lake Victoria
TANZANIA
MALAWI
ANGOLA
ZAMBIA
R. Zambesi
GROOTFONTEIN ZIMBABWE-
RHODESIA MALAGASY
REPUBLIC
BOTSWANA MOZAMBIQUE
JOHANNESBURG SWAZILAND
NAMIBIA DURBAN
SOUTH
AFRICA LESOTHO
CAPE TOWN

SYRIA IRAQ
LEBANON UNITED ARAB EMIRATES GULF
ISRAEL KUWAIT OF
JORDAN OMAN
OMAN
Suez Canal
R. Nile
Lake Nasser
RED SEA SAUDI
ARABIA NORTH YEMEN
SOUTH GULF OF ADEN
YEMEN
DJIBOUTI

ATLANTIC OCEAN

INDIAN
OCEAN

LAGOS

Key
- Towns/Cities
- Light Horse
- Pony
- Heavy Horse

Ice/Tundra

Mountains/Uplands

Tropical forest

Forest/Woodland

Grassland

Savanna

Scrub

Desert

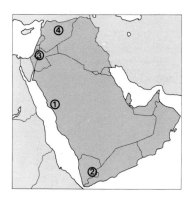

1. Arabia has never had many horses because of its unsuitable climate, but it has lent its name to the most famous of the world's breeds.
2. The Giawf pony is bred in Yemen.
3 & 4. Famous Arabian stud farms exist in Jordan (3) and Syria (4).

The Middle East

Arabian

The Arabian desert horse has exerted its influence on breeds of horses throughout the world for many centuries. A good Arabian horse is distinguished by its beauty, speed and staying-power, hardiness and endurance, intelligence and generous temper. It has a strong constitution that enables it to withstand heat and cold, hunger and thirst, and the fatigue of very long rides.

The Arabian is rather small in size, short-coupled, and usually 14 – 14.2hh (142–147cm), more rarely up to 15hh (152cm). Its head is fine, with a wide forehead, dished profile, large eyes and nostrils, and deep, lean and clearly marked jaws. As in many other desert animals, the ears are long and slender. The neck is arched, the chest broad and muscular, with sloping shoulders but low withers. The back is short, the loins are strong, the ribs well sprung, and the croup is long and level with a high-set tail that is carried in an arch. The legs are clean, with prominent tendons, sloping pasterns and round durable hoofs. The bone is of dense material. The principal colours of the desert Arabian are bay, brown, chesnut, and grey.

However, it should not be thought that every horse in Arabia comes up to a high standard of soundness and beauty. There are many pure-bred Arabian horses in which the conformation of the withers, back and loins, and especially of the hocks, leaves much room for improvement. The majority have remarkable powers of endurance and speed, but the ideal of the breed is approached by few of them. The great explorer and scholar Burton (1821–90) wrote of the pure-bred horses of inner Arabia: 'They are mere "rats", short and stunted, ragged and fleshless, with rough coats and a slouching walk. But the experienced glance notes at once the fine snake-like head, ears like reeds, wide and projecting nostrils, large eyes, fiery and soft alternately, broad crown, deep base of skull, wide chest, crooked tail, limbs padded with muscle, and long elastic pasterns. And the animal put out to speed soon displays the wondrous force of blood.'

The Bedouin value only their mares. Stallions are not ridden, for in the past their neighing at a mare could betray a raiding party. The Bedouin know long pedigrees of pure-bred mares by heart and judge the animals not so much by their conformation as by their descent. They are loath to part with a good mare, and may deprive their infants of much needed camel milk in order to give it to a filly.

Right: *The sleek Arab is one of the world's most beautiful horses. This one has a ceremonial collar round its neck.*

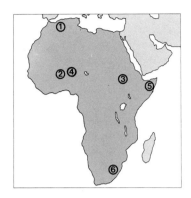

1. *The horses of North Africa are a mixture of Barb and Arab: Barb blood is more predominant in the mountains and Arab in the plains.*
2. *The northern horses spread south to the Sahel countries of West Africa, mingling with the local breeds. Collectively they are now known as West African Barbs.*
3 & 4. *Sudan (3) is the home of the Kordofani or Western Sudan ponies. It also produced the Dongola which spread west to the river areas of eastern and southern Sahel (4). Forming many different types and varieties they are now known as West African Dongolas.*
5. *Somalia has its own breed of ponies.*
6. *The Basuto pony from Lesotho has become very rare.*

Right: *Oriental horses are well known for speed and stamina over difficult terrain.*

Africa

The Oriental Horse in Africa

In Africa the Oriental type is most conspicuous in regions south and west of Egypt. Egypt itself is a poor horse-breeding country. Horses are not employed there in agricultural work but only as cart and riding animals in the towns. Horses bred in Egypt from pure Arabian sires and dams lose a great deal of their Arab quality by becoming long-legged and weedy.

There were apparently no horses in east Africa before the great Arab invasions of the eleventh century AD. Messudi, who travelled along the coast in AD 917, found only riding oxen for military use. The Arab invaders took a fair number of Arabian horses into the Sudan whence they were introduced into the Horn of Africa and Ethiopia.

The same Muslim invasions took the Arab horse to the west as far as Morocco. In Tripolitania, which consists almost entirely of desert and poor steppe inhabited only by nomads and semi-nomads, the population is Arab proper, and many horses are of true Oriental derivation. In Tunisia, Algeria and Morocco the Oriental type is prevalent near the coast.

On the fringe and in the mountains and oases of the Sahara, where the environment is similar to that of the Arabian desert, the Oriental type is occasionally encountered in a nearly pure form. Among the horses of the Tuareg and Berber tribes in Niger and Mali a desert type closely resembling the Arabian is found. The breed of the Tuareg of Aïr is famous for its endurance, staying power and speed on hard and rocky ground. These horses are commonly fed on millet and camel milk. They are of a small size, averaging 13.3hh (140cm), of a harmonious conformation and high-spirited elegant appearance. The head is short, with a wide square forehead, straight profile, alert ears, and lively eyes. The neck is carried high and has an abundant silky, sometimes curly, mane. The back is straight, short and firm, the croup horizontal and the tail-setting high; the chest is wide, the ribs are well-rounded, and the flank is short. The legs are often fine, but commonly straight and of firm bone with hard hoofs. The coat is grey.

From the Sahara, horses of Oriental type have spread to the south and west, deteriorating in size and conformation under the unfavourable conditions existing near the equator and on the coast of the Atlantic.

Horses did not penetrate the tropics to reach the south of Africa because of sleeping sickness and nagana, diseases affecting man and domestic animals caused by the trypanosome parasites spread by the tsetse fly. All horses and ponies now found in the southern part of the continent are descended from stock imported by Europeans since the first four horses were shipped from Java to the Cape in 1653.

Right: *The Barb originated along the notorious Barbary coast of North Africa, principally in Morocco, where the Royal Stud produces clean-bred stock, and Algeria. The Barb is hardy and docile but due to cross-breeding the pure-bred is becoming quite rare.*

Barb

The term 'Barb' is often applied to the horses of Morocco, Algeria, Tunisia and Libya in a general sense, but not all North African horses warrant this term, as there are many Oriental horses in the Maghreb or Atlas countries. The Barb is up to a hand (10cm) taller than the Arabian. It commonly has a long and coarse head, high withers, flat shoulders and thighs, rather weak back and loins, long legs, drooping croup, and a thick and bushy, low-set and tucked-in tail. Its most characteristic feature is the convex profile of the head. The predominant colours are grey, white and brown. Owing to its larger size, many horsebreeding tribes of North Africa prefer the Barb to the Arab; formerly the French used it in large numbers in their colonial armies too.

The characteristic conformation of the Barb points to its derivation from an ancestral stock other than of Oriental type. This is evident from the appearance of the Arabian horse which, reared under unfavourable environmental conditions, does not generally lose its refinement, but merely decreases in size. This characteristic is shown by several pony breeds of Oriental type. The Barb's coarse head, convex profile and totally dissimilar conformation suggest that it is derived from horses of Occidental type. Similar horses

were bred in the Iberian peninsula during the Iron Age. Recent Barbs tend to be of mixed ancestry, with a variable proportion of Occidental blood.

In Libya the purest Barbs occur in the most inaccessible mountains. In Morocco, Algeria and Tunisia too the Barb is dominant in the mountain regions of the interior. The Berbers preserved their own horses. In the west of Morocco, which was reached by only a small number of Arab invaders, the Barbs are purer than in the east; the western Barbs have little or no trace of Arabian blood in their appearance or general characteristics.

From Algeria and Morocco Barb horses have spread into West Africa, where the majority are distinguished by a grey coat. This is most conspicuous in the northern breeding areas, while towards the south bay and chesnut horses are also found. In many parts the horses represent a mixture of Barb and Oriental; many have straight facial profiles, an indication of the Arabian blood which the Barb has absorbed since the Arab conquest of North Africa. But the long, often heavy head and drooping croup of the true Barb, which are quite foreign to the Arabian, have been retained by nearly all West African Barbs.

Dongola

The original breeding centre of the Dongola horse in the Sudan forms an enclave in an otherwise purely Oriental horse-breeding country. The Dongola seems to have arrived there from North Africa via the caravan routes of the central and eastern Sahara. In Dongola and Sennar this originally Occidental breed has absorbed a considerable share of Oriental blood. When the Scottish explorer James Bruce visited Sennar in 1772, he observed very fine horses which the King of Sennar had obtained from Dongola. They were all above 16hh (163cm), as strong as British coach-horses, but light in their action. However, less than a century later a German traveller recorded that the original Dongola horse was nearly extinct, chiefly owing to the ravages of African horse-sickness and the requisitioning of large numbers of Dongola horses by the Turks. Now there are very few horses left in that area. In the Sudan there are a few thousand, and in the western lowlands of Eritrea a few hundred, but in West Africa the type is widespread.

The Dongola is an old breed that seems to have been common in Upper Egypt and the Sudan during the early centuries of the Christian era and the Middle Ages. The great kingdoms which developed in the eastern and central Sudan were

dominated by a mounted aristocracy, and mailed cavalry formed the nuclei of their armies. Rock drawings in the Nubian Desert portray the Dongola with its characteristic features, its markedly convex facial profile, arched neck, high withers, steep shoulders, narrow and weak loins, drooping croup and low-set tail. In many respects it resembles the Barb, but the colour of the coat is commonly a deep reddish-bay, sometimes chesnut or black, with white markings on the forehead and fetlocks. The breeders prefer animals with a white face and four white legs.

The present Dongola can be up to 15.2hh (157·5cm), but it is clumsy, soft in constitution and possesses almost every fault of conformation known in horses. It has been described as large, flashy, ugly and useless, and its originally small and now rapidly diminishing numbers are no cause for regret.

In West Africa the Dongola has interbred with Barbs as well as with Oriental horses to give a considerable number of distinct breeds and varieties, some being of Dongola-Barb and others of Dongola-Arab type and still others a mixture of the three. Apart from the convex profile of the head and drooping croup, common to both Dongola and Barb, the presence of Dongola blood is apparent in the colour of the coat.

Above: *Horses watering at Lake Awassa, Ethiopia. Most of the horses found on the African continent were taken there by the early European settlers and missionaries.*

African Ponies

The term 'pony' is usually restricted to horses not over 14.3hh (147cm). In the United States the bronchos, mustangs and cayuses (Indians' ponies) are sometimes called ponies regardless of size. In a more limited sense the term is applied to small breeds of a particularly stocky build.

With regard to north-equatorial horses in Africa, the term is used for a number of small breeds, not exceeding 13.3hh (140cm), which are found either in the south at such distances from the equator at which horses can still survive, or in equally unfavourable climatic conditions in the inundation areas of the Niger and on the coast of West Africa. As these breeds are of very different racial types, either Oriental, Barb or Dongola, or combining Oriental and Dongola, Oriental and Barb, or Dongola and Barb features, their small size may be attributed solely to their poor environment. In view of the marked racial differences between the various pony breeds of Africa north of the equator, it is evident that their ancestral stocks were derived from different sources and introduced at different times.

The Somali ponies are of pure Oriental descent. They are sturdy animals, about 13hh (132cm). Burton (1856) described them as follows: 'The head is pretty, the eyes are well opened, and the ears are small; the form is also good, but the original Arab breed has degenerated in the new climate. They are soft, docile, and – like all other animals in this part of the world – timid; the habit of climbing rocks makes them sure-footed, and they show the remains of blood when forced to fatigue.'

Another type, with a large share of Occidental blood, is the Kordofani. It is believed to have been introduced from the north-west, probably sometime during the Middle Ages. It is a first-class pack-pony, capable of great endurance, sturdy, square-built and usually less than 14hh (142cm). It has a coarse head with a convex profile, resembling in this respect the Barb and Dongola, poor straight shoulders, a heavy belly, drooping croup, low sickle hocks, and short upright pasterns, but bones and hoofs of strong durable material. The coat colour is usually light bay or chesnut.

Below: *An African villager looks on at a group of ponies grazing by a lake in Lesotho.*

The pony breeds of West Africa vary considerably in size, but all have a heavy head, thick short neck and an unharmonious conformation. The Kirdi of Chad and the Cotocoli of Togo are only 10 – 12hh (102–112cm). West African ponies may be either bay or chestnut in colour. Although most of them have absorbed a Barb strain and some may actually be degenerated Barbs, they never have a grey coat.

Basuto Pony

In Lesotho (Basutoland), the southern African country situated between the South African provinces of Cape Province, Orange Free State and Natal, the African people have developed an indigenous breed of pony. It is descended from horses of European farmers, which were mainly derived from breeding stock imported by the Dutch East India Company from their possessions in the east and subsequently from Thoroughbreds brought over from Britain.

During the period of wars and incursions which began in 1822 with the Zulu invasions and lasted for many years, the Bantu tribes of what is now Lesotho and the adjoining country obtained horses for the first time. Later, the local Bantu people were employed by the Boers as farm hands and were paid for their labour in stock, especially in horses. In addition, European traders, who had heard of the Basutos' interest in good horses, entered Basutoland with large droves which they exchanged for cattle. Thus a hundred years ago practically the whole Basuto nation was mounted on ponies.

The typical Basuto pony is a small, rather thick-set animal with short legs and very hard hoofs. Its conformation, character, action and great powers of endurance are derived from ancestral stocks which had adapted to the harsh conditions of Basutoland. Lesotho is the most mountainous and coldest part of southern Africa. Shelter and feed other than natural grazing are rarely provided, and the breeding stock live in the mountains throughout the year, exposed to the extremes of heat and cold. The ponies are galloped up and down precipitous mountains, thereby becoming extraordinarily fearless and sure-footed.

Below: *These young horses seem to be making their own way along the Frootfonjkin–Rundu Road in Namibia (South-West Africa).*

Asia

Wild horses once roamed throughout the grassland zone extending from the Atlantic coast of the Iberian peninsula in the west to the shores of the North Pacific Ocean in the east. It is probable that all of them belonged to a single species, remnants of which are known to us as *Equus przewalskii* or Przewalski's Horse. However, judging from the amount of skeletal and dental variation found, it is likely that they belonged to many different inter-breeding types and groups of horse.

The first historical use of horses was as draught animals in north-east Asia Minor and northern Mesopotamia, hitched to vehicles with wheels of solid discs composed of three wooden planks. The domestication of the horse had first occurred to the north of this area, and the use of onager-drawn chariots and wagons had been introduced from the south. The combination of the two with the replacement of the onager by the faster horse was a logical step, and led to the increasing domestication of the horse in the region north of the Black Sea between 3000 and 2000 BC. However, exploitation of the horse for meat and milk was widespread in the grassland zone from an early time. The eating of horse meat was prohibited by Pope Gregorius III in 732 as a remnant of pagan worship.

The invention of the horse-drawn war chariot with much lighter spoked wheels provided a powerful military engine which allowed its early possessors to invade the ancient cultures in the south and east – Greece, Asia Minor, Mesopotamia, Iran, India and China. In all of these, horse-drawn chariots made their appearance between 2000 and 1500 BC.

The social and economic importance of the horse increased tremendously and the knowledge of it was speedily diffused through Asia and Europe. It resulted in the absorption of every wild race into the domesticated stock within the space of 3,000 years with the exception of a few in inaccessible desert regions. Many wild horses were also hunted down and destroyed by horse breeders whose business was harmed by the abduction of domesticated mares by wild stallions. Wild horses were still being captured a century ago according to Russian reports. At foaling time the Mongols rode with two horses each into the desert, and having found a herd of wild horses they followed it until some of the young foals fell down from fatigue. Another report from about the same time records the capture of ghor-khar (half-ass) foals in the Bikaner desert on the borders of Punjab in Pakistan and Rajasthan in India. In this barren region parties of mounted Baluchis used to ride down ghor-khar foals during the foaling season; about two-thirds of the young animals died in captivity, but the rest were tamed.

Left: *Buzkashi (or Kokburi) is a tough mounted game originally played by the nomadic tribes of the steppes and now played in Afghanistan. The object of the game is to gain possession of a dead goat or sheep held between the rider's knee and saddle.*

This map of the basic physical divisions of the region indicates the areas where major horse breeds originated.

Heavy Horse
1. Kazakh

Light Horse
2. Arabian
3. Baluchi
4. Harzai

5. Improved Chinese breeds
6. Iomud
7. Karabakh
8. Oriental Horse
9. Shirazi
10. Thoroughbred
11. Turkoman

Pony
12. Caspian
13. Jaf
14. Kathiawari

15. Kazakh
16. Kurdi
17. Manchurian
18. Marwari
19. Mongolian
20. Przewalski's Horse
21. South China Pony
22. Spiti
23. Tarai
24. Tibetan Pony
25. Tsinghai
26. Yabu

Key

● Towns/Cities

Light Horse

Pony

Heavy Horse

Ice/Tundra

Mountains/Uplands

Tropical forest

Forest/Woodland

Grassland

Savanna

Scrub

Desert

1. Przewalski's Horse was first discovered in Dzungaria in 1881.
2. Rock drawings of similar horses from the Old Stone Age have been found west of Lake Baikal in the USSR.
3–5. Mongolian ponies are found in the steppe land north of the Gobi (3), in the Gobi desert itself (4) and in Inner Mongolia (5), part of China.

Mongolia

Przewalski's horse

Wild horses are nearly extinct. The few remaining animals live in a restricted desert or near-desert area in the Takhin Shara-Nuru (Yellow Wild Horse Mountain Chain), on the border between the Mongolian People's Republic and Sinkiang, where they are protected by law. However, it would be erroneous to regard the wild horse exclusively as a denizen of the steppe for the history of the horse demonstrates its great adaptability to steppe, forest or tundra. Man and his domestic animals have crowded it out from more favourable pastures.

The wild horse now named *Equus przewalskii* Poliakoff was discovered by the Polish explorer Przewalski in Dzungaria in 1881. The first Przewalski horses were introduced into Europe in 1899. All attempts to rear captured wild foals failed until a number of domestic mares were served so that they foaled at the time that another batch of young wild foals was caught. The wild foals were suckled by the foster mares whose own foals had been killed, their hides being placed on the wild foals so that these would be accepted by the mares. In 1901 five Przewalski colts and seven fillies reared in this manner were acquired by the Duke of Bedford from Hagenbeck and taken to Woburn. In 1902 the London Zoo obtained two pairs from the same importer, of which one pair was later transferred to Manchester. Now many pure-bred Przewalski horses are kept in zoological gardens throughout the world, and these are registered in their own stud book.

Equus przewalskii is a small horse, fairly compact in build and rather low on the legs, standing about 13–14hh (132–142cm). It is a little higher at the croup than at the withers, and the length of its body is about equal to its height. The head, especially the facial part, is large, with a relatively broad prominent forehead. The muzzle is very broad, and the upper lip hangs a little over the under lip. There is practically no forelock. In summer the mane is short and erect, but in winter it grows longer, tending to bend to the side of the neck. The pelvis is more horizontal than in the ass and zebra, and the bone is of strong material. The hoofs are small and almost cylindrical, with contracted heels. Chestnuts, similar to those of domesticated horses, are present on all four limbs. The coat is long, shaggy and dun coloured, becoming lighter towards the lower part of the body.

Equus przewalskii is represented in three late palaeolithic rock drawings near the source of the Lena river, west of Lake Baikal, USSR. During the Palaeolithic Age before 10,000 BC, horses of Przewalski type ranged into western Europe. Some of the bones found at Solutre in the Dordogne and in the Madeleine rock shelter are indistinguishable from those of Przewalski horses. Drawings of horses in the cave of La Madeleine show the same relatively heavy head, long face, absence of forelock, upright mane and short back.

Mongolian ponies

In the Mongolian People's Republic and in Inner Mongolia, China, the ponies stand approximately 12–13hh (122–132cm) when fully grown at the age of seven or eight years. The Mongols keep them in large droves in the steppe, milking and riding them.

Mongolian ponies vary considerably in conformation, especially in cranial type. Generally they are distinguished by a long, rather heavy head with a wide forehead, fairly long broad ears, and strong teeth. The head is usually carried low, in some animals below the level of the withers when walking. The neck is light and badly set on straight shoulders and the withers are low. The majority are well muscled, thick-set and of compact build. In the grassland zone ponies of a fairly refined type are encountered; in some the head is reminiscent of an Arab's. In the scrubland and semi-desert of the Gobi the ponies often have coarse heads and necks, and resemble the wild *Equus przewalskii*. The leg bones are small, and animals with crooked hind legs or sickle-hocks are common, but the hoofs are of good quality.

Mongolian ponies have long flowing manes and forelocks, and long bushy tails. The coat consists of strong coarse hair, which in winter grows long and woolly. All colours found in domestic horses are present in the Mongolian; bay and brown are probably the most common. Grey predominates in the Mongolian People's Republic, but on the grasslands of Inner Mongolia white ponies are frequent, and are often selected for riding. Grey or yellow-dun ponies occasionally have striped legs and an indistinctly defined shoulder bar. Bays and duns usually have a dark dorsal stripe.

In the fertile grassland in the eastern part of Inner Mongolia an improved type of Mongolian pony standing 13–14hh (132–142cm), called Wuchumutsin, has long been bred for riding and draught work.

The Mongolians milk the mares for three months after foaling. Milking is done by the women, while the men keep a hold on the foals. The milk is fermented into koumiss, and from this a fairly strong alcoholic spirit, resembling vodka, may be distilled.

Left: *A Mongolian pony stallion in the Gobi. Many of these ponies are exported to China.*

Below: *The ancient Przewalski horse.*

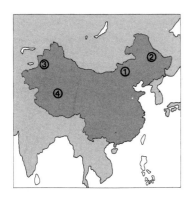

1. Several improved breeds such as the Hailar and Sanpeitze, come from the east of Inner Mongolia.
2. Heilungkiang in Manchuria produces its own type of Mongolian pony as well as the Sanho light horse.
3. Kazakh and Kirgiz ponies are bred in Sinkiang in the areas bordering Kazakhstan and Kirgizia.
4. Three breeds of ponies come from the mountainous Tsinghai province: the Sining, Khetshui and Tatung.

Below right: A Heilungkiang riding pony stallion. The possible influence of the Mongolian pony can be seen in the head.

Below: The Kazakh, a dual purpose pony used on collective farms in Kazakhstan.

China

Chinese horses

With the exception of the south-eastern provinces where paddy is cultivated and the buffalo is the principal draught animal, horses are bred in nearly every part of China.

The domestic horse was introduced into northern China from the west in the first half of the second millennium BC. By the middle of the second millennium the horse was used to draw war chariots of a similar type to those introduced at about the same time to other cultures. The pictograph (the symbol in picture writing) for chariot shows that at that time a team consisted of two horses. Later, four, or even six horses were used. From the eighth century BC the importance of a state was measured by the number of horse-drawn war chariots it could muster. Horses were acquired mainly from Mongolia, Shansi, Shensi and eastern Tibet. Horse flesh was often eaten; the tribes west of China reared horses specially for this purpose. Later the eating of horse meat became uncommon in China, and at the present time it is restricted to the Mongol minority in Inner Mongolia.

Manchurian ponies

Most Chinese horses are pony sized, although in the north several breeds of Siberian derivation are larger, as are the pure-bred or crossbred descendants of the Vladimir Draught, Baltic Ardennais, Akhal-Teke, Russian Saddle, Kabardin, Karabair and Hucul horses from the USSR distributed in northern and central China

in 1950. In the north-western part of Heilungkiang province, which lies alongside the breeding area of Mongolian ponies, a local variety of the latter is bred. It stands 12.2–13hh (127–132cm), usually has a large head with a moderately convex profile, a poor neck, prominent withers, broad chest and long slightly hollow back. Its legs are of good bone, with strong hoofs, and its mane and tail are long and full. It is usually light dun, bay, white or grey.

The Heilungkiang pony is mainly used for light draught and is occasionally ridden. The breed is very disease-resistant, and hardy enough to withstand the extremely cold climate of its breeding area which has only 100–115 frost-free days a year. The ponies graze from June to September, and are fed on hay for the rest of the year.

In Kirin province, sturdy Mongolian-type ponies are bred in several grassland areas and a similar type is bred in Hopeh.

Kazakh pony of Sinkiang

The Kazakh pony is bred in the eastern and north-eastern parts of Sinkiang, bordering on Kazakhstan, Kirgizia and Tadzhikistan, USSR. Large droves of these small hardy ponies used to be exported to the south, as far as the plains of India. They seldom exceed 14.3hh (150cm), can withstand the very low winter temperatures of their breeding area and are suitable for pack work on mountain paths.

The Kirgiz pony, bred by the Khalkas of Sinkiang, in the border area, is a local, smaller variety of the Kazakh.

Tibetan pony

The Tibetan pony or Nanfan is bred in the grassy areas of the tableland. It is very compact, stands 12–14hh (122–142cm) and is heavier than the

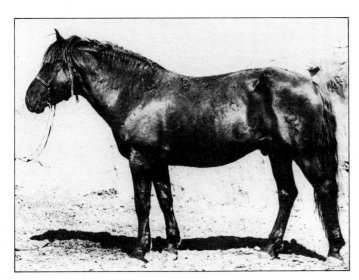

Mongolian though generally not so coarse. It has a relatively short head with a prominent forehead and concave facial profile. Most Tibetan ponies are white, a few yellow dun with a dark dorsal stripe, or fawn and brindled. Tibetan ponies are tough and wiry and good climbers at high altitudes. Because of the scarcity of pasture they are fed pig's blood and raw liver in winter, or raw dried beef and hard cheese. In the cold regions of central Asia meat used to be regarded as a necessary feed for horses.

Tsinghai ponies

In Tsinghai province, a mountainous region south of Sinkiang and Kansu, three pony breeds are found: Sining, Tatung and Khetshui.

The Sining comes from the eastern part of Tsinghai and the adjacent region of Kansu. It is believed to be derived from Tibetan and Mongolian stock, and is commonly kept on mountain pastures above an altitude of 2,000m (6,500ft). The Sining is the best pony of north-west China, being strong and sturdy. It is used along the pack trails into Tibet.

The Tatung of north-east Tsinghai is also used as a mountain pack animal. At a stud founded with the aim of improving the Tatung pony, Kabardin stallions from USSR are used in order to breed a larger and heavier type.

The Khetshui is bred in south-east Tsinghai and western Kansu. It is larger and stronger than the Mongolian and is widely used in Tsinghai and adjacent provinces for the improvement of local pony stock with the aim of producing a draught and saddle pony at least 14hh (142cm).

South China ponies

Ponies are bred in moderate numbers only in the upland areas of southern China. They are usually given the name of the province where they are bred. The smallest, standing 10hh (102cm) is bred in Yunnan, while in Sikang it may exceed 13.2hh (137cm). South China ponies are sure-footed and can carry great weights over long distances.

Improved Chinese breeds

These are found mainly in the northern part of the country, and include the Sanho of Heilungkiang and the Hailar and Sanpeitze of Inner Mongolia. These breeds were developed from crossbreds of Mongolian pony mares and Orlov, Anglo-Arab and Thoroughbred stallions introduced into these regions by Russian immigrants in Tzarist times. They make good riding horses but are now used also for draught. Their breeding area is bleak and they are fed on hay for seven months of the year.

India, Pakistan & Iran

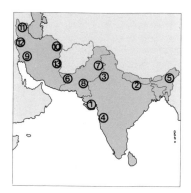

1. *The Kathiawari, or Cutchi, is an ancient breed found in Gujarat.*
2 & 3. *The Tarai survives the heat of Uttar Pradesh (2) and Bihar and resembles the Dhanni from the Punjab (3).*
4. *Bombay's native breed, the Deccani, is nearly extinct.*
5. *The Manipuri is a local breed from Assam.*
6. *Pakistan's Baluchi horse is bred in Baluchistan.*
7 & 8. *Others of Pakistan's breeds come from the Punjab (Unmol, 7) and Sind (Makra, 8).*
9. *The main strains of the Persian Arab, the Bakhtiari, Sistani and Qashqai, are bred in Khuzistan in western Iran. The Shirazi, named after the city of Shiraz, is also found there.*
10. *The Turkoman, related to the Akhal-Teke is bred in the north on the borders of Turkmenistan and Afghanistan. This area also produces the Chenarani and Iomud.*
11. *Karabagh or Karabakh horses developed from stock over the Soviet border in Azerbaijan.*
12. *The Kurdi and the Jaf come from Kurdistan.*
13. *Yabu ponies are used as pack ponies in the mountainous east.*

Horses of India and Pakistan

Horses first entered India during the Aryan invasions of the middle of the second millennium BC. While the racial type of the earliest horses of India is not known, several Indian sculptures from a later period represent horses similar to the Arab. However, by the end of the first millennium AD, the Rajput kingdoms that existed in northern, western and central India had large cavalries consisting of heavier, stronger and sturdier horses. The most conspicuous feature of these animals was the convex profile of their heads.

Indian horses now tend to be of pony size and lightly built. They are descended from interbred mixtures of ponies of Mongolian type from the north and imported Arab horses. Marco Polo recorded that vast numbers of horses were imported into India from the Persian Gulf and Arabia. During the period of British rule many Thoroughbreds were imported from Britain.

Indian ponies

The Kathiawari or Cutchi, bred in the Kathiawar peninsula of Gujarat in western India, still shows the convex profile of the ancient equine stock of the Rajputs. Typically the ears are turned in. The breed is very variable in height and is lightly built. Despite its rather poor conformation, however, it is capable of fairly heavy work. Its coat is either dun, rufous, grey or bay.

The Marwari or Mallani of Rajasthan, north of Gujarat, resembles the Kathiawar, and is usually chestnut or bay in colour.

In the northern plains of Uttar Pradesh and Bihar the Tarai pony is used in towns and villages to pull the light, two-wheeled tangha cart. It is probably of debased Arab stock and can stand the heat in this part of India far better than horses from the north. The Tarai stands 11–12hh (112–122cm) is of slender build, with a long, narrow head, straight profile, short ears and generally poor conformation. Tarai ponies are bays, usually with a black mane and tail.

Similar in type are the Dhanni, a light horse of the Indian Punjab; the grey or dun, occasionally black or bay Spiti pony of the Kangra valley of north-east Punjab; the Shahabad pony of western Bihar; and the now nearly extinct Deccani or Bhimthadi of Bombay. The Manipuri of Assam is typical of several south-east Asian pony breeds. It is a small animal, standing 11–13hh (112–132cm), which for centuries has been used in its home country as a polo pony.

Pakistan horses

In Pakistan the majority of horses are light and larger than ponies. They include the Baluchi or Baloch of Baluchistan and Derajat, which, like the Kathiawari, has turned-in ears; the white or grey Hirzai of Baluchistan, thought to be of nearly pure Arabian origin; the Waziri of north-west Pakistan and Afghanistan; the nearly extinct bay or grey Unmol of the north-western Punjab, and the dun Makra of Sind.

Persian horses

The principal breeds of Iran are the Persian Arab and the Turkoman. There are three main strains of the Persian Arab, which is widely bred in Khuzistan, western Iran, namely, Bakhtiari, Sistani and Qashqai. Generally the Persian Arab has a height of 14–15hh (142–152cm). It has a wide prominent forehead, straight profile, large eyes and nostrils, and deep jaws. The neck is arched, the chest broad, the shoulders are well sloped, the back is short and strong, and the croup either level or only slightly sloping to the high-set tail. The legs are slender but strong, and the hoofs are small and of hard material. The principal coat colours are bay, chestnut and grey, seldom black.

Above: *The modern form of polo developed in India. The polo club at Silchar in Cachar district, which was started in 1859, is the oldest polo club in the world.*

Above left: *A painting by Manohar of Emperor Shah Jahan and one of his sons' riding escort. Most Kings and Emperors liked to be depicted riding stallions, riding a mare, it was thought, was undignified.*

The Turkoman is bred in Khurasan, north-east Iran, from where its breeding area extends into the adjacent regions of Afghanistan and Turkmenistan, USSR. It stands 15–16hh (152–163cm), has a heavy head, long neck and narrow chest; its withers are of moderate height, its back long, and its hindquarters are poor and drooping to the low-set tail. The legs are long and slender, but the hoofs are of weak material, unfit for work on stony hills. On level desert ground the Turkoman shows strength and endurance. Its coat colours are similar to those of the Persian Arab.

The Shirazi or Darashoori is bred in Fars, south-west Iran. It is a light docile riding horse, probably descended from native mares crossed with Arab stallions. Large numbers of the breed have been exported to India where they are known as Gulf Arabs. They stand 14–15hh (142–152cm) and show the influence of Arab blood in their conformation. Their legs are often faulty, but their hoofs are sound.

Other Persian riding horses include the Chenarani of north-east Iran and the Iomud, which extends from its main breeding area in Turkmenistan into the adjacent border region of north-east Iran. The Iomud is similar to the Akhal-Teke of Turkmenistan but smaller in size standing 14–15hh (142–152cm). Its body is rather heavy, with a long neck and low withers, but the legs are well shaped. It is usually grey, but occasionally dun.

Carriage-horses in Iran are commonly of the Karabakh breed which was developed in Azerbaijan and improved by being crossed with Arab and Turkoman stock in the eighteenth century. The Iranian Karabakh, or Karadagh, is 14–15hh (142–152cm), strong and muscular with a rather coarse head, short heavy neck, broad chest, moderately long back and straight or slightly sloping croup.

The Caspian pony, believed to be the survivor of Iran's prehistoric horse, is still found in small numbers on the forested shores of the Caspian. Until 1965 it was thought to have been extinct for a thousand years, and great excitement was aroused when several were found pulling carts in nearby towns and grazing on the shore line. In build the Caspian is more like a small horse, standing 10–12hh (102–122cm).

The Jaf and Kurdi of Kurdestan and the Yabu of eastern Iran and Afghanistan are small ponies used mainly for pack work in the mountains, being sure-footed on difficult terrain.

Australasia

Australia and New Zealand feature strongly in the modern horse world although their equine history is comparatively short. They have bred very similar horses, despite the differences in the two countries. Australia is a huge, mostly flat and arid land mass of ancient undisturbed rock, with an indigenous population of marsupial mammals isolated for millions of years from the placental mammals evolved later.

New Zealand, on the other hand, is a more modern country in geological terms, consisting partly of limestone from the old sea bed where the limestone was formed originally from the remains of sea creatures, and partly of volcanic rocks, mainly on North Island. The climate is equable enough for grass to grow throughout the year, and this, combined with the limestone so beneficial in promoting good bone growth, makes New Zealand such a first-class breeding ground for horses.

The Thoroughbred yearlings at the annual sales are magnificently grown youngsters with almost faultless conformation. At the top 1979 sale, out of the 350 yearlings sold, 200 went to Australia and well over fifty to other countries. Out of what remains New Zealand still manages to win her fair share of Australian Stakes races, including several Melbourne Cups. New Zealand horses have a reputation for being top-class stayers, a quality shown by the great Balmerino

who culminated his victorious tour of Italy, England and America by running second in the Prix de l'Arc de Triomphe in 1977.

In comparison Australia generally lacks the necessary conditions for breeding horses. Although it has an economy based largely on pastoral products, much of the land is virtual desert and is sparsely inhabited. The best pastoral land is the most heavily populated, with the best climate, and this includes the south-east and south-west, the eastern coastal strip and Tasmania. These areas are all ideal for breeding horses. The climate is extremely hot and humid in the north, and although there are horses there, they do not prosper.

Below left: *Australian rider Jeff McVean riding the New Zealand-bred mare Claret. McVean and Claret toured the European showjumping circuit in 1978 winning the British Open Championship and the coveted King George V Gold Trophy at the Royal International Horse Show, London.*

Below: *The Australian continent has never had a strain of horse or pony as a natural inhabitant. But today it has very much become a land of the horse with the Australian Thoroughbred gaining a world-wide reputation.*

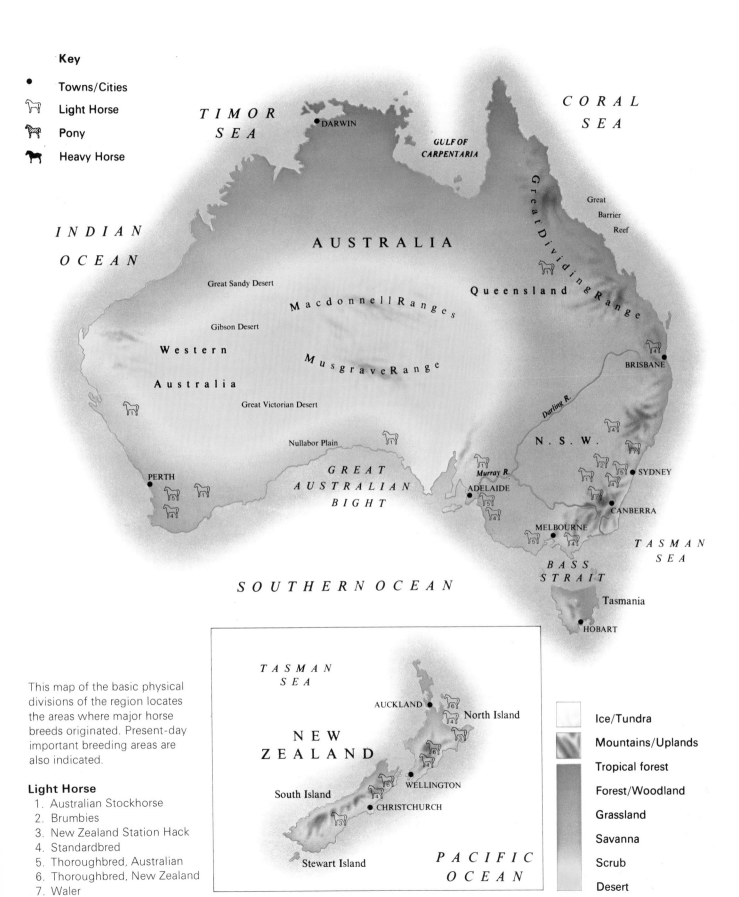

Key

- Towns/Cities
- Light Horse
- Pony
- Heavy Horse

TIMOR SEA

DARWIN

GULF OF CARPENTARIA

CORAL SEA

INDIAN OCEAN

AUSTRALIA

Great Barrier Reef

Great Sandy Desert

Macdonnell Ranges

Queensland

Great Dividing Range

Gibson Desert

Western

Musgrave Range

BRISBANE

Australia

Great Victorian Desert

Darling R.

N. S. W.

Nullabor Plain

PERTH

GREAT AUSTRALIAN BIGHT

Murray R.

ADELAIDE

SYDNEY

CANBERRA

MELBOURNE

TASMAN SEA

SOUTHERN OCEAN

BASS STRAIT

Tasmania

HOBART

This map of the basic physical divisions of the region locates the areas where major horse breeds originated. Present-day important breeding areas are also indicated.

Light Horse

1. Australian Stockhorse
2. Brumbies
3. New Zealand Station Hack
4. Standardbred
5. Thoroughbred, Australian
6. Thoroughbred, New Zealand
7. Waler

TASMAN SEA

AUCKLAND

North Island

NEW ZEALAND

South Island

WELLINGTON

CHRISTCHURCH

Stewart Island

PACIFIC OCEAN

Ice/Tundra

Mountains/Uplands

Tropical forest

Forest/Woodland

Grassland

Savanna

Scrub

Desert

Australia

1–4. Australia's best horse-breeding country comprises New South Wales (1), the eastern coastal strip (2), the south-west (3) and Tasmania (4).

Below: *A herd of Brumbies being rounded up in the Australian Alps in south-eastern New South Wales.*

The Horse of Australia

In 1788 the first horses ever to tread Australian soil were shipped from the Cape of Good Hope in South Africa with Governor Phillip's first batch of convict settlers. Other horses followed, some from Valparaiso in Chile, a few from India but most from the Cape. These were the days of sail when journeys were long and exhausting, often against prevailing winds. Many horses died.

The type of horse in the Cape at that time was described as a cross between a Persian or Arab horse and the Barb of North Africa, the result much resembling the Spanish horse. It had a large head, straight shoulders, poor front leg and particularly bad foot, but was, however, extremely hardy, tough and brave, qualities which remain in the Australian-bred horse to this day, and it doubtless met the needs of the early penal settlers as far as communication and transport were concerned.

As immigration to Australia increased, faster horses were needed for long overland journeys, and Thoroughbreds were imported to improve the quality of the existing animals. The expanding agricultural economy made a much stronger type of horse necessary, so Clydesdales were imported from Scotland to replace the bullocks used hitherto. Many Cleveland Bays from Yorkshire

Left: *A typical Australian Waler. During World War I more than 2,000 were exported to the Allied armies in India, Africa, Palestine and Europe.*

were also sent on the long, often fatal voyage to Australia in order to improve the size and type of carriage-horse.

A shipment of two Thoroughbreds and an Arab from England and a Thoroughbred from France in 1840 were the first recorded imports of either breed. Racing became a regular and rapidly expanding sport and these imports were followed by many more. It was not long before enough Thoroughbreds had been bred and imported to start an Australian Thoroughbred Stud Book.

During the next fifty years the horse population of Australia expanded even faster than the human. A certain number of horses, known as Brumbies, had become wild and bred amongst themselves and many thousands roamed unbranded throughout Australia. The vast cattle and sheep stations also bred large numbers of horses which were rounded up annually to provide replacements for stock work.

Almost the only entertainment stockmen had in the remote outback was from horses. They would catch Brumbies and have buck-jumping competitions which later grew to the full-scale rodeos now held all over Australia. Australian cowboys are amongst the best in the world today. Bush race meetings are also very popular, and some large properties have their own racecourses.

At one period the best type of horse wild or otherwise was to be found in New South Wales. Around the 1880s when strong, hard, durable horses were being pressed into army service, New South Wales supplied many Walers, as they became known.

In 1884 Australia sent her first shipment of horses to India. This was the forerunner of a trade which reached large proportions particularly when journey times were cut as steamships started operating in the 1880s. Horses were purchased by the British as well as the Indian Army for the artillery and cavalry, Walers being far superior to horses that could be obtained in India, and particularly popular as officers' chargers and for playing polo. Heavier horses were also in demand for the artillery. By the early 1900s the horse population of Australia had reached the three million mark, so by the outbreak of World War I Australia was in a position to swell this market by tens of thousands.

At this stage horses were being used for everything. Large numbers of pack horses were required by gold prospectors and miners and the horse still powered all forms of transport, whether town trams or the faster, lighter mail coaches. The horse was totally indispensable to the stockmen who were constantly mustering and driving vast numbers of cattle and sheep sometimes many hundreds of miles to the saleyards. A good horse was essential, for if the huge mobs of cattle stampeded it had to be fast and bold enough to gallop to the head of the rushing cattle and turn the leaders.

Very recently a decision was made to establish this useful type of animal as a breed, and as the term Waler is now no longer used, the Australian Stock Horse Stud Book was opened. The horses registered are almost all Thoroughbred or near Thoroughbred under 16.1hh (165cm) and they are carefully selected for type and performance. Once accepted they are branded thus Ȧ.

Mechanization in the 1920s gradually reduced the demand for horses, the three million horse population dwindled to a mere half million by the 1930s and the export trade to India ended.

However, the horse is now increasingly used for sport and recreation; polo, showjumping and eventing are very popular, while racing and trotting have an enormous following, the famous Melbourne Cup being the most coveted award in the Southern hemisphere. Many other breeds including the British native ponies, Arabs and Quarter horses have been imported and the Pony Club has the reputation of being the largest in the world. Ideal for use in the Pony Club is the Galloway, a good type of miniature horse standing 14.2–15hh (147–152cm) which has developed in Australia over the years. The Australian Stock Horse has developed into a much sought-after and versatile type of horse well known for its jumping ability.

Australians have always performed extremely well in world Three-Day Event and showjumping competitions. An excellent record of well over 8 feet (2·44m) has been maintained for years in national high jump competitions. Only South America has unofficially claimed a greater height. Australian showjumpers, among them Bonvale, April Love and Claret compete successfully at international level.

However, it is the Australian Olympic Three-Day Event record which is really impressive. In 1956 in Stockholm the team was fourth. In 1960 in Rome it took home the team Gold medal, the individual Gold medal (Laurie Morgan on Salad Days) and the individual Silver medal (Neale Lavis on Mirrabooka).

Above: *A Quarter Horse brood mare and her foal running out at the Muskoka Stud, Hawkesbury River, New Zealand.*

New Zealand

1. Clydesdales were used extensively on the rich agricultural country of the Canterbury Plains.
2. The first Thoroughbreds were imported at Wellington from Australia.

Right: *Working horses at the Strathaven Clydesdale Stud, near Fairlie, New Zealand. There is evidence of the Clydesdale being taken to Australia around the beginning of the 19th century.*

Above: *The famous trotter Cardigan Bay is celebrated on one of New Zealand's postage stamps.*

Ranches are called stations in Australia and New Zealand and from that the New Zealand horse gets its name. Evolving in the same way as the Australian Stock Horse, as the horse of the shepherd and stockman, today the New Zealand Station Hack is popular as a hunter and a showjumper.

Early importations of Thoroughbreds led to the compilation of the first Thoroughbred Stud book in 1862. Such quality animals introduced from abroad gave rise to traffic in the other direction as the excellence of the New Zealand breeding grounds proved itself. Carbine was one of the first great race-horses. In 1904 Moiffa won the Grand National in England and in 1928 Pharlap was called the 'racing phenomenon of the century' for his exploits in Australia.

Trotting became a popular sport from the 1860s and the first registered trotting horses were imported from America in 1882. The most famous New Zealand trotter was Cardigan Bay who when racing in America became the first horse raced in harness to win more than a million dollars in stake money.

Of other imported breeds the main one has probably been the Arab, the first of which was imported in 1850. A Lipizzaner stallion, Eaglescliff Emperor, arrived from Piber in the 1920s, while American Quarter horses and Standardbreds, Percherons and Cleveland Bays from England and Australia have all left their mark on the development of the Station Hack.

Glossary

Action: style of the horse's movement, regularity of stride and good balance.
Aids: signals used by rider to convey instructions to horse. Natural aids: voice, seat, legs and hands. Unnatural aids: whip, spurs, etc.
Airs: paces other than normal gaits of walk, trot, canter, etc; e.g. *Passage* and *Piaffe*.
Amble: irregular trot produced by using both limbs on the same side simultaneously.
Artificial airs: *Passage*, *Piaffe* and High School movements.
Ascot Gold Cup: the principal long-distance race of the English flat season. Founded in 1807.
Asil: horse of noble lineage (Arabic).

Barrel racing: racing between and around barrels, popular in Australia and USA.
Blaze: white mark between the eyes and covering much of the forehead, reaching down to the muzzle.
Bloodstock: collective term used in relation to clean-bred horses and breeding stock.
Blue dun: black horse with blue sheen.
Blue Grass Country: horse breeding area in Kentucky, USA.
Blue Riband: term usually applied to classic flat-races; e.g. The British Epsom Derby Stakes.
Bone: measurement of bone immediately beneath knee or hock.

Cadence: rhythm and tempo of a horse's paces.
Camp drafting: Australian sport based on cattle cutting, usually performed at agricultural shows.
Cannon: bone of foreleg below the knee, ending at fetlock joint.
Canter: easy gallop, used originally by pilgrims on their way to Canterbury.
Chestnut: small horny prominence about three inches (7·5cm) above knees on forelegs and on inner and lower hock joint on hind leg.
Classics: term applied to a series of important races for three-year-old colts and fillies.
Classics (Britain): five races for three-year-olds: the 2,000 Guineas and 1,000 Guineas (fillies) at Newmarket; the Derby and the Oaks (fillies) at Epsom; the St Leger at Doncaster.
Classics (USA): four races: the Kentucky Derby, Preakness Stakes, Belmont Stakes and the Coaching Club American Oaks (fillies).
Clean-legged: without feather hair.
Cob: well-established type of big-bodied short-legged horse or pony no higher than 15.3hh (155cm).
Coldblood: heavy horse of northern forest type used mainly in agriculture.
Collected: horse having maximum control over its movements, ready to respond to the rider and aids.
Colt: entire male horse under four years old.
Combined Training: Three-day Event, Two-day Event or One-day Event.
Conformation: description of shape and build of horse.
Coronet: band surrounding top of foot at edge of hair growth.
Croup: upper line from loins to root of tail, usually convex.

Dam: female parent of a horse or foal.
Demi-sang: first Thoroughbred cross.
Dock: part of tail on which hair grows.
Dorsal stripe: continuous stripe of black or brown down the back from neck to tail.
Draught horse: horse used for pulling vehicles or loads; usually a heavy horse, but not invariably.
Dressage: from the French 'to train'. Term applied to the systematic training of a horse. As a competitive event, a test of obedience and suppleness.
Dun: greyish brown, mouse-coloured.

Eastern: oriental horses of Arabian, Turkish or Syrian breeds.
Entire: uncastrated male horse.
Extended paces: the lengthening of the normal gaits without increase in speed.

Feather: fetlock hair, especially when long as in the Shire.
Fetlock joint: joint between cannon bone and pastern.
Filly: female horse under four years old.
Flat race: race without obstacles.
Flea-bitten: horse of grey colour flecked with darker tones.
Foal: horse under one year; e.g. colt-foal, filly-foal.
Forehand: that part of the horse which is in front of the saddle or roller.
Forelock: continuation of mane between the ears, hanging over forehead.
Forward seat: position of rider over natural centre of gravity of free moving horse, giving unity of movement to horse and rider.
Fox-trot: four-beat gait unevenly spaced. The stride is shorter and slower than the running walk.

Gait: pace of horse, usually walk, trot and canter.
Gelding: castrated male horse.
Girth: circumference of body measured behind the withers around lowest point of body.
Grand National: main steeplechase event in Britain, staged at Aintree, Liverpool, over 4½ miles (7·2km).
Grand Pardubice: steeplechase held in Czechoslovakia over 4¼ miles (6·9km).
Grullo: slate or mouse-coloured (USA).

Hack: type of riding horse.
Hack (vb): to go riding.
Hamstring: the Achilles' tendon running down back of second thigh to point of hock.
Hand: one hand = 4 inches (10·16cm). Unit for measuring horse's height.
Hand gallop: steady, smooth canter.
Haras: French for stud farm.
Haute Ecole: High School. Classical art of riding as practised by the Spanish Riding School in Vienna and the Cadre Noir of the French Cavalry School, Saumur. It includes the performance of various 'airs above the ground' such as *levade, pesade, capriole, ballotade, courbette* and *croupade*, and the airs 'on the ground' *passage* and *piaffe*.
hh: hands high.
Heavy horse: one of the big draught varieties such as Ardennais, Clydesdale or Shire.

Hock: joint corresponding to human ankle between second thigh and hind cannon.
Horse of the Year Show: international horse show staged in London every October.
Horse Trials: Three-Day Event, Two-day Event and One-day Event.
Hot blood: one of the eastern horses or Thoroughbreds.
Hunter: horse used for hunting, of a type suitable for the terrain over which it is ridden.

Liberty horses: circus horses unridden.
Light horse: horse group comprising hunters, hacks and riding horses in general, usually warm-blooded.
Loins: the back either side of the spine just behind the saddle.
Lungeing: early stage in training when the young horse is controlled by a single webbing or rope rein about 30ft long (12m).

Mare: female horse four years old and over.
Melbourne Cup: One of the most important Australian handicap races run over two miles.
Military or Militaire: old term applied to Combined Training.
Morocco: primary colour white, the other colour black, brown, dun or sorrel. (USA)

National Horse Show: premier horse show in USA staged at Madison Square Gardens, New York.
Nations' Cup: *see* Prix des Nations.
Newmarket: generally known as the headquarters of British flat-racing. Records of horse-racing near the town go back to 1622.

Outcrossing: mating of unrelated or distantly related horses.
Overo: bay, black, brown, dun, roan or sorrel with white as second colour, in irregular pattern. (USA)

Pan American Games: events based on Olympic format held before the Games every four years for horses of South, Central and North America.
Pari-Mutuel: French system of betting, (PMU).
Pastern: part of leg between fetlock joint and coronet.
Piebald: colouring where skin has large irregular patches of white with black as the other colour.
Point-to-Point: steeplechases confined to amateur riders and horses that have been regularly hunted.
Pony: an equine up to 15hh, 14.2hh (147cm) or less for show Ponies. Possibly a descendant of the Plateau horse (Mongolia).
Posting: rising from the saddle at the trot.
Prix des Nations: International Team Showjumping competition, teams consisting of four riders from the same country. Points championship for the President's Trophy.
Pur sang: pure-bred.
Pur Sang Anglais: Thoroughbred.

The Queen's Plate: Canada's oldest race for Canadian three-year-olds.

Remounts: general term for all horses used in an army unit.
Rosettes: show-ring awards. Red and blue usually signifying first and second place respectively in Britain and Canada, the reverse in USA.
Rount: roan or flesh-coloured with white or peach. (USA)
Royal International Horse Show: one of the premier horse shows staged in London.
Royal Winter Fair: international horse show staged in Toronto, Canada.

School paces: collected paces, higher and more regular than ordinary paces.
Second thigh: Gaskin. Portion of hind leg above the hock up to the stifle.
Skewbald: colouring where skin has large patches of white hair in an irregular pattern with any other colour but black.
Snowflake: white spots on darker background.
Sock: white marking on legs from coronet upward extending only a short way.
Sorrel: chestnut colour with lighter red or gold. (USA)
Spanish walk: artificial air in which the horse lifts its forelegs high. Favoured in circuses.
Stallion: entire male horse four years old or more.
Star: any white mark on forehead.
Steeplechase: race with fences and ditches; sometimes with water jumps.
Stifle: junction of patella and tibia, corresponding to human knee.
Stocking: white leg from coronet to knee or hock.

Tap root: original source of a breeding line.
Three-Day Event: competitive event consisting of a dressage phase, speed and endurance phase, steeplechase and cross-country phase and showjumping. Usually completed over three days.
Tobiano: primary colour white, with other colours black, brown, dun or sorrel; all legs white. (USA)
Tote, Totalisator: British term for Pool betting.
Triple Crown (British): victory in the 2,000 Guineas, the Derby and the St Leger.
Triple Crown (USA): victory in the Kentucky Derby, Preakness Stakes and the Belmont Stakes.
Trot: natural two beat gait on diagonals, e.g. sequence of near fore, off-hind, off-fore, near hind.

Warmblood: light horse used for riding. Also used to indicate presence of Arab or thoroughbred ancestry.
Withers: ridge between the shoulders.
Wrangler: cowboy or cowhand. (USA)

Yearling: colt or filly between one and two years old.
Yellow Dun: yellowish pigment in horse's hair with black skin, mane and tail.

Breed list

This is a comprehensive list of breeds, types and variations of horse found throughout the world. Synonyms, if any, are given, together with the country where the horse was originally bred and the countries into which it has been introduced. The latter are marked with asterisks.

Abbreviations used in this section

syn synonym
var variation of
L Light Horse
H Heavy Horse
P Pony
H/L indicates the breed can be in either the Heavy Horse or Light Horse category
L/P indicates the breed can be in either the Light Horse or Pony category

L Akhal-Teke (syn Turki, Turkoman) *Afghanistan*, Iran, Pakistan*, USSR*
P Albanian *Albania*
P Altai (syn Oirot; var Siberian) *USSR*
L Altér Real *Portugal*
L American Albino *USA*
L American Quarter Horse (syn Kentucky Whip) *Australia*, Canada, New Zealand*, South Africa, USA*
L American Saddlehorse (syn Saddlebred, Kentucky Saddle, Five-gaited Horse) *Australia*, USA*
L American Trotter (syn Standardbred, American Trotting Horse) *Australia*, Canada*, New Zealand*, Switzerland*, USA*
L Amur *USSR*
P Anatolian Native *Turkey*
L Andalusian (syn Andulasian-Barb, Andalusian-Lusitanian, Bético, Spanish) *Australia*, Spain*
P Andean (var Peruvian Criollo) *Peru*
L Anglo-Arab *Australia*, Austria*, Belgium*, Brazil*, France, GB*, Italy*, Netherlands*, New Zealand*, Norway*, Poland*, Portugal*, Spain*, Sweden*, Turkey*, USA*, USSR**
L Anglo-Argentino (syn Argentine Horse) *Argentina*
L Anglo-Don *USSR*
L Anglo-Kabardin *USSR*
L Anglo-Karachaev *USSR*
L Anglo-Kozakh *USSR*
L Anglo-Norman (syn Norman; var French Saddle) *France*
L Anglo-Normando *Argentina*
L Anglo-Teke *USSR*
L Appaloosa (syn Palouse) *Australia*, USA*
L Arab *Algeria, Argentina*, Australia*, Austria*, Belgium*, Brazil*, Bulgaria*, Canada*, Chile*, Czechoslovakia*, Denmark*, Egypt, France*, Germany*, GB*, Greece*, Hungary*, India*, Iran*, Iraq, Ireland*, Israel, Italy*, Jordan, Libya, Morocco, Netherlands*, New Zealand*, Norway*, Pakistan*, Peru*, Poland*, Portugal*, Romania*, Saudi Arabia, South Africa*, Spain*, Sweden*, Switzerland*, Syria, Tunisia, Turkey*, Uruguay*, USA*, USSR*, Yemen, Yugoslavia**
L/P Aragon *Spain*
H Ardennais (var Belgian) *Belgium, Canada*, Hungary*, Poland**
L Argentine Criollo (syn Argentine Landrace) *Argentina, Uruguay*

P Ariègeois *France*
P Assateague *USA*
P Australian *Australia*
L Australian Stock Horse (syn Waler) *Australia*
H Auxois *France*
L Avar (var Dagestan) *USSR*
L/P Avelignese (var Haflinger) *Italy*
LP Azerbaijan *USSR*

L Bagual *Argentina*
L Baguezané (syn Kinaboutout) *Niger*
L Bahia *Brazil*
P Bahr-el-Ghazal (syn Kreda, Ganaston; var Dongola) *Chad*
L Bakhtiari (var Persian Arab) *Iran*
L Baladi (syn Egyptian Arab) *Egypt*
P Balearic Island *Spain*
H Baltic Ardennais (syn Latvian Ardennais) *USSR*
L Baltic Trotter *USSR*
L Baluchi (syn Baloch) *Pakistan*
L Bandiagari (syn Gondo, Macina) *Mali, Niger*
L Barb *Algeria, Libya, Morocco, Tunisia*
L Barouèli *Mali, Niger*
P Barra (var Highland) *GB*
P Bashkir *USSR*
L Basque-Navarre (syn de la Barranca, Navarre) *Spain*
L Basseri (var Persian Arab) *Iran*
P Basuto *Lesotho, South Africa*
P Batak (syn Deli) *Indonesia*
L Bélédougou (syn Banamba; var West African Barb) *Mali*
H Belgian (syn Belgian Heavy Draught, Brabant, Brabançon) *Belgium, Denmark*, Italy*, Poland*, USA*, Yugoslavia**
P Belgian Warmblood *Belgium*
P Bhirum (syn Pagan) *Nigeria*
P Bhotia (syn Bhutan) *Bhutan, India, Nepal, Sikkim*
P Bimanese (var Sumbawa) *Indonesia*
H Bityug (syn Beetewk, extinct) *USSR*
L Black Forest *Germany*
L Black Sea *USSR*
P Bobo (syn Bobodi, Minianka) *Mali, Upper Volta*
L Boer (syn Boerperd) *South Africa*
L Bokhara *USSR*
P Bolivian (syn Sunicho; var Criollo)
P Borana (syn Galla Pony) *Ethiopia*
L Bornu (var West African Dongola) *Nigeria*
P Bosnian (syn Bosnian Mountain) *Yugoslavia*
H Boulonnais *France*
L Brandenburger *Germany*
L Breton (1) *France*
H Breton (2) (syn Trait Breton) *France*
L Breton (3) (syn Postier Breton) *Brazil*, France*
L Breton Saddlehorse (syn Corlay) *France*
L British Spotted *GB*
L Brumbie *Australia, New Zealand*
L Budyonny (syn Budennyi) *USSR*
P Bulgarian Colonist (syn Bessarabian, extinct) *Bulgaria*
H Bulgarian Heavy Draught *Bulgaria*
L Bulgarian Mountain (var Bulgarian Native) *Bulgaria*
L Bulgarian Native *Bulgaria*
H Burgdorf *Switzerland*
L Burguete *Spain*

L Calabrese *Italy*
L Calvinia *South Africa*
P Camarguais *France*

P Cambodian *Cambodia*
L Campolino (var Mangalarga) *Brazil*
L Canadian *Canada*
L Canadian Cutting Horse *Canada*
L Canadian Hunter *Canada*
P Canadian Pacer (formerly var French Canadian) *Canada*
P Canary Island *Spain*
P Canik (var Anatolian Native) *Turkey*
L Cape Harness *South Africa*
L Cape Horse (syn South African, extinct) *South Africa*
L Carthusian (syn Andalusian-Carthusian, Cartuja) *Spain*
L Castillian *Spain*
P Catalan (syn Hispano-Breton) *Spain*
P Cayuse (var Indian Pony) *USA*
L Charentais (var French Saddle) *France*
L Charolais (var French Saddle) *France*
L Chenarani *Iran*
L Chilean (var Criollo) *Chile*
P Chincoteague *USA*
L Chumysh *USSR*
P Chuvash *USSR*
P Chyanta (var Bhotia) *Nepal*
L Cleveland Bay (syn Chapman Horse) *GB, USA**
H Clydesdale *Argentina*, Australia*, Canada*, GB, New Zealand*, South Africa*, USA**
P Cob Pony (var Welsh Pony) *GB*
L Colombian Criollo *Colombia*
L Colorado Ranger *USA*
H/L Comtois *France*
L Conestoga (extinct) *USA*
P Connemara *Australia*, Ireland, Sweden*, USA**
L Corsican *France*
L Costeno (var Peruvian Criollo) *Peru*
P Cotocoli (syn Koto-koli, Togo Pony) *Benin, Ghana, Nigeria, Togo, Upper Volta*
L/P Criollo *Argentina, Bolivia, Chile, Colombia, Mexico, Paraguay, Peru, Uruguay, Venezuela*
L/P Crioulo *Brazil*
L Cuban Trotter *Cuba*
L Cukurova *Turkey*
P Cushendal (extinct) *Ireland*

L Dabrowa-Tarnowska *Poland*
P Dafur (var West Sudan) *Sudan*
L/P Dagestan *USSR*
L Dales *GB*
L Danube *Bulgaria, Romania**
P Dartmoor *GB*
P Davert (extinct) *Germany*
L/P Deccani (syn Bhimthadi) *India*
L/P Deliboz *USSR*
P Deli-Orman (var Bulgarian Native) *Bulgaria*
P Devon Pack Horse (extinct) *GB*
L Dhanni (possibly extinct) *India*
P Djerma *Benin, Mali, Niger, Nigeria, Upper Volta*
L Dobruja (var Romanian) *Romania*
L/P Døle Gudbrandsdal (syn Østland) *Norway, Poland**
L Døle Trotter *Norway*
L Don (syn Trans-Don) *USSR*
L Dongola (syn Dongolawi) *Chad, Nigeria, Sudan*
P Dülmener (syn Münsterland) *Germany*
L Dutch Draught (syn Holland Heavy, Netherlands Draught, Zeeland) *Netherlands*
L Dutch Warmblood (WPN) *Netherlands*

L East Bulgarian *Bulgaria*
L East Friesian *Germany*
P East Kazakh (var Kazakh) *USSR*
L Einsedeln (syn Swiss Anglo-Norman, Schwyz; var Swiss Halfblood) *Switzerland*
L Erlenbacher (syn Simmenthal; var Swiss Halfblood, extinct) *Switzerland*
P Estonian (syn Klepper) *USSR*
H Estonian Draught *USSR*
LP Ethiopian-Galla (syn Abyssinian, Galla, Yellow) *Ethiopia*
P Exmoor *GB*

P Faeroes Pony *Faeroes*
P Falabella *Argentina, GB*, USA**
P Feldmochinger (extinct) *Germany*
P Fell *GB*
H/L Finnish *Finland*
P Fjord (syn Fjordhest, Nordfjord, Norwegian, West Norwegian) *Czechoslovakia*, Denmark*, Germany*, Netherlands*, Norway, Sweden**
H Flemish (syn Flanders, extinct) *Belgium*
L Foutanké (syn Fouta) *Senegal*
L Frederiksborg *Denmark*
L Freiberger (syn Freiberg Saddle, Franche Montagne, Jura) *Switzerland*
H French Ardennais (syn Trait du Nord) *France*
L French Canadian (extinct, revived as Canadian) *Canada*
L French Coach (extinct) *USA*
L French Saddlehorse (syn Selle Français) *France*
L French Trotter (syn Norman Trotter) *Belgium*, France*
L Frencher (extinct) *Canada*
L Friesian *Netherlands*
L Fula (syn Adamona; var West African Dongola) *Cameroun*
L Furioso (syn North Star, Mezöhegyes Halfbred; var Hungarian Halfbred) *Austria, Czechoslovakia, Hungary, Romania, USSR**

P Galiceno *Mexico, USA**
P Galician (syn Asturian) *Spain*
P Galloway (1) *Australia*
P Galloway (2) (extinct) *GB*
P Garrano (syn Minho, Portuguese Galician) *Portugal, Spain*
P Garron (var Highland) *GB*
H/L Garwolin *Poland*
P Gayoe *Indonesia*
L Gelderland *Netherlands*
L German Bessarabian (syn German Colonist, extinct) *Bulgaria*
L German Coach (extinct) *USA*
L German Trotter *Germany*
P Gharkawi (var West Sudan Pony) *Sudan*
P Giawf *Yemen*
L Gidran (var Hungarian Halfbred) *Bulgaria*, Czechoslovakia*, Hungary, Poland*, Romania*, Yugoslavia**
P Goonhilly (extinct) *GB*
P Gotland (syn Russ Gotland, Skogsbagge) *Sweden, USA**
L Graditz *Germany*
P Greek *Greece*
L Groningen *Netherlands*
L Guarapuavano *Brazil*
L Hackney (syn Norfolk, Norfolk Trotter, Yorkshire Heavy, Yorkshire Trotter) *Australia*, Canada*, GB, Italy*, Netherlands*, USA**

P Hackney Pony *Australia*, Canada*, GB, Netherlands*, South Africa*, USA**

P Haflinger *Austria, Belgium*, Czechoslovakia*, France*, Germany, GB*, Netherlands*, Italy, Switzerland**

L Hailar *China, Mongolia*

P Haiti Pony *Haiti*

L Hanoverian *Austria*, Belgium*, Denmark*, France*, Germany, Netherlands*, Sweden*, Switzerland**

L Hausa (var West African Dongola) *Niger, Nigeria*

P Heilungkiang (syn Manchurian, Pony of North-east China; var Mongolian) *China*

L Herati *Afghanistan*

P Highland *Australia*, GB*

P Hinis (var Anatolian Native) *Turkey*

L Hirzai *Iran, Pakistan*

L Hodh (var West African Barb) *Mali, Mauritania*

L Holstein *Australia*, Germany, Sweden*, Switzerland**

P Hokkaido (mainland var Japanese Native) *Japan*

P Hucul (syn Carpathian) *Bulgaria*, Czechoslovakia, Poland, Romania, USSR*

L Hungarian (syn Hungarian Native) *Hungary*

H Hungarian Draught *Hungary*

L Hungarian Halfbred (var Anglo-Arab) *Hungary, Romania*

L Hunter (usually var Thoroughbred) *GB*

L Ialomita (var Transylvanian, extinct) *Romania*

P Iceland Pony *Iceland, Sweden**

L Ili *China*

P Indian *USA*

L Iomud *Iran, USSR*

L Irish Cob *Ireland*

H Irish Draught *Ireland*

L Irish Hobby (extinct) *Ireland*

L Irish Hunter (syn Irish Halfbred) *Ireland*

L Irish Thoroughbred *Ireland*

H Italian Heavy Draught *Italy*

L Italian Trotter *Italy*

L Jabe (syn West Kazakh) *USSR*

L Jaf (var Persian Arab) *Iran*

P Japanese Native *Japan*

P Jumla (extinct) *India*

H Jutland (syn Danish) *Denmark*

L Kabardin *USSR*

P Kabuli *Afghanistan, India, Pakistan*

L Kalmyk *USSR*

P Kaminiandougou *Mali*

L Karabair *USSR*

L Karabakh *USSR*

L Karacabey Halfbred Arab *Turkey*

L Karachaev (var Kabardin) *USSR*

L Karadagh (syn Karabakh) *Iran*

P Karakachan (var Bulgarian Native) *Bulgaria*

P Karelian *USSR*

L Kathiawari *India*

P Kazakh *China, Mongolia, USSR*

P Khetshui *China*

L Kielce *Poland*

P Kirdi (syn Lakka, Logone, Mbai, Pagan, Sara) *Cameroun, Chad, Congo*, Nigeria*

P Kirgiz *China, USSR*

L Kisbér Halfbred (var Hungarian Halfbred) *Hungary*

P Kiso (mainland var Japanese Native) *Japan*

L Kladruber *Czechoslovakia*

L Knabstrup *Denmark*

P Koniakar *Mali*

H Kopczyk Podlaski *Poland*

P Kordofani (var Western Sudan) *Sudan*

L Kouroumé *Mali*

L Kozakh (syn Old Don, extinct) *USSR*

L Krakow-Rzeszow *Poland*

P Krk Island (syn Veglia, extinct) *Yugoslavia*

L Kumyk (var Dagestan) *USSR*

L Kurdi *Iran*

L Kushum (syn West Kazakh Saddle-Draught) *USSR*

L Kustanai *USSR*

L Kuznetsk *USSR*

P Landais (syn Barthais) *France*

L Latgale Trotter (var Baltic Trotter) *USSR*

L Latvian Coach (syn Latvian Carriage, Latvian Draught) *USSR*

P Lezgian (var Dagestan) *USSR*

P Liebana (extinct) *Spain*

L Limousin (var Anglo-Arab) *France*

L Lipizzaner *Austria, Czechoslovakia, Greece*, Hungary*, Yugoslavia*

H/L Lithuanian Draught *USSR*

L Ljutomer Trotter *Czechoslovakia, Yugoslavia*

P Lofoten (extinct) *Norway*

L Lokai *USSR*

P Long Mynd (extinct) *GB*

P Losa *Spain*

L Lovets *USSR*

L Lower Amazon (var Northeastern) *Brazil*

H Lowicz *Poland*

L Lublin (syn Lublin Thoroughbred) *Poland)*

L Lublin-Kielce *Poland*

P Lundy (var New Forest) *GB*

L Lusitanian (syn Portuguese) *Portugal*

P Lyngen (syn Nordland) *Norway*

P Macassar *Indonesia*

P Macedonian *Yugoslavia*

L Makra *Pakistan*

H/L Malakan *Turkey*

L Malopolski *Poland*

P Manchurian (syn Heilungkiang) *China*

L Mangalarga (syn Sublime) *Brazil*

P Manipuri *India*

P Manx (extinct) *GB*

L Marchador (syn Mineiro; var Mangalarga) *Brazil*

L Maremma *Italy*

L Mariesmeno (extinct) *Spain*

L Marwari (syn Mallani) *India*

P Maziri *Afghanistan*

L Mazury (syn Trakehner) *Poland*

L M'Bayar *Senegal*

L Mecklenburger *Germany*

P Mérens *France*

L/P Mexican *Mexico*

P Mezen *USSR*

P Mimoseano *Brazil*

P Mingrelian (syn Megrel) *USSR*

L Minusinsk *USSR*

P Mira *Portugal*

P Misaki (mainland var Japanese Native) *Japan*

L Missouri Fox Trotting Horse *USA*

L Miyato *Japan*

L/P Moldavian (var Romanian) *Romania*

P Mongolian *China, Mongolia*

L Morgan *USA*

L Morocco Spotted *USA*

P Morochuquo (var Peruvian Criollo) *Peru*

H Morvan (extinct) *France*

L Mossi *Upper Volta*

P M'Par (syn Cayor) *Senegal*

H Mura (var Yugoslav Draught) *Yugoslavia)*

H Muraköz *Hungary, Poland*, Yugoslavia**

H Mur Island (extinct) *Hungary, Yugoslavia*

L Murgese *Italy*

L Mustang *USA*

P Mytilene *Turkey*

P Myzeqeja (var Albanian) *Albania*

P Namaqua (extinct) *South Africa*

P Nanbu (mainland var Japanese Native) *Japan*

P Narimsk (var Siberian) *USSR*

L Narragansett Pacer (extinct) *USA*

P Nefza *Tunisia*

L Netherlands Trotter *Netherlands*

P New Forest *Australia*, Canada*, Denmark*, France*, GB, Netherlands*, New Zealand*, Sweden*, USA**

L Nogai (extinct) *USSR*

L Nonius *Austria*, Bulgaria*, Czechoslovakia*, Hungary, Romania*, Turkey*, Yugoslavia*

P Nordkirchen (extinct) *Germany*

H Noriker (syn Noric, Pinzgauer) *Austria, Germany, Yugoslavia**

L Norman Coach Horse (syn Old Norman, extinct) *France*

L Norman Cob *France*

L Northeastern (syn Curraleiro, Sertanejo) *Brazil*

L North Swedish *Sweden*

L North Swedish Trotter *Sweden*

L Novokirgiz (syn New Kirgiz) *USSR*

P Ob (syn Priobsk, Ostyak-Vogul) *USSR*

L Oldenburger *Austria*, Czechoslovakia*, Denmark*, Germany, Netherlands**

P Onega (var Karelian) *USSR*

L Orlov-Rostopchin (syn Russian Saddlehorse) *USSR*

L Orlov Saddlehorse (extinct) *USSR*

L Orlov Trotter (syn Russian Trotter, Orlov-American Trotter, Russo-American Trotter) *USSR*

L Pahlavan *Iran*

L Palomino *Australia*, USA*

P Panje *Poland, USSR*

L Pantaneiro (var Northeastern) *Brazil*

L Paso Fino *Colombia, Puerto Rico, USA*

L Paulista (var Mangalarga) *Brazil*

P Pechora *USSR*

P Peneia (var Greek) *Greece*

H Percheron *Argentina*, Australia*, Brazil*, Canada*, Chile*, France, GB*, Japan*, South Africa*, Spain*, USA*, USSR*, Uruguay**

H Percheron local varieties: Augeron, Berry, Bourbonnais, Loire, Mayennais, Nivernais, Saone-et-Loire *France*

L Persano *Italy*

L Persian Arab (syn Plateau Persian) *Iran*

P Peruvian Criollo *Peru*

L Peruvian Stepping Horse (syn Peruvian Paso Horse, Peruvian Ambler) *Peru*

P Philippine Pony *Philippines*

P Pindos (var Greek) *Greece*

H Pinkafeld (extinct) *Austria, Hungary*

L Pinto (syn Paint) *USA*

L Pleven (syn Plevna) *Bulgaria*

H Po (syn Cremonese) *Italy*

H Poitevin (syn Poitou) *France*

P Polesian *USSR*

L Polish Arab *Poland, USA**

P Polish Konik *Poland*

L Polo Pony (usually var Thoroughbred) *Argentina, GB, USA**

P Pony of the Americas *USA*

P Pony of the South *Mali, Senegal*

L Portuguese (syn Lusitanian, Bético-Lusitano, National, Peninsular) *Portugal*

H Posavina (var Yugoslav Draught) *Yugoslavia*

P Pottok (syn Basque) *France*

L Poznan *Poland*

L Przedswit *Czechoslovakia, Poland*

P Przewalski's Horse *China, Mongolia, USSR*
P Puno *Chile*

L Qashqai (var Persian Arab) *Iran*
L Quatgani *Afghanistan*

H Rhineland (syn Rhenish, Rhenish-Belgian) *Germany*
P Riding Pony (var Welsh Pony) *GB*
P Rila Mountain (var Bulgarian Native) *Bulgaria*
L River Horse (syn Fleuve) *Mali, Senegal*
L/P Romanian *Romania*
P Romanian Mountain (var Romanian) *Romania*
L Rottaler *Germany*
H Russian Draught (syn Russian Ardennais) *Bulgaria*, USSR*

P Sable Island *Canada*
L Sacz (syn Sadecki) *Poland*
L Sahel (var West African Barb) *Mali*
H St Lawrence (extinct) *Canada*
P Saishu Island (syn Korean) *Korea*
L Salerno *Italy*
P Sandalwood (syn Soemba, Sumbanese) *Indonesia*
L Sanho *China*
L Sanpeitze *China, Mongolia*
LP Sardinian *Italy*
H Saxony Coldblood (var Rhineland) *Germany*
L Saxony Warmblood *Germany*
H Schleswig *Germany*
L Selle Français (syn French Saddlehorse) *France*
P Senner (possibly extinct) *Germany*
P Serrano (syn Salteno; var Peruvian Criollo) *Peru*
L Shagya (var Arab) *Czechoslovakia*, Hungary, Romania*, USA*, Yugoslavia**
P Shahabad *India*
P Shan (syn Burmese, Pegu) *Burma*
P Shetland (syn Sheltie) *Australia*, Belgium*, Canada*, Denmark*, France*, Germany*, GB, Netherlands*, New Zealand*, Sweden*, USA**
L Shirazi (syn Darashoori; var Persian Arab) *India*, Iran*

H Shire (syn English Cart-horse) *GB, USA**
P Siamese (syn Thai) *Thailand*
P Siberian *USSR*
L Sicilian *Italy*
P Sikang *China*
L Silesian *Germany*
H Silesian Coldblood (var Rhineland) *Germany*
P Sining *China*
L Sistani (var Persian Arab) *Iran*
P Skyros (var Greek) *Greece*
H Slaski *Poland*
H/L Sokolka *Poland*
P Somali *Somalia*
L/P Songhai (var West African Dongola) *Mali*
P Sorraia *Portugal, Spain*
P South China Pony *China*
H/L South German Coldblood *Germany*
H Soviet Draught *USSR*
P Spiti *India*
L Standardbred (syn American Trotter) *USA*
L Stara Planina (var Bulgarian Native) *Bulgaria*
L Station Hack *New Zealand*
L Strelets *USSR*
H Suffolk (syn Suffolk Punch) *Argentina*, Australia*, GB, USA**
L Sulebawa (var W. A. Barb) *Nigeria*
P Sumbawa *Indonesia*
H Swedish Ardennais *Sweden*
L Swedish Warmblood (syn Swedish Halfbred) *Sweden*
L Sweyki (syn Schweike, extinct) *Germany*
L Swiss Halfblood *Switzerland*
H Sztum *Poland*

P Taishu (island var Japanese Native) *Japan*
P Tanghan (var Bhotia) *Bhutan, Nepal*
L Tarai *India, Nepal*
L Tarbais (extinct) *France*
P Tattu (var Bhotia) *Nepal*
P Tatung *China*
P Tavda *USSR*
L Tennessee Walking Horse (syn Plantation Walking Horse) *USA*
L Tersk *USSR*
L Thessalian *Greece*

L Thoroughbred (syn English Racehorse) *Argentina*, Australia*, Belgium*, Brazil*, Bulgaria*, Canada*, Czechoslovakia*, Denmark*, France*, Germany*, GB, Greece*, Iran*, Ireland*, Italy*, Japan*, Netherlands*, New Zealand*, Norway*, Poland*, Portugal*, South Africa*, Spain*, Sweden*, Switzerland*, Turkey*, USA*, USSR*, Venezuela**
P Tibetan (syn Nanfan) *China*
P Timor Pony (syn Flores) *Indonesia*
P Tiree (var Highland, extinct) *GB*
P Tokara (island var Japanese Native) *Japan*
L Tomsk *USSR*
L Toric (syn Tori) *USSR*
P Torodi *Benin, Niger*
L Trakehner (Polish syn Mazury) *Germany, Poland, USSR**
P Transbaikal (syn Buryat, Buryat-Mongolian) *USSR*
L Transylvanian (var Romanian) *Romania*
L Tsushima *Japan*
L Turkish Arab *Turkey*
L Turkoman (syn Akhal-Teke, Turki, Turkmenian) *Afghanistan*, Iran, Pakistan*, USSR*
L/P Tushin *USSR*
L/P Tuva Coach *USSR*

L Ukrainian Saddle *USSR*
L Unmol *Pakistan*
L Upper Yenisei *USSR*
L Uzunyayla *Turkey*

L Vendée *France*
P Venezuelan Criollo (syn Andadores, Llanero) *Venezuela*
P Vietnamese (syn Annamese) *Vietnam*
H Vladimir Draught (syn Ivanovo-Clydesdale, Russian Clydesdale, Vladimir Clydesdale) *USSR*
H/L Voronezh Coach (syn Voronezh Draught) *USSR*
P Vyatka *USSR*

L Waziri *Afghanistan, India*, Pakistan*
L Welsh Cob *GB*

Above: *Kabardins grazing in the Caucasus*

Above left: *Lipizzaners enjoying the freedom of the Austrian mountains.*

Above far left: *Examples of mixed breeding, such as this caravan horse, are found all over the world.*

P Welsh Mountain Pony (var Welsh Pony) *Australia*, GB, New Zealand**
P Welsh Pony *Australia*, Belgium*, Denmark*, France*, GB, Netherlands*, New Zealand*, South Africa*, Sweden*, USA**
L West African Barb *Mali, Mauritania, Niger, Nigeria, Senegal*
L West African Dongola *Mali, Niger, Nigeria, Upper Volta*
P Western Isles Pony (var Highland) *GB*
P Western Sudan Pony *Sudan*
L Westphalian Coldblood (var Rhineland) *Germany*
L White Russian Coach *USSR*
L Wielkopolski (syn Mazursko-Poznanski) *Poland*
L Wuchumutsin (var Mongolian) *China, Mongolia*
L Württemberger *Germany*

P Yabu *Afghanistan, Iran*
P Yaeyama *Japan*
P Yagha (syn Liptako) *Upper Volta*
P Yakut *USSR*
L Yorkshire Coach Horse (var Cleveland Bay, extinct) *GB*
H Yugoslav Draught *Yugoslavia*
L Yugoslav Nonius *Yugoslavia*

P Zaniskari *India*
L Zapateros *Spain*
P Zemaitukai (syn Lithuanian Landrace, Samogitian) *USSR*
L Zweibrücker (syn Palatinate Warmblood) *Germany*

Index

Acknowledgements

Material reproduced in this book was obtained from the sources listed below whose assistance is gratefully acknowledged. Pictures are listed by page number, additional numbers read in order from top to bottom and left to right.

Ardea London 60/1 (Bunge), 83/1, 112/1, 137/1
Australia News and Information Bureau 150/1, 151/1
Barnaby's Picture Library 59/1, 115/1, 122/1
J Allan Cash 47/2
Cooper Bridgeman Library 32/2 (The Sir Alfred Munnings Art Museum, Dedham)
Compix 138
Gerald Cubitt 135/1, 139/1

Professor H Epstein 143/1, 144/2
Robert Estall 48/1, 64/1, 68/1, 103/1, 109/1
Mary Evans Picture Library 16/1, 18/2, 19/1, 21/2, 23/1, 48/2, 147/1
Robert Harding Associates 47/1, 114/1, 123/2
Michael Holford Library 20/1, 145/1, 146/1
Alan Hutchinson Library 132/1, 140/1
Mansell Collection 15/2, 22/1, 22/2, 24/1, 27/2, 31/1, 32/1, 50/1
Tony and Marion Morrison 61/2
Novosti Press Agency 131/2
Oxford Scientific Films 49/1
Fritz Prenzel 148/1, 152/1, 153/1
W W Rouch and Co 36/1, 40/1
Spectrum Colour Library 12/3, 16/2, 28/1, 37/1, 59/1, 61/1
Elizabeth Weiland/Vision International 17/1, 92/1

Western Americana Picture Library 6/1, 20/1, 21/1, 24/2
Zefa Picture Library 12/1 (Heydemann), 12/2 (Revers), 33/2, 42/1 (Bordis), 95/1 (Reinhard Tierfoto)

The remaining pictures are all from Sally Anne Thompson and Animal Photography Ltd to whom a special debt of thanks is owed.

Maps on pages 44, 45, 65, 77, 85, 108-109, 117, 124-125, 133, 141, 149 produced by Nick Farmer for Chris Milsome Ltd.
© Chris Milsome Ltd. 1980.

The following artists are responsible for the artwork in the book:
Marion Appleton
Harriet Bailey-Watson
Jim Marks
Nigel Osborne
Thumb Design Partnership Ltd
Kathy Wyatt

Thanks are also due to the following for their assistance:
Dr Alan Gentry from The British Museum, Natural History
Jim Jennings, the American consultant, Editor of Quarter Horse magazine
R G Stevens of Fairey Surveys for the map on page 39